Living on the Edge of America

A · WARDLAW · BOOK

Living on
the Edge of America

AT HOME ON THE TEXAS-MEXICO BORDER

·

Robert Lee Maril

Texas A&M University Press

COLLEGE STATION

The paper used in this book meets the minimum requirements
of the American National Standard for Permanence
of Paper for Printed Library Materials, Z39.48-1984.
Binding materials have been chosen for durability.

Library of Congress Cataloging-in-Publication Data

Maril, Robert Lee.
  Living on the edge of America : at
home on the Texas-Mexico border /
Robert Lee Maril.
      p.   cm. – (A Wardlaw book)
    ISBN 0-89096-505-6
    1. Lower Rio Grande Valley (Tex.) –
Rural conditions – Case studies.   2. Mexi-
can Americans – Texas – Lower Rio Grande
Valley – Social conditions – Case studies.
3. Mexicans – Texas – Lower Rio Grande
Valley – Social conditions – Case studies.
4. Whites – Texas – Lower Rio Grande
Valley – Social conditions – Case studies.
I. Title.   II. Series.
HN79.T42R57   1992
305.8′6872′07644 – dc20   91-46457
                                        CIP

For Andrea, Travis, Lauren, and Jordan

Contents

Preface

This book is about the people whose home is the Lower Rio Grande Valley of Texas, the Valley as they name it. This book is about what it is like to live in this border region, the poorest in the United States. It is about the everyday lives of Valley Mexican Americans, Anglos, and Mexicans. It is about their individual victories, standoffs, and defeats in a land of extreme social inequality.

Mexican Americans and Anglos who live in the Valley are in general hard-working individuals who want to improve their lives and the lives of their families. Mexicans, who comprise a significant minority of all Valley peoples, have identical interests; some have illegally resided in the area for many years, seeking a better life on the north side of the Río Bravo, the river we call the Rio Grande.

In these pages are described the personal braveries of the Valley people, their small and important triumphs, their struggles in the face of daily emotional and physical brutalities brought about by extreme poverty. Poverty and the human suffering created by it are not gracefully endured in the Valley; they are violently, actively resisted. While extreme poverty constrains the lives of many Valley people, it does not completely define them. There are here a richness of culture, blends of language, attitude and posture towards life, and history all set within a subtropical background of sea breezes and warm, clear moons.

The images of the Valley which the electronic and print media choose to send throughout the rest of this nation are often grossly misleading, elliptical. There are drug smugglers to be sure, and undocumented workers and, at times, freakish crimes and criminals, but these elements no more define the region than they do any other. An accurate depiction of the people of New York, Chicago, or Los Angeles would include more than statistics on street crime or descriptions of infamous murders.

This book is also about my own life on the Texas border with Mexico, about the thirteen years I spent in the Valley, first finding and making a home, then raising and maintaining a family and household, then becoming more actively involved in the community. This book is about sharing a life with those who are very poor and with those who are affluent and isolated from the poverty which surrounds them; it is about how I, and sometimes they, changed as a result. In this effort I have not attempted to artifically separate my life in the Valley from those whom I describe. I have, nevertheless, tried to be honest and objective about what happened; the people in these pages are real and only superficial characteristics about them have been changed in order to protect their privacy.

In *Poorest of Americans: The Mexican Americans of the Lower Rio Grande Valley of Texas* I documented in some detail certain aspects of life in the Valley and along the Texas-Mexico border. I emphasized that the majority of Valley Mexican Americans, a name which they strongly prefer to any other, are by all commonly accepted definitions of poverty among the poorest of American poor. In contrast, the Anglo Valley minority, a label that is most often used by residents of this region, is disproportionately affluent, holds the better jobs, enjoys the highest quality of Valley life, and maintains a stronghold on social and political power. There remain exceptions, of course, a small number of Anglos who are impoverished and a small number of Mexican Americans who are members of the upper classes.

One unfortunate constraint in the kind of analysis that I used in *Poorest of Americans* is that the value and character of the individual life was necessarily deemphasized in favor of a focus upon much larger patterns of human behavior since the original colonization of the region in the 1750s. Reliance on census figures and other kinds of secondary data (data which may be ideal in clarifying general trends in, for example, relationships between class and race) may, in fact, overlook or distort the individual life. This is particularly the case with regard to the important contributions of women to Valley life and history; there is a real paucity of research and data that focus upon issues of importance to Valley women.

Here, in contrast to *Poorest of Americans*, I focus upon the individual and his or her life on the Texas-Mexico border. It is the individual who must, through the living out of a life, make and remake the decisions that help to determine the exact nature of the social arrangements in which he or she lives from one sunrise to the next. It is the individual who bears the ultimate responsibility for his concept of self, for his present, and for his future. It is within the crucible of the individual life that one acts and reacts, that one experiences each second of his or her life as an original event. This is not to neglect the larger forces that influence people, sometimes beyond their immediate control; rather, it is to draw attention to the diversity of peoples who live in the Valley and to the richness and importance of their experiences. It is from the individual and the living out of the individual life that we may at times learn the most.

Hispanics today are an increasingly significant American minority. There is, as suggested, a considerable diversity among these peoples, a diversity which is frequently disallowed. Television, for example, would have us believe that Hispanics are most often undermotivated maids, gardeners, or members of street gangs who speak heavily accented English. This book actively disclaims these worn-out stereotypes, offering in their place a wide range of individuals whose lives along the Rio Grande are varied and rich. I do not mean to suggest in these pages, however, that Valley Mexican Americans are identical to other Hispanics who live in cities and towns across this nation.

Finally, I wrote this book because I fear there are still many Americans who believe that the poor in this nation are, in essence, inexorably different from themselves. There are many reasons to take pride in the differences that do obtain among Americans, in the diversities of cultural expression and human experiences that prevail in the United States. But it is not these cultural differences that necessarily create or determine poverty and poor people, it is other forces that are central to our American economy and social structure. If Valley Mexican Americans can be poor so, too, can you or I. The poverty that Valley peoples confront is, I would suggest, ultimately ours, as are their many triumphs.

I would like to thank Estellie Smith, Tom Pilkington, Jay Hill, and Andrea Fisher Maril for their help with the manuscript in its various drafts. Any errors that remain are, of course, my own.

Publisher's Acknowledgment

The Texas A&M University Press is privileged to add its imprint to this Wardlaw Book. The designation claims a special place in the list of Texas A&M publications.

Supported with funds inspired by the initiative of Chester Kerr, former head of Yale University Press, this book, along with its companion volumes, perpetuates the association of Frank H. Wardlaw's name with a select group of titles appropriate to his reputation as man of letters, distinguished publisher, and founder of three university presses.

Donors of these funds represent a wide cross-section of Frank Wardlaw's admirers, including colleagues from scholarly presses throughout the country as well as those from other callings who recognize and applaud the many contributions that he has made to scholarship, literature, and publishing in his four decades of active service.

The Texas A&M University press acknowledges with profound appreciation these donors.

Mr. Herbert S. Bailey, Jr.
Mr. Robert Barnes
Mr. W. Walker Cowen
Mr. Robert S. Davis
Mr. John Ervin, Jr.
Mr. William D. Fitch
Mr. August Frugé
Mr. David H. Gilbert
Mr. Kenneth Johnson
Mr. Chester Kerr
Mr. Robert T. King
Mr. Carl C. Krueger, Jr.
Mr. John H. Kyle
John and Sara Lindsey
Mrs. S. M. McAshan, Jr.
Mr. Kenneth E. Montague
Mr. Edward J. Mosher
Mrs. Florence Rosengren
Mr. Jack Schulman
Mr. C. B. Smith
Mr. Richard A. Smith
Mr. Stanley Sommers

Dr. Frank E. Vandiver   Ms. Maud E. Wilcox
                    Mr. John Williams

Their bounty has assured that Wardlaw Books will be a special source of instruction and entertainment to the reading public for many years to come.

PART ONE

Skindiving at the Surface

At the End of the Long Road

The Valley was a long, long way away. At the end of the road. It took a long time to get there.

Texas is a large state and the Valley was not just over the next rise, not just beyond the backs of the stock silhouetted against the broad sky. When you hit the Texas state line, whether coming east from Arkansas and Louisiana, north from Oklahoma, or west from New Mexico, there is still a long, long way to go. San Antonio is two hundred and seventy miles south of Dallas, in what most people would consider South Texas. The Valley is more than two hundred and fifty miles due south of San Antonio, as far south as you can get and still stand on the American mainland.

There are only two reasonable roads to take to the Valley. One is State Highway 281 which runs south from San Antonio to Edinburg. I usually followed State Highway 77 south from Corpus Christi because it was a slightly shorter route. The asphalt was two lane most of the trip, but it's been recently widened to four lanes except for a few patches.

There was never much to see south of Corpus Christi. The sand, sea, and refineries of Corpus gave way to immense vistas of brushland and mesquite. In spring, summer, and fall the daytime heat rose off the pavement of Highway 77 in desert waves, distorting the bodies of the small, crushed animals that lay alongside the gravel shoulders and in the nearby ditches.

This time, once out of the city limits of Kingsville, I pushed my car into the upper seventies, jammed the knob of the air conditioner to the far right, and hoped against reason that the unit would pull from its bowels an Alaskan breeze. I sucked on ice cubes from a ten-pound bag nestled in a cooler to the right of my feet. I thought cold thoughts in a vain attempt to avoid the heat and tried, once again without much luck, to find a static-free radio station.

By around ten that night the temperature had fallen to a tolerable eighty-five degrees. The wind blew from the southeast, bringing with it the smell of saltwater bays and inlets that line the Gulf of Mexico. Since San Antonio the humidity had grown thick as fog; I was less than twenty miles away from the sea. The radio stations, after a long silence, began to come in loud and clear. I glided southward on Highway 77, through the wet heat that surrounded the stunted mesquite, buffel grass, and prickly pear, my speakers blaring *cumbias*, *rancheros*, and American Top Forty from a clear-channel station in Matamoros.

Solitary car and truck lights could be seen from miles away on the lonely highway. Brief shadows of coyotes and other night creatures flickered by. In darkness the turkey vultures worked the shoulders of the highway, scattering in silent, prearranged patterns as my car approached their huddles.

I pulled over to the far side of the road, a few feet beyond the shoulder. I stretched my legs, my boots crunching through the gravel until I reached the low grass that bordered the highway. A few yards off into the prickly pear, beyond my sight in the night shadows, a small animal rustled through the brush. Far down the road towards Brownsville and the Rio Grande, I heard a diesel ranging up through its gears. The night was clear, the stars bright, the sea wind soft and suggestive. I removed the sunroof from my car, stored it carefully in the trunk, and climbed back into the driver's seat. Despite my minimal efforts, I was sweating heavily as I put the key into the ignition.

Five more miles down the highway, past the lone eighteen-wheeler headed north towards Corpus Christi and the rest of the United States, I turned the headlights off for a few, brief minutes. I followed the contours of the road easily, the starlight bouncing off the luminescent lines that marked the driving lanes and the shoulders. Radio silenced, Gulf wind roaring around and through the car, I could almost smell the border.

In the shadows to either side of me I glimpsed the outlines of standing cattle as I pushed the car up to seventy and beyond. I sped across a low bridge that spanned a dry creek bed. Here the water from rare spring and summer showers was soaked up immediately by the parched soils. Only during the infrequent squalls spawned by the hurricanes did the water stand sluggishly about, turning algae green in the summer months, slate gray in October. The legs and wings and heads of thousands of migrating tropical birds dotted the waters in the late fall.

I turned the headlights back on, eased up on the gas pedal, passing in the night the one-light crossings at Sarita, Armstrong, and Norias.

This land and the people who worked it belonged to the King Ranch or to the other large ranches, each blanketed by seas of mesquite and ebony and prickly pear interspersed with islands of short grasses and the rare stock pond overlooked by a solitary live oak. During daylight the oil rigs were visible down narrow roads cut into the brush, behind the rusting barbed wire, cattle guards, and small trailers (air conditioners hanging out the single window) that served as security stations. During the oil boom in the early 1980s, the rigs towered over the landscape, at night throwing an eerie light across the tops of the stunted trees, backlighting the standing cattle and the turkey vultures.

The Valley officially begins at the northern border of Willacy County, but there were no signs of human habitation as I sped by the green county line marker. The endless barbed wire bordering the ramrod-straight highway was a temporary wall holding back the aggressive mesquite, three taunt metal strings against fibrous tentacles leeching into the roots of the soft asphalt, down into the tender bed of the road. Five miles farther the lights of Raymondville glowed softly against the southern night horizon. From out of nowhere a brightly lit billboard announced the excellent fishing in Port Mansfield, ten miles to the east. Then in quick succession there was a line of billboards waiting patiently behind the barbed wire, one announcing the opening of a new Wal-Mart in Raymondville, another pronouncing the community "The Gateway to the Rio Grande Valley."

Highway 77 took a rare, lazy curve to the east. Alongside a two-lane access road, darkened citrus stands stood filled to the brim with baskets and net bags of oranges and grapefruits stacked under their open porches. Farther back from the access road I glimpsed, under cover of mesquite and thick vegetation, small wooden houses, each outlined by dim lights from utility poles. Swarms of flying insects covered the lights in shimmering sheets. I had seen no other houses in eighty miles of travel. The smell of citrus, from both the fruit stands and the fields, sweetly tinged the air.

Beyond in the night were six hundred and twenty-five thousand Valley people, not including the uncounted workers from Mexico and Central America. This population was scattered over a four-county area that included Willacy, Cameron, Hidalgo, and, to the west along the Rio Grande, the even more isolated Starr County.

I drove on past immense cotton and sorghum fields waving gently in the night breeze. Coming over a final rise to Harlingen, in Cameron County, I saw the metal pyramids of the cottonseed plant and smelled, for the first time, pesticides riding on the air. Scattered stands of stunted mesquite bordered many of the fields, their thick entanglements of trunks, branches, thorns, and leaves impenetrable to all but the rat-tlers, rodents, and the rare, catlike jaguarundi. The trunks of planted palm trees loomed along the roadside like large popsicle sticks. The lights from the front porches of small, wooden-framed houses now dotted the borders of the highway. Behind them were acre after unending acre of field and grove, irrigated to lushness by the waters of the Rio Grande.

I rolled into Brownsville around one-thirty in the morning, exited off Highway 77 onto Boca Chica (small mouth) Boulevard, then took a few side streets until I pulled into the driveway at 24 Poinsettia Place. The Rio Grande flowed less than a mile and a half from my front door, an ugly stream which separated the richest nation in the world from one of the poorest.

I had reached the end of the long road, where one country collided with another, where individuals were often catapulted and bent into frontier permutations, all against each other—Anglo against Mexican, Mexican against Mexican American, Mexican American against Anglo, then back again. There was a crudeness in this exchange of people, a bravado, a hopefulness tinged by cruelty, both a blending and a pu-rity of old and new cultures, each altered. From the window of my second-story bedroom I smelled the underbelly of the Texas-Mexico border, a hyperventilated blend of rich desert air, diesel fumes, orange blos-soms, human sweat and, at base, the aroma of thick stands of mesquite resistant under the stars.

In the Beginning

My wife, Andrea, and I first moved to the Valley in 1975. I'd visited Andrea's parents in Harlingen before we got married but knew very little about the Valley except that I liked the cheap Mexican food, the sandy beaches at South Padre Island, and the warm December days.

And that the Valley was very different from western New York. We'd spent a stiff winter in one side of a huge old stone house (it had at one time been a small hotel), which overlooked Canandaigua Lake, one of the five Finger Lakes just southeast of Rochester. Although we had no jobs waiting for us in the Valley, Andrea quit her part-time teaching job at the Community College of the Finger Lakes and I gave up my tenure-track position at nearby Brockport State, a branch of the State University of New York. We dreamed of a new life along the border.

I badly wanted, and needed, a new start. I thought I had survived the turbulence of the sixties and early seventies, the drugs, Vietnam, changes brought on by the women's movement, and all the rest of it which was crammed into such a short span of years. But I had only partially survived, although I didn't know it at the time. I had stayed in school, earned my degrees, and kept my mouth shut when necessary. I had avoided sexually transmitted diseases, drug overdoses and freakouts, and getting bashed on the head or gassed at demonstrations and protests. I had looked the other way when necessary, keeping my nose to the student grindstone, getting good grades and pleasing my professors. But I also found bits and pieces of time to engage in the politics and the social changes which washed over the midwestern campuses where I studied, first at Grinnell College, then Indiana University, and finally Washington University in Saint Louis.

Only once was I partially found out. After turning in my Master's thesis at Indiana, I received a letter from the chairman of the sociology department which informed me that I had not been accepted into the doctoral program for further study. I went to talk with the professor. He seemed very uncomfortable when he told me that he did not think I was serious enough about being a professional sociologist to warrant continued study at Indiana. I protested that my grades were among the highest in my peer group. He agreed, but told me, again, that in his opinion I would never make a good sociologist. In a way he was right. For all my efforts, I really was just drifting along, at times numbed by all that was taking place around me. I continually hedged my bets, refused to make political or professional commitments, forgot whose side, if anyone's, I was on.

Many times during my final years of graduate school at Washington University I assured myself that earning a Ph.D., taking a job as an assistant professor of sociology, tying myself into an academic community, all would, at last, settle my doubts and confusions. But my two years at Brockport State, my first position, were even less satisfying in some ways than graduate school. I enjoyed teaching my students, but found all the rest that was required of a full-time professor to be useless or boring. The second year I spent more time in the gym—Brockport State had fantastic facilities—than in any academic efforts. I had absolutely no tolerance for department committee meetings, even less for the effort required to publish academic articles which I knew no one read. Every time I pulled out my dissertation, my head began to spin, my stomach churn. I couldn't sit reading for more than an hour at a time. Writing was out of the question because I couldn't seem to, or want to, concentrate. I was full of ideas for new research but had no motivation to begin. Instead I spent my time under the inscrutable eyes of a real judo master, swimming laps in the olympic-sized pools, lifting weights, or learning to ski cross-country. That spring the chairman at

Brockport State was as relieved as I was when I told him that I was going to resign before my three-year contract was up.

At first we lived with Andrea's parents in Harlingen while we both looked for jobs. Andrea, although she had gone to graduate school in anthropology, wanted to be a social worker. She spent her days taking tests and being interviewed by various program staff in the Texas Department of Human Services. Eventually, after three or four months, she was hired as a case worker in protective services; she spent her first years in the Valley tracking down potential cases of child abuse in Harlingen and other nearby communities.

Not surprisingly, no one was very anxious to hire me. I had no marketable job experience outside the academic world and was too overqualified, although I tried, to get hired by the public schools. Without much success I worked as a newspaper reporter at the *Valley Morning Star* in Harlingen. I was almost hired to work as a reporter at Channel Four. After several months of sitting by the phone, I finally got a nibble at the vocational school.

Texas State Technical Institute (TSTI) sat on several acres of palms and tropical vegetation directly across the street from Harlingen's three-gate airport. A few of TSTI's facilities were housed in vintage World War Two hangars, very large metal structures painted in bright colors, which had once been part of the air force base. But the majority of the campus in 1975 was brand new and expanding. Attractive one-story brick classroom and office buildings dotted the new parts of the campus. I parked my car next to a beautiful blooming acacia and walked up the sidewalk to the Administration Building. Inside I was greeted by a friendly Mexican-American secretary who introduced me to the chairman of the department of support services, the man I hoped would soon be my new boss.

"We need a sub for Johnny Cavazos," Michael McDonald began rather hesitantly after motioning me to sit down. He was tall, angular, and handsome in his brown suit, but what at first surprised me, catching me completely off guard, was the dark coffee color of his skin. Blacks were rare in the Valley; I hadn't seen a black man since I left New York.

"Johnny's leaving next Tuesday to go back to school. Texas A&I in Kingsville, just up the road from here. Somebody has to take his classes, keep them going, you know, that kind of thing."

Badly in need of a job, any job, I talked hard and fast about my education and teaching experience. McDonald listened to me patiently, nodding his head, following along as I led him through my vita.

"Johnny teaches all our reading courses. Most of the students are migrant farm workers who came here under a special government program. Some of them graduated high school a few years back. They need to polish up on their reading, you know, improve their skills so they can go out and get a good job."

My heart did a flip-flop off the high dive. I was totally unqualified for the position. I had spent my years in graduate school learning how to be a researcher and a university teacher. All my university students already knew how to read before they signed up for my courses in classical sociological theory and mass communications. I'd never met a farm worker in my life. I knew one Chicano, a radio announcer I'd worked with in Saint Louis, when I was doing my dissertation on a listener-supported station in down-and-out Gaslight Square. Twice a week David Gonzales played Mexican music from one to four A.M.; we used to drink coffee together after I got off my morning shift. Six months later he moved back to El Paso and I never saw him again.

McDonald didn't seem to care that I wasn't qualified for the job. He gave me a tour of the campus, one he had obviously given many times before. He had short speeches to make at each building where we stopped. What impressed me most during the hour-long tour was the friendliness of the students and the teachers. I asked what I hoped were appropriate questions as he showed me countless labs, equipment displays, and students intently practicing their crafts.

McDonald told me, after a warm handshake, to call him in a day or two. I called him Thursday, Friday, and Saturday morning at his home. Each time he said that he had not yet reached a decision on the position. I asked him if there were other candidates he wanted to interview. He said there were not. I offered to come in Monday morning to meet Johnny Cavazos and observe his classes before he left for Kingsville.

"Okay, that might be a good idea. That way Johnny could meet you, see what kind of teacher you are." Was he hiring me or not? I couldn't tell.

I drove over to the campus after lunch and sat through three of Johnny Cavazos's classes. He had a reading class for dental assistants, one for welders, one for diesel mechanics. The students, ninety-five percent of whom were Mexican Americans, were graduates of Valley public high schools or had passed a series of tests and earned their General Educational Development (GED) diploma. They appeared polite, attentive, and respectful, and they obviously enjoyed Cavazos's classes. He was a good teacher. He put them through reading and writing drills, exercises in public speaking, all the while giving them plenty of positive, cheerful reinforcement. Occasionally he would prod a student in Spanish or make a joke which I didn't understand. The diesel mechanics whizzed through the class period, the welders plodded, the dental assistants fell somewhere in between.

"You'll do fine," Johnny Cavazos told me later in his office. "Even with the gasoline mechanics. I've got them in the morning and they can be a handful. But I can tell about you. Believe me, you'll do fine." He flashed a big smile at me, then shook my hand hard. Everyone in the Valley seemed to believe in pumping my hand until my elbow wore out. Then Johnny Cavazos began pushing large piles of material towards me. I caught flashes of reading exercises, spelling lists, and educational games among the stacks; all were mimeoed in smudged blue ink or written in his large, bold strokes.

I left Johnny Cavazos's office confused. Was I officially hired or not? I looked for Michael McDonald, but his secretary told me he had gone home for the day. No one had as yet actually offered me the teaching position, not to mention the details of the job description, salary, benefits, and all the rest of it.

In fact, I never was really offered the job or officially hired. I showed up the next morning at eight-thirty sharp, a Tuesday, and just sort of began working there. I took over Johnny Cavazos's classes where he had left off, encouraged by the note he had left me on his desk. Three months later a contract appeared in my TSTI mailbox. By then, of course, I had already figured out my salary at TSTI from the paychecks I'd been receiving. The other teachers filled me in on the health and insurance benefits, the rules, both written and unwritten, and all the rest. Periodically I received, along with the other staff, cryptic memos from the director of TSTI about the length of coffee breaks, the correct dress of faculty, and other minutia which everyone, including myself, ignored.

At TSTI I earned only half as much as in New York, and I had twice the teaching load and other work to do. But I wasn't about to complain. I was more than greatful to have at last found a job in the Valley, one that I thought I could learn to do and one that, oddly enough, I already knew I would enjoy. I had a new start.

Guero

That semester Johnny Cavazos wrote me four letters from Kingsville. Each inquired about particular students. Most of the male students at TSTI preferred to be called by their nicknames. There were Four Wheel Drive, Mr. T., O. J., Two Timer, and Ratchet. Johnny asked me in the first, second, third, and fourth letters how Rolando Muniz, they called him Guero, was doing.

It was a loaded question. All of my classes seemed to feel compelled to test the new teacher at least once. I persevered the first few weeks, gradually taming each of the classes one by one, first the secretaries, then the diesel mechanics, the dental assistants, and the welders. But the gasoline mechanics were different. Very different.

Rolando Muniz was called Guero, which means blond, because he was light-skinned compared with the rest of the Valley Mexican Americans and because, unlike the others with black hair, he had dark brown hair. On first impression, Guero also looked frail and sickly. He was about average in height, but very thin. Fragile wrists emerged from the camouflage shirts he liked to wear to class. He couldn't have weighed over one-twenty. Cheekbones rode high on his intelligent face, emphasizing the contrast between the color of his dark brown hair and his paler skin.

But, as Johnny Cavazos well knew, Guero was about as frail as the starting noseguard for the Dallas Cowboys. From the start, Guero ran my class of gasoline mechanics. He didn't seize control of the class in some battle of the wills, he simply had control of it before I ever entered the doorway to the classroom. Of course I didn't know it at the time, not for several weeks. I did know I was in deep trouble, but I didn't know exactly why or how. Hence the letters from Johnny Cavazos, who in his large and bold script hinted from the beginning at possible problems with the gasoline mechanics. By the third letter, when I had not replied, he asked me outright if Guero was causing any trouble. In my letter to Johnny Cavazos I falsely reassured him that all was in order, that I had Guero twisted around my little finger.

Notes in hand, I ran the class the best I knew how. The eighteen young gasoline mechanics sat quietly in their four rows of desks, nodding pleasantly at me for fifty minutes. They responded when requested, were polite, but I knew they weren't learning one iota. Always seated at the back of the class, Guero didn't say a word the whole period.

One morning after class Guero walked slowly up to the chalkboard as I stood erasing the new list of spelling vocabulary.

"Hey teacher," Guero said as the others filed out of the room.

"Yes?" I said, surprised that he still was there.

"I don't think anybody in this room knows what you been talking about."

So I went home that evening, piles of Johnny Cavazos's materials under my arm, and planned for the next day. The next morning I entered the classroom with flash cards, more vocabulary lists, copies of yesterday's editorial in the *Valley Morning Star*, and other supplements. I was determined to teach this class of future gasoline mechanics how to read at the college level. I had three and one-half months to do it.

That day and the next and the next did not go as I intended. The gasoline mechanic students went through the motions of the drills and the exercises as if sleepwalking. In contrast, the dental assistants, welders, diesel mechanics, and the others all seemed to fall into line; progress was not swift, but there were signs that some kind of learning was taking place.

I finally realized, especially after rereading Johnny Cavazos's third letter, that Guero, not I, was the center of attention in my classroom. With facial expressions, hand gestures, occasional comments, and other cues, many of which I undoubtedly missed altogether, Guero maintained control of my class from one day to the next. I remained just a temporary inconvenience, someone who stood at the front of the class and made unnecessary noise.

Every other day I gave vocabulary tests. Students had to correctly define ten words from a list that I had given them the previous day. The gasoline mechanics lost their lists from one day to the next. I mimeographed new ones. They lost the new lists. I mimeographed new lists yet again. They lost them yet again. There was no pitched battle, no confrontation in the classroom, just their uninvolvedness mixed with a substantial amount of passive resistance. If Guero was not orchestrating the effort, he was at the very least marching his peers in the direction they wanted to go. I grew more confident with each passing day of my abilities to teach the majority of vocational students at TSTI, yet more frustrated with the gasoline mechanics who refused to learn.

At the suggestion of Johnny Cavazos in one of his letters, I gave all my classes a standardized reading test. To my surprise, the average gasoline mechanic tested at a sixth-grade reading level. The majority of other students in my other classes didn't score much higher. But the test scores were a little misleading, especially in my class of gasoline mechanics, because they averaged in two students who were reading at the college level with the rest, artificially raising the class average. Four Wheel Drive read at the third-grade level, so did Two Timer and Ratchet. Guero tested out at the second-grade reading level. Every student in the class of gasoline mechanics and the other reading classes was a recent graduate of a Valley public high school or held a GED. I was shocked.

I went to Michael McDonald, test scores in hand.

"You're not going to believe this," I told him, "but my reading class of gasoline mechanics averaged sixth grade on the Nelson-Denny reading test. And that includes Guadalupe Garcia and Fernando Cortez, who are reading at college level."

"I'm not surprised. You have a big job to do." Then he sat there, arms crossed, and didn't say a thing. After a few moments of silence, I left his office, puzzled.

Six weeks of classes passed by. I was close to giving up on Guero and his friends. Without much success I had talked to their other instructors, attempted to talk again to Michael McDonald, and even gone in search of the reading specialist. I found out, much to my amazement, that I was the reading specialist.

I did discover the TSTI Reading Laboratory. It was an empty room in another classroom building. On the floor, in one corner, were a stack of dusty reading exercises. In the closet were two broken tape recorders.

I was giving the mechanics their regular vocabulary test one Wednesday morning when Michael McDonald poked his head in the door and said he needed to talk to me. I told my class to finish the quiz, that I'd be just outside the door in the hallway. McDonald had some employment forms for me to fill out. We talked about nothing in particular for five minutes or so, then I returned to my class.

The room was strangely quiet. To a person, except for Guero, the students were looking at a spot somewhere on the ceiling.

I had learned, through trial and error, to grade the papers immediately and return them to the students. The idea was to give them immediate feedback on their accomplishments, a concept that was completely foreign to me as a university teacher. It was very easy to grade the stack of papers. The tests were all perfect, not one error. The test answers were also all the same, exact duplications of the answer key I had left on my desk when I had gone out to the hallway to talk to Michael McDonald.

I handed back the papers without a comment. The bell rang and the mechanics filed slowly out, slapping each other on the back in congratulations.

Two days later I gave the class another vocabulary test. Five minutes into the test I announced that I had to give the dean an important piece of information and would return shortly. No one said a word as I hurriedly left the room.

I gave them a full fifteen minutes, then returned. I graded the papers in less than a minute. Every student had, as before, copied from the answer key on my desk. All of the answers were wrong on my answer key and wrong on their papers. They all got zeros.

I handed back the tests. They sat there looking stunned, then looked at each other and, finally, at Guero. I didn't say a word. The bell rang and they quickly left the room.

The class changed after that, although not in ways an observer would have necessarily noticed. I blundered on through the semester, at times boring them, at times piquing their interest. But now I had their attention, most of the time, and their goodwill. They no longer lost their vocabulary lists and the other materials I gave them. They even began laughing at my corny jokes.

About six weeks after the cheating incident the gasoline mechanics invited me and their other teachers to a party. They called it a *pachanga*. It was held one steaming December afternoon at the Harlingen Municipal Park, a few blocks from the TSTI campus. There was plenty of shade under the concrete pavilion, a large barbecue pit fashioned from a fifty-gallon drum, fajitas, chicken, tortillas, guacamole, picante, and all the trimmings.

About fifty people—students, their girlfriends, teachers, friends, and other hangers-on—were standing or sitting in small groups. Laughter bounced off the ceiling of the pavilion as the food was consumed. Occasionally two or three students would go to their pickup trucks in the parking lot, then return fifteen minutes later. Music blared from two ghetto blasters tuned to the same station.

Guero motioned me over to where he sat at one of the concrete picnic tables with a few of his friends.

"You want to take a walk over to my truck?" he asked.

"Sure," I said.

We ambled over to a red, battered fifteen-year-old Ford. I admired, for his benefit, the extra-large tires and, on the rear window, the stenciled design of three cacti, a sunset over a beach, and the words in silver "Rio Grande Valley."

"It still needs some work on the body," Guero told me. "Here, help yourself."

Guero handed me a cold beer from his cooler on the floor of the cab. Alcohol was forbidden at TSTI functions, but I didn't see the harm in accepting his offer. I took a couple of draws on the can.

"You're going to make it," Guero told me, not wasting his words.

"So are you," I said. Guero nodded.

"My friends wanted me to ask you something. You know the other day when we zeroed all those tests. Well, they were wondering why you didn't say anything about it. You know, we could have gotten kicked out or something."

"What zeros?" I said.

Guero looked over across the bucket seats at me, smiled, then pulled out a big joint from the front pocket of his jeans.

"No thanks," I said. "I can't."

"You got a name now," Guero said after a moment, taking a big hit on the joint.

"Give it to me," I said, expecting the worst. I knew the importance of nicknames at TSTI. They revealed much and were irrevocable.

Guero exhaled slowly, playing the whole thing out, enjoying making me wait in the heat that was beginning to burn a hole in the top of my head.

Finally he said, "John Boy."

"John Boy?"

"You know, like on the Waltons on TV. John Boy."

"You mean the guy with the blond hair?" I said, disbelieving and a little offended. "You mean the do-gooder, the nerd?"

"Yeah, that's the one. But he's not a nerd, man, he just does what he can do."

"But I don't even have blond hair," I protested, unwilling to accept the name. My hair was somewhere between light and medium brown.

"It's blonder than mine," Guero said, laughing suddenly and for the first time I could remember, showing big bright teeth. He ran his hand carelessly through his dark brown hair.

Guero was right. My hair was blonder than his. They called me John Boy. After a while, I got used to it.

Diesel and Gas, Olivia and Fred

There was a huge difference at TSTI between the diesel mechanics program and the gasoline mechanics program. I noticed the differences from the very beginning. Even after Guero gave me back my class, the diesel students, like Rick (short for Rickshaw), Cougar, Spike, and Manny, were much more motivated in the classroom than their gasoline counterparts. The diesel mechanics carried their homework and pens in identical, well-organized notebooks, took pride in receiving high grades on their quizzes, and openly competed in my class to see who was the best reader. Although their reading scores on the standardized test were not higher to start with, by the end of the semester the diesel mechanics handily out-performed all my other classes.

One day after lunch I walked over to the large metal structure that housed the diesel mechanic program. The two assistant teachers, Juan Muñoz and Jaime Salazar, were nowhere to be seen, but I found Jack Sturdivan, the director, just returning from his lunch. Red-faced, sweat dripping down the front of his white, short-sleeved shirt, Sturdivan showed me proudly around his shop. Each student had a workplace, complete with table, workbench, and his own tools. The equipment looked up-to-date and well-maintained. In the center of the large room were several different, and huge, diesel equipment engines in various stages of repair.

As Sturdivan's students returned from their lunch break, he corralled them one at a time with his hairy and tanned right arm, slapping them hard on the back with his meaty hand. From beneath the shirt covering his left arm the colors of his marine tatoo briefly appeared.

"This one here, Manny, he's a good one. He works real hard at it, stays after a job 'til he gets it right. If he can't figure it out, he's not afraid to ask for help. He's going to make a damn good mechanic."

Manny looked over at me, embarrassed by the open praise from his teacher, but obviously proud of his talents. Sturdivan gave him a friendly push and grabbed onto Spike. Spike at first acted as if he were resisting his teacher's outstretched arm, then allowed himself to be tugged in our direction. Spike was a good head taller than Sturdivan and outweighed him by fifty pounds.

"Now Spike, you have to keep an eye on him all the time. If you let him, he'll go lazy on you. But if you push him a little, he really can outdo them all. There's not a better mechanic in this class. Spike has talent for these engines, only you got to keep on him some. No way he won't get picked up by one of the factory people and get some free schooling in Detroit. Spike can make a real good living as a factory mechanic. If he starts sliding on you, just give me a call. Right, Spike?"

Spike looked pained at Sturdivan's disclosure to his reading teacher, but smiled anyway. So far Spike, in contrast to the other diesel mechanics, had been doing a good job at holding back in my class. Unlike the rest of the students, Spike was reading at the college level. But he rarely demonstrated his skills in class, probably because he didn't want to get labeled as an egghead or, worse yet, the teacher's pet. Each was unlikely. Spike fit his nickname. Brawny, tough, he'd made all-district as a linebacker for the Harlingen Cardinals and even been given a serious look by the University of Texas.

Sturdivan toured me around again for the next twenty minutes, roping in his students when he could, openly praising their talents, preaching at them with an enthusiasm that was appealing. Finally he led me into his office and offered me a cup of coffee, which I turned down for a cold Coke.

"This program wasn't worth dogshit when I started here, Maril," he told me first thing. "Took two years to get them the right kind of equipment to train on, then word-of-mouth did the rest. The administration here doesn't do anything unless you yell in their faces real loud. The folks in Houston and Dallas hear I got well-trained Mexican-American kids who will work their tails off. They come down here, interview the kids, decide which ones they want. Or sometimes, if the kid is really special, they'll pay his way up for a visit.

"At the other end of it, you got these kids graduating from all around the Valley and they start hearing about the money they can make if they take the diesel mechanic program at TSTI. Word gets around fast. They'll hear it from their father or an older brother or a school counselor, somebody they trust. But we're selective here. I only take the best ones who apply. We got twenty spaces every eighteen months. I tell a kid from day one what is expected. If they can't cut the mustard, then they're out on the street again."

"So there are jobs waiting for them?" I asked, sipping on the coke.

"Jobs? Shoot, we got tons of jobs waiting for a trained diesel mechanic. Of course, there aren't any jobs for them here in the Valley, not ones that pay more than $3.35 an hour. Up north they start them out at $18,000 and run 'em up higher when they learn a little more. Now you got to remember that $18,000 is a bunch of money to a kid from the Valley. More money than their dad's ever seen, that's for sure. So right from the start the kids here are motivated. They know that with some hard work they can get out of this place and find a first-rate job."

I told Sturdivan about the difficulties I'd had with my class of gasoline mechanics.

"They're as different as night and day. Everybody and his dog can work on their car here in the Valley. It's one of the things that you learn how to do growing up poor. We got ten men looking for every one job at a dealership in Harlingen or Brownsville. A certificate from TSTI in gasoline mechanics don't mean doo-doo. If they end up making $4.10 an hour after five years, then I'd personally consider them lucky.

"Look, Maril, you're new so you don't know the system yet. At this place you got yourself two hot-shot programs, my program and laser technology. All the rest suck eggs. If you know what I mean?"

I told Sturdivan that I got the idea, finished my Coke, and went back to my office.

Olivia, my student-assistant, quickly jumped up from my desk chair and asked if I had any work for her to do. Olivia was driving me crazy. I sent her off to the cafeteria to get me an ice tea. I didn't want anything to drink, but it got her out of my office for a few minutes. She told me, from the hallway, that if it was alright with me she'd stop by on her way to see Fred. Fred was her boyfriend. I waved and she was quickly off and down the hallway.

All the instructors at TSTI had student-assistants. Olivia had worked for Johnny Cavazos and now she worked for me. She was in her second year of the TSTI secretarial program, already excited about her impending graduation in June. She was a bundle of energy, very quiet with big, expressive eyes and a pleasant smile.

The first week I'd been at TSTI Olivia had proved very useful. She'd helped me clean out Johnny's office, rearrange the few pieces of office furniture, and carry in books and papers from my car in the faculty parking lot.

But after that Olivia felt like an anchor around my neck. She couldn't type worth a nickel even though she'd passed three typing courses at TSTI. At her suggestion I finally timed her one day. She typed twenty-two words a minute, not counting numerous errors. It was no wonder, then, that it took her four hours to type a one-page reading exercise for my dental assistants.

Olivia could just barely read. Although she had received B's and C's at San Benito High School, where she graduated, the standardized reading test I finally gave her showed she had the reading skills of a fourth grader.

I really didn't know what to do with Olivia. If I gave her work, I found myself spending more time correcting her errors than I would have spent if I had done the work myself. I was feeling overwhelmed as it was. I had five different reading courses each day, not counting a night class twice a week that met for three and a half hours. I had a total of 150 students and what seemed like an ocean of papers to grade.

Fred, Olivia's boyfriend, kept her company at TSTI when he could. I often found them earnestly talking in my office when I returned from a class. Olivia was good-natured, optimistic about life, and willing to learn. She had plenty of friends besides Fred who often stopped by to see her when she was in my office. But I didn't think it was my responsibility to teach her the skills she should have learned in the two-year secretarial program. I had 150 other students demanding my attention. I resented my office being turned into the center of Olivia's social activities at TSTI.

I went to Bob Freede for some advice. I had given up on Michael McDonald doing much except agreeing with me and being pleasant. Bob was retired Air Force and had taught at TSTI for six years. I asked him if he had any difficulties with Becky, his student-assistant.

"Nope," he said with his usual confidence, "none at all."

"So Becky can actually type, file your paper work, that kind of thing," I said, coveting Becky's office skills.

"No. Not really. Not worth asking her to spend time helping me out. She just sits with the others and shoots the breeze until she gets her hours in," he said matter of factly. "Sometimes I send her off on an errand, but that can be a problem too. Mostly she just sits over in the hallway there. See, there she is right now."

I looked in the direction Bob's finger was pointing. Becky waved back at the two of us.

I could not just let Olivia vegetate. She could be learning valuable skills which could prove helpful when she got her first job placement. I started giving her classroom materials to type. I corrected them, handed them back to her, then re-corrected them. I gave her magazine and newspaper articles to read and sent her off to the library where she would not be disturbed by her friends.

I tried to explain my actions, but before I could finish the sentence Olivia said, "It's okay. I like keeping busy. It passes the time by quicker."

One useful thing that Michael McDonald did tell me was that the placement office at TSTI was "lazy." Graduates of TSTI, with the exception of those from the diesel mechanic and laser technology programs, got little help in finding their first job. Occasionally teachers, according to McDonald, helped land their students work. I asked Olivia one morning what her job prospects were.

"I don't have anything waiting for me but the first thing I'm going to do is look real hard. I'll look in the papers and ask my friends if they have heard anything about jobs. I know I can get a good job now that I've got a degree from TSTI."

Several weeks before graduation at TSTI my father-in-law, who practiced medicine at one of Harlingen's pediatric clinics, mentioned to me that he was going to need a new secretary. His old one had quit work to have her baby and did not plan to return. I told him about Olivia, that she was willing to learn, highly motivated, and would eventually make a good secretary or receptionist. I also told him the truth, that Olivia's job skills were limited. My father-in-law was still interested and asked when he could interview her.

Olivia was very excited about the job interview. She told me how she had practiced job interviews in her classes, about the importance of wearing the right kind of clothes for the job interview. She was determined to make a positive first impression. She said she'd always wanted to work in a doctor's office.

My father-in-law hired Olivia in May, one week after she graduated, and fired her in July. Puzzled, I asked him one night after dinner what went wrong.

"Olivia is a very sweet girl," Tom said, sipping his strong coffee. "But she doesn't seem to know the first thing about being a secretary. She can't type worth a hoot, she can't take phone messages without getting them confused, and she can't file. I gave her every chance to prove herself, but the other secretaries couldn't find a job she could do without messing it up. She never got any better at it. Marta was spending more time straightening out Olivia's foul-ups than she was doing her own job."

I ran into Olivia several months later. She was working as a sales clerk at Wal-Mart. She told me she liked her job but her boss only let her work twenty-five hours a week. She was making $3.35 an hour, minimum wage, and regretted not having health insurance or retirement benefits. Olivia was living with her family, looking for an apartment to share with her two girl friends. She told me that she and Fred were still together and had seriously started planning for the future.

Months later I saw Olivia at Burger King. She was working behind the cash register.

"How are things?" I asked, grabbing my fries, burger, and drink from her.

"I'm getting married. I'll send you an invitation. In three months." She stepped to the side and let another girl handle the customer in line behind me.

"Fred and you?" I asked, sure of her answer.

"Of course Fred and me. He's going to graduate in December, so as soon as he gets a job we'll get our own place. Right now I'm living with Luly and Becky in a two-bedroom. I don't think you know Luly, but Becky used to work for Mr. Freede."

I was happy for Olivia and Fred. But I couldn't remember what program Fred was in at TSTI. There were more than fifteen hundred students enrolled at the school and, while I'd seen him around the campus since Olivia had graduated, I'd never known exactly what he was studying.

"Fred's a mechanic," Olivia told me when I asked, adjusting her Burger King cap. "He's going to graduate in December from the gasoline mechanics program."

Roaches and Other Wildlife

Alone, I sat in my in-law's small rose garden in Harlingen, enjoying the night air, eyeing the stars through the palm fronds that hovered twenty feet above my head. The rose blooms were fading quickly now, their petals shriveling from the day's heat. Tom, my father-in-law, faithfully groomed his twelve hybrid roses each evening, telling me with some faith that the bushes would bloom again before the end of the year. My in-laws both had green thumbs and an array of household plants which, nurtured to gigantic proportions, filled the spaces between the roses and escaped between the slats of the wooden fencing that backed onto the neighbors' yards. These carefully tended plants produced pound after pound of leaves, stems, blooms, and roots along with their different scents, scents which now dwelt pleasantly in the low-hanging air that surrounded me.

I sipped carefully from a big glass of ice tea, a thick slice of lime jammed onto its rim, and thought about nothing in particular. I wormed more closely into the comfortable patio chair, then fought without much effort against a warm and fragrant sleep in the small rose garden. I thought, finally, about going inside to catch the ten o'clock news, about an unfinished Travis McGee mystery that lay on the kitchen counter, about my classes the next morning at TSTI.

As I drifted among the heavy fragrances, I caught a movement out of the corner of my eye. A dark, unclear shape moved slowly across the white plastic end table that stood near my feet. I opened my eyes wide, focused again on the movement, registered the shape and the size. The blob had crawled down the leg of the plastic table, between two potted barrel cacti, and around another flowerpot filled with flowing wandering Jew.

Five feet away from me, headed in my direction, was the biggest damn cockroach I'd ever seen. The creature was at least four inches long, two or more inches at the beam. Instinct overcoming repulsion, I grabbed the shoe from my left foot and hammered hard at the monstrosity on the ground.

In my excitement, I missed the target. The ugly blimp rose up into the air above my head, paused briefly there in the wavering beams cast by the patio lighting, then disappeared into the shadows far above me.

"Jesus Christ," I screamed so loudly that all the neighbors could hear, "it flies!"

I ran into the house to tell Tom the bad news.

"Yeah," he said calmly, "they're pretty big, aren't they. But there's not much you can do about them. Actually, they're not roaches. Everybody around here calls them palmetto bugs. They nest in the palm trees."

I was no novice to the American cockroach, but the idea of baseball-sized roaches-on-the-wing did not endear my new surroundings to me.

Calling them palmetto bugs didn't fool me one bit; obviously that was a ploy by the local Chamber of Commerce to make an asset out of an indigenous toxic insect dump. The creatures rightly belonged in a freak show, not in the tops of trees which swayed above the rooftops of half the Valley houses.

The giant roaches were, in fact, less intimidating than they first appeared. They were as inept on their six feet as could be, an easy target once I lost my initial awe of them. When approached, they seemed to hesitate a bit, their dullard nerve-ending-of-a-brain unable to synthesize the simplest of information. If they did not exactly trip over their own cumbersome feet, they came close, poor raw material for the Texas Two Step or the Cotton-Eyed Joe. They were a lethargic herd, perhaps so inbred during their time in the tropics that the elephantine species hoped to survive by the act of simple gross-out. Maybe it worked on their natural predators. Perhaps the Valley birds took one look at the displacement quotient of these creatures and flew on to tidier meals.

On the other hand, their slovenliness tempted a more direct approach to their slaughter which, in the long run, undoubtedly worked much in their favor. I've used various methods on urban, streetwise roaches, from chemical bombs to elaborate traps that provided these insect hyenas with what I hoped was a slow, torturous death.

Armed with a two-pound hammer, I took to prowling my in-laws' rose garden before I settled in for a relaxing evening on the patio. I reasoned that my brief scouting maneuvers would scare away any of the flying fortresses, allowing me to enjoy the night air in peace. While I thought I had outfoxed the six-legged fauna, I had in fact fallen into an evolutionary sleight-of-hand.

Stalking the boxcar crawlers one night, big Sears hammer cocked and ready, I soon spied my first trophy in a dewy puddle by the garden hose. I fired once, twice, three times, in quick succession, smashing the hose to smithereens then pulverizing a Mexican flowerpot, then a decorated tile that my mother-in-law used as a coaster for glasses.

As this same monstrosity lumoxed across the packed earth of the rose garden, I fired volley after volley until I finally hit pay dirt. The evolutionary Houdini then made his bow. The gore sprayed in all directions, antennae, leg joints, and abdominal juices raining on an area six feet in diameter. In a few brief seconds I had succeeded in destroying half the rose garden and spraying the rest with palmetto bug fallout. I had no trophy to take to the taxidermist; I had, instead, a jigsaw puzzle of pieces that only a demented entomologist could love.

From then on it was quite clear that these Valley anomalies took their own sweet time when out for a stroll because they knew damn well that their only human adversaries were the uninitiated who had not spent their time cleaning gore off themselves and their formerly pleasant surroundings. These unsubtle creatures didn't need to hide or run in fear when seen; the wise Homo sapiens simply looked the other way.

The real villain, of course, was the Valley climate. Freezing temperatures would have iced these jumbos dead in their tracks, turned their exoskeletons to frost. These same tropical temperatures also bred oversized ruby-red grapefruit that tasted sweeter than any orange, omnipresent gangs of fleas that raised red welts on my ankles and legs, and houseplants that belonged in the Little Shop of Horrors. This flora and fauna all thrived under a steaming Valley sun, all growing to a size far beyond the outer limits of reasonable expectation.

Further up the food chain, giant hummingbirds wintered in the Valley before returning to the novels of Gabriel Marquez. These incredible creatures, along with the rich array of other migratory birds, including an assortment of waterfowl regularly hunted in the Valley wetlands, were unfortunately allocated to second-class citizenship. Grackles, Mexican crows, manipulated the Valley's bird population like so many shoppers at a Wal-Mart.

Grackles, I soon discovered, have no song. Instead they produce a constant and random effluvia from their throats which sounds as if a clever Hollywood producer had merged the audios of "I Love Lucy" with the chase scenes from "Robo Cop Two," then run it backwards. I am convinced that in the bird world of real estate, concrete evidence of the first grackles moving into the neighborhood has the same impact on Valley birds as would a family of diseased Zulu vampires setting up a household in a white, middle-class suburb.

Valley grackles are very protective of their space, which they seem to define as that area which stretches from the ground to five hundred feet into the sky. They appear to dislike any human beings, even birders bearing gifts from the Audubon Society. I was dive-bombed on numerous occasions as I ran through the early morning coolness of the Harlingen streets, before the heat had taken over, or in the evenings when the Gulf breeze began to blow away the day's accumulation of stagnant air. The birds flew right at my face, veering off at the last second as I yelled obscenities into their toothless beaks. The next morning the same birds, waiting in the same palm trees, would once again sweep down from their perches. If I saw them coming, I could usually get a hand up to protect myself, but often the cowards advanced from the rear, sweeping past my head with a rush of feathers. I was left with the backwards sound ringing in my ears of Robo Cop icing Lucy with his best death ray.

Only my big red dog Morgan seemed successful at ignoring the nuisances. He ran far in front of me as I jogged down the side streets of Harlingen, zig-zagging a course that took him from one garbage can to another, always ready for an impromptu breakfast of secondhand food. His large, feathery tail followed him wherever he went. It was an excellent bombing target, and the grackles sighted in on it numerous times. But Morgan couldn't have cared less what was happening to the rear part of his anatomy; instead, he lived for what foods he consumed through his mouth. I don't think he even noticed the grackles as they swept down upon him in synchronized air-to-ground attacks.

Morgan thrived on the Valley flora and fauna. He sucked up the baseball-sized roaches from their hiding places as if they were the choicest tart or mousse on the after-dinner dessert cart. He was also not averse to a gecko aperitif if one could be found. The small, friendly lizards were everywhere, inside and out. At night the albino version herded near lampposts, patio and garage lights, and lighted windows, feasting on the nighttime flying insects that abounded. I learned, the hard way, to slowly reach into the mailbox, to slowly switch off a garage light and, when working on my MG, to lift the hood delicately, then air out the engine of all sleeping geckos, roaches at rest, and all the other weird creatures.

The geckos in particular were full of surprises. They liked to sit in windowsills during the day, waiting patiently for a fly or spider to come by. But sometimes they roamed in our dresser drawers, or the bottoms of my cowboy boots, or were trapped in guitar cases. I reached for a shirt or a pair of socks and, instead, out leaped a five-inch-long creature of bulging pink eyes, mouth open and ready. Hitting the floor running, it would quickly disappear under a nearby bed or chair.

I made concessions and compromises. I made peace with the geckos, preferring to side with the lizard family rather than align myself with disease-bearing insects. When I came upon a gecko I could capture, I escorted him to the sidewalk outside my door, knowing full well that he, along with his brothers and sisters, would soon again be enjoying the shelter of my home rent-free. In contrast, fleas left in specially designed body bags, victims of advanced chemical warfare. Andrea and I tried, in vain, to give the roaches no reason to venture inside, keeping the counters spotless, the floors food-free.

I retired my two-pound hammer as a serious tool for roach hunting. I relied, with some reservation, on the most evil pesticides that American technology could invent, knowing full well that there was a very thin chemical line between ridding my house of roaches and other vermin, on the one hand, and on the other, obliterating my own progeny. There was no way to really get rid of the mutant baseballs with spindly legs, or the other less threatening creepies, crawlies, and flyies that went bump and zoom in the Valley night. I learned to live among these Valley grotesqueries as best I could. I had no other choice.

The Night Class

"Can we go home now?" a student asked me for the seventh time. It was barely eight-thirty and the night class didn't end until ten.

"No," I repeated, my patience wearing thin.

I dismissed the class at ten sharp and the forty students rushed for the door. I had assumed this TSTI class would be different than the day classes. The students were much older, most had families, many held full-time jobs during the day. I began stuffing my papers and books into my brief case, tired and frustrated.

One student stayed behind. Quietly, and timidly, he approached my desk. He looked to be about fifty-five, and was dressed in gray slacks and a blue *guayabera*. Pablo Calderón gracefully introduced himself. We shook hands. Getting directly to the point, he said, "You're a hard man, right?"

I didn't say anything. It had been a long day. I had taught the gasoline mechanics, the dental assistants, the diesels, and the welders from eight to five, with time off at the TSTI cafeteria to down a *papas y huevo con queso* and a large ice tea. Then I'd driven fast down 77 Sunshine Strip to my arroyo apartment, greeted Morgan, the large, red dog, and Isabella, the cat, at the front door, turned on the a.c. full blast while I watched the national news on the tube, embraced Andrea with as much enthusiasm as I could muster when she returned, gobbled a quick sandwich, and then driven back to TSTI.

"What do you mean?" I finally got out.

"You keep us here all night just like the schedule says. The other teachers let us go by eight, sometimes earlier. If the Dallas Cowboys are playing on ABC Monday Night Football, they they let us go by seven forty-five so we can get back home to see the kick- off. We all got to work the next day. Do you have a family?"

"You're kidding, right?" I said, disbelieving. "I'm not keeping you here to be mean. The schedule says I teach from six-thirty to ten every Monday and Wednesday nights. So I'm following the schedule."

Pablo ignored my answer. "The men think you are being hard on them for some reason. They want to know why. Sometimes the other teachers cancel a class, like for the whole night, if there's something important they have to do. You could do that, too, if you wanted. We've all got families and we don't get to see them much. Life is short."

I told Pablo I appreciated his comments. I finished stuffing my briefcase and headed for the parking lot, too worn out to be really angry.

The next day I talked to the other TSTI teachers. Jim Sturdivan was the only exception to what I heard. He said, "I don't care if there is a damn hurricane going on outside this building. I keep them the full time and if they don't like it, it's just too bad."

But Bob Freede summed up the prevailing attitude. "Look, you have to realize that some things just aren't going to change. You can't teach them how to read in a semester. The Valley is the way it is. So let them out a little early. Nobody gets hurt. That way they are happy and you get to go home, have a beer, whatever. You should have figured it out by now. Don't be such a hardass, Maril."

Wednesday night I walked into class, determined to be a hardass. My arms were full of books, papers, reading games, and mimeoed exercises. I had enough material to keep them busy for a week. A loud groan escaped their lips as soon as I entered the room.

"We're staying here until ten o'clock, just like we did Monday," I began, dropping the bulk of the materials onto my desk for extra emphasis. "No one asks me if they can go home early. When it's ten o'clock, we all go home."

I gave the students a fifteen-minute break at eight. The room cleared quickly, except for Alejandro, at twenty-eight one of the youngest in the class. I knew by his records that he was a Vietnam vet. Alejandro remained at his desk, a big smile on his face, eyes covered by large sunglasses he wore at all times. He talked very little except when answering my questions, spent most of his time nodding his head during the drills and exercises. From the first week of classes I knew Alejandro was in a different world, mentally visiting the classroom on occasion, most often somewhere else. His actions didn't seem to bother the other students; he was an accepted part of the night class, like the chalkboard or a piece of the classroom furniture.

A hand quickly shot up after the students had returned.

"Can we go home now?" one of the students asked in a pleasant voice.

"I've already answered that question," I said, forcing my voice lower, suppressing my anger. I continued with the class. Three more times I was asked the same question, each time by a different student.

"I told you, and I mean it. We will stay here until ten, like the schedule says. Not eight-thirty, or nine, but ten. Please don't ask me that question again."

At ten I dismissed the class and the room emptied, except for Alejandro, in a matter of seconds. Then Pablo Calderón stepped back inside the door.

"Why do they still keep asking me to leave early?" I asked him before he could speak.

"They were sure you would change your mind," he said quickly.

"But I told everybody what the class policy was. I'm not going to change it."

"They were sure that the policy was just for the higher-ups. If you are not trying to be hard on us, then you will let us go home. All the teachers do it." Pablo nodded, wished me a good week, and left.

Raul, the oldest student in my class at sixty-eight, put it another way, a way I was to hear many, many times from a variety of Valley people. "You got to go along to get along," Raul said carefully, with no bitterness. "That's always been the way it is in the Valley. You'll change after you've been here awhile. You'll start to fit in more, then you'll see what I'm talking about."

Raul was a retired mailman living on his pension and on Social Security. By Valley standards he was considered a rich man. Raul got a certain amount of respect because of his age and wealth, but he was also considered somewhat of a chump. Few in my class could understand why Raul was wasting his time taking classes when he could be fishing, playing golf, or anything else he pleased.

Raul knew what the others thought about him, but believed that most of the others were still too green to know much about life.

"What about Alejandro?" I asked him.

"Alejandro is still in Nam. He won't change till he gets off the dope," he said knowingly, as if he'd seen the same thing ten thousand times before.

During break one Wednesday night, Raul, stuffing the pictures he showed me of his kids, grandkids, and great-grandkids back into his thick wallet, told me about himself.

"I was a mailman for a long, long time. The way I got my job was some luck, some knowing how the system works. Back after the war, that's World War Two, us Mexicans, now we call ourselves Mexican Americans, couldn't get jobs carrying the mail. What counted most for me was I went to the county commissioner who knew me from when I was a boy. He knew my family. My father had worked for him and one of my uncles, too. He's the one that fixed it for me to get the job. A couple of my friends got mad at me over it, but they'd have done the same thing. They forgot about it after awhile and things between them and me went back to the way they had been."

"I'd get tired of the job," I told him, being honest about it.

"You've got it wrong there. Tired didn't have nothing to do with it. I didn't put in the years because I liked the work. Of course I got tired of it. Some people don't even watch out after their own animals. Their dog runs right up to you in the street and tries to bite your leg off. I did it for the money. You act like you been used to taking money for granted. But we can't do that in the Valley."

A week later, the three of us, Pablo Calderón, Raul, and I, were sitting in the TSTI cafeteria drinking coffee. Raul shifted heavily in his plastic chair and took a gulp from his styrofoam cup.

"One good thing about carrying letters is I had time to think. I felt cheated about my education. Shit, I learned ten times more in the marines than I ever did at Harlingen High School. School was always a joke. Nobody took it seriously, not even the teachers. We didn't learn one thing. I taught myself to read in the corps and I read like a son-of-a-bitch, everything I could get my hands on. I promised myself then that I would get a real education when I came back. But when it was all over and I came back here I got married first thing and had to support a family. But my wife has always backed me on this. I'm going to get a college diploma and she's one hundred percent behind me on it."

Raul had returned from World War Two with big plans, but eventually he went to work in the fields because it was the only work he could find. When the opportunity with the post office came along, he'd seen his chance and taken it.

"What you got to understand is this," he told me, looking me straight in the eye, then quickly glancing away. "Nobody wants to work in the fields. If you ever worked in the fields, you'd know what I mean. It's honest work, but you don't get paid nothing for it and what you have to put up with, you wouldn't believe. Everybody is always trying to cheat you one way or the other. They won't just leave you alone. They're always after you for something, to cheat you from what is right. But what choice does a man have? You do what you have to."

Pablo Calderón, Raul, and I began staying later and later after class. We talked about world events, personal experiences, or nothing in particular. Sometimes Alejandro joined us, although he seldom said anything and I didn't know if he was understanding what we said or just taking up space. Alejandro would nod occasionally, point his finger at one of us when he seemed to agree with what we said. At least I think that was what he was doing. One night I didn't get home until eleven-thirty. We'd been talking about our childhoods. I described to Pablo, Raul, and Alejandro the private high school I had attended, the small liberal arts college in Iowa, and the graduate schools. When I'd finished, they'd looked at me as if I came from Mars or Venus.

Finally Raul said, "You wouldn't last one day in the fields. Not one day. Probably not even a morning." He gave a knowledgeable wink in the direction of Pablo, who was sitting on the corner of my desk. Alejandro pointed his finger at me, then walked off without saying a word.

"Why not?" I asked.

"Your attitude. You can't control yourself. You let things get to you. Whatever it is you're thinking, the next minute out it comes. I've known people like you before, in the marines. You got to learn when to talk and when to keep it to yourself. You couldn't cut it in the fields. You'd be mouthing off to the boss and he'd fire you before the sun set."

Pablo Calderón laughed loud and long, then slapped me gently on the back.

"You know I'm not lying to you," Raul told me. "Shit, I'm too old to have the energy to lie to you." I knew he wasn't lying.

The Dallas Cowboys were playing good ball that year. They were four and two before their first appearance on Monday Night Football. Everyone that knew football knew the Cowboys couldn't miss making the playoffs. Monday night they played the Washington Redskins, a team that Dallas fans loved to hate. I had two weeks to go before the end of my night reading course and I'd carefully filled the remaining classes with exercises, drills, and discussions of the material. I never seriously considered canceling the class.

Five minutes into the night class that Monday a hand shot up.

"Can we leave early tonight to catch the Cowboys?" asked an anxious student.

"No," I said firmly, silently cursing professional football. But then I looked over at Pablo Calderón, Raul, Alejandro, and the other men whom I had gotten to know over the weeks and months. The students, with heads bent, pens to paper, were in the middle of a written exercise that tested their ability to recognize the main ideas in a paragraph. Not a few, including Pablo Calderón and Raul, had progressed rapidly through hard work and determination. They weren't Harvard material just yet, but they were on their way. The hands of the big clock at the back of the gray-walled classroom approached the eight o'clock kickoff.

"This class is dismissed," I said through the thick silence, surprising myself. "But this time, this one time only."

The class of forty men applauded loudly and briefly. Then they were out the door, Alejandro leading the way, sunglasses off, racing for his old blue Chevy truck in the parking lot.

The White Flash

The major reason I got along with my boss Michael McDonald was because we both liked to play basketball. We shot some hoops in a pick-up game one Saturday afternoon near my apartment. A few weeks later Michael asked me if I wanted to play on a Harlingen City League team. I never hesitated.

I drove into the parking lot at Harlingen High School just as the sun was beginning to set behind the enormous football stadium. I locked up my car and, gear in hand, headed for the basketball gym. Built on the same scale as the football stadium, the three-story-high, silver-colored steel structure was an imposing edifice, witness to many decades of Texas high school basketball.

I had intentionally arrived thirty minutes early so I could warm up before Michael's team began its practice. I stripped off my sweats and began taking jump shots from the corner and the top of the key. The bounce of my ball reverberated throughout the empty, cavernous building. Banks of lights shone down from the wooden beams and rafters, bouncing their rays off the gleaming slats of the worn wooden floor. At one point I took a brief break, finally finding the water fountain in the boys' locker room. The smell of forty years of basketball practices and games followed me out onto the floor, reminding me of my junior high and high school years in Oklahoma.

Michael and a friend of his drifted in about twenty minutes later. Michael's friend was six-four, broad-shouldered, no more than twenty years old. The beams of the rafter lights bounced off the ebony skin of Michael's friend, giving it an illusionary sheen. I kept shooting, wondering what I had gotten myself into as the other players, alone or in twos, began to take the floor. To a man they were tall, intimidating, strong. It was just me, already feeling very old at twenty-eight, and twelve black basketball players.

Michael McDonald introduced me to Coach Chuck. The man took my hand in one of his meathooks and squeezed it very gently. Coach Chuck was large, barrel-chested, and carried an extra fifty pounds around his belt line. In silence he took his hat off, appraising me like beef at auction.

Coach Chuck ran us through twenty-five minutes of basketball drills, then followed it with a half-hour of scrimmaging. At the end of practice I slowly walked off the court, breathing heavily, sweat pouring off me in buckets. I had no regrets about my play. Unlike the rest of the team, I knew I could not bench press five hundred pounds, slam dunk the ball, or rebound two feet above the rim.

Michael McDonald walked over with Coach Chuck.

"Well, Coach, what do you think?" Michael asked him.

Coach Chuck then muttered more words than I would hear from him in the next three months.

"The guy is short, slow, and can't shoot worth a shit. And he's white. But what the heck."

With that blessing I became an official member of the team. For my sweat and hustle the rest of the basketball season I received, in return, the right to sit on the bench until midway through the third quarter (by which time we always led by more than twenty points), the privilege of wearing an ugly green-on-green uniform, and the distinction of always leaving the court victorious.

I had joined the best team in the city of Harlingen. I had also become a member of the only formerly all-black team. The other teams were Mexican American, except for a team I heard about called the White Team.

For my exertions on the court I also got the privilege of a ringside seat to racism in Harlingen. Just behind the public face of this city lay the curses, slurs, and all the rest of it—racism ready to raise its ugly head in the middle of the normal sweat, groans, pushes, and elbows of a basketball game. Basketball is a noncontact sport only to the uninitiated who sit on the last rows of the upper deck, those who cannot properly see or hear what takes place during the normal course of a game. But from courtside the game is revealed as a running war of elbows, knees, pushes and shoves, taunts and jibes, challenges and answers, all held tenuously in check by the competency of the refs.

All our games began in the first quarter with the same unreasonable hope, the hope of the other team that a miracle could take place under the lights of the Harlingen High School Basketball Gymnasium. That hope was soundly thrashed from the opening tip-off when six-foot-six Ronald Washington, a dry-waller by day, gracefully put the ball into the hands of Max Jones, Jr. Max, our starting guard, then charged down the court and slammed the ball through the hoop two-handed. By the start of the second quarter we had them, even on a bad night, by fifteen.

The other team would always regroup over the halftime break, their coach temporarily able to convince them that their twenty-five-point deficit was a function of our lucky shooting and their bad-luck offense.

For the first two minutes of the second half you could see these illusions swimming around in the heads of the other team's players as they slashed down the court, drove for the basket, lost the ball, then watched the backs of Ronald and Max, Jr., grow smaller as the two broke down the court toward the undefended basket. Or it was Dwayne, or Davis, or a man they called Silk, all of whom blocked shots and forced opponents into a charge or a walk.

In defense of my team, our players really did hold back in the second half. Instead of a sixty-three to thirty-five score, we could easily have topped a hundred if Coach Chuck had left the starting five in. As it was, he left two starters in the game, subbing frequently from his bench.

The Mexican-American teams were often very quick, at least until they ran out of steam in the third quarter, but rarely did they have the shooting skills, ball handling, and discipline of my black team. More important, my team played a hard defense, smothering opposing teams, causing twenty or more turnovers a game.

This mismatch in levels of skills between our team and the others in the Harlingen City League, when combined with the not-so-latent racism, usually brought hostilities to a peak midway through the third quarter. By that time the other team's illusions of winning had been thrashed, their halftime speech by their coach a valiant memory. It was then that I was likely to hear the racial slurs against my teammates, particularly when I was stupid enough to try to rebound the ball in the paint.

The other team members were, however, not altogether foolhardy. Their comments were rarely shouted; more often they were muttered as they picked themselves off the floor after being outplayed, outleaped for a rebound, or run back on defense after Max, Jr., picked their pocket. The Mexican-American players were careful about what they said, when they said it, and whom they said it to. My team was so much bigger and stronger than the other teams that only a fool would have yelled "nigger" under the spotlights in that Harlingen basketball gym.

It was very clear to me after a few of these games that the Mexican Americans came into the building already hating blacks. When the game was over, they hated them even more. As the only white on a black team, often the only white in the gym, I got to listen to the Mexican-American players saying things to me about my teammates—even though I wore a green-on-green uniform—that they would never have said to the black members of my team. They assumed, however incorrectly, that because I was an Anglo I would naturally side with them against the blacks.

I was at first very surprised when I heard these racial slurs because my other Mexican-American friends, in moments of confidence, would not hesitate to complain about the frequent discrimination they received from Valley Anglos. They would describe particular situations in which Anglos had racially discriminated against them, situations they remembered in great detail. Yet here they were themselves, making racial slurs against a team that had fairly beaten them. The Anglo minority in Harlingen dumped on the Mexican-American majority, who then, in turn, dumped on the minute number of Valley blacks who were at the very bottom of the social ladder.

"Wait till they play the White Team," one Mexican-American player told me as I was putting on my sweats after the game. Revenge was obviously on this man's mind as he savored the thought of my team's defeat.

To his credit, Coach Chuck remained stone-patient through the season, ignoring the slurs when they occasionally reached his ears. The only time I saw him get mad was when we were drubbing a team by thirty in the fourth and Max, Jr., got cut down going up for a slam. Coach Chuck called a time-out, checked on Max, Jr., then put the rest of the starting five back in the game until the final buzzer. It was the first and only time we broke a hundred.

We played the White Team the next-to-our-last game. Their front line was six-five, six-six, and six-eight, made up of former Texas A&I players from Kingsville. Those three had enough knee pads, leg braces, ace bandages, and elbow pads to stock a hospital. Their starting point guard was the only Mexican American on their team. Rumor had it that he had played for Pan American University in Edinburg his freshman year, but flunked out of school during the winter semester.

It was a good game to watch. The White Team actually out-rebounded us the first half, a first for the season, and their Mexican-American guard poured it in from the top of the circle. Their front line was tough and used their height to their advantage. It was rough under the basket, but the play was clean. At the end of the first half we held on to a seven-point lead, but five minutes into the second half we began to pull away from them. The White Team's big front three seemed to wear out, no longer able to block out, set good picks, or make the outlet pass on the fast break. When I went into the game at the start of the fourth, we led by twenty-three.

After the buzzer at the end of the game, the White Team refused to shake our hands. They gathered near their bench, dressed back into their sweats, and left the gym in a small group. Coach Chuck stood there watching them leave, hands on his hips, staring hard at their

backs as they quietly walked past our bench and out the double fire
door.

I went partying with Michael and the other players after that game.
We went to a disco not far from Baptist Memorial Hospital. I could
feel the negative response from the patrons as I walked in the front
door between two large black men. The young Anglos and Mexican
Americans were not pleased to see us. Several of the women made racial comments that were meant for us to hear.

Leaning against the bar I looked at Michael McDonald to see if he'd
heard the words that had been aimed our way. If he had, he never
let on.

Although I had a few good guesses, I never was sure why Coach
Chuck tolerated me on his team. I think it might have had something
to do with him, and the other players, wanting me to see what they
had to put up with in Harlingen. I do know there was no hope of my
ever joining the starting five. By the end of the season I was still shorter
than the others on my team, no quicker getting down the court than
the first practice, and my shooting remained inconsistent. And I was
still white.

Valley Heat

Andrea and I found an apartment in a white stucco complex that bordered Harlingen's Arroyo Colorado. The arroyo was a large and wide
ditch that was bone dry much of the year, except during hurricanes
and other occasional downpours. One of the selling points of the third-
story apartment was the brisk breeze that blew through our rooms in
the early evenings, partially cooling the Valley heat that had baked
into the walls, carpet, and furniture during the day. Off the living room
and adjoining kitchen a small balcony looked south towards the arroyo and its scattered, stunted trees. Harlingen's major artery, 77 Sunshine Strip, passed in front of our complex, then spanned the arroyo
by way of a four-lane bridge. With the windows open to the breeze,
we could look down on the quiet arroyo and the traffic that passed
by on the busy street below us.

During my first days at TSTI I regularly returned home for lunch,
but I soon found the apartment heat oppressive. Morgan greeted me
at the door, heavy pink tongue casting bits of thick saliva around the
room. I refilled his water dish, poured myself a glass of ice water, trying
without much success to ignore Isabella the cat rubbing against the

leg of my pants. Lunch with two hot animals in a small, baking apartment wasn't much fun.

It was not long before the temperature of a Harlingen restaurant became far more important to me than the quality of its food. New friends and old family told me to not concentrate on the heat, to "think cold." So I tried, without much luck, to think cold. New Valley friends repeatedly told me, "You think it's hot here, you should live in Rio Grande City."

It was very hot when we first arrived in the Valley. But August is hot in many places. It stayed hot through the early and late fall. In October the palm fronds fell with a thump to the ground or lay in the middle of the streets until city workers got around to picking them up. The micro-leaves of the mesquite disappeared one afternoon in a strong wind, revealing the gnarled branches and thorns beneath. The tiny leaves sifted like snow into unlikely places; I found them under the dust cover of the gearshift in my car, between the pages of my textbooks, and in the folds of the sheet that covered my bed.

In December I finally put on a sweater, more out of habit than necessity. Christmas day ended with the temperature at a frigid eighty-four degrees, the humidity at seventy percent. I watched the professional football players stomp each other in the snows of January, stuffing my face with tortilla chips and guacamole in front of my in-laws' large color television. A few days later I went for a swim at the beach.

In January there was an attempt at winter, but only a mild attempt. When the temperature dipped into the high forties, Harlingen mothers swaddled their small children in snowsuits and covered their faces with scarfs. Full summer swaggered down 77 Sunshine Strip in mid-March, bringing with it nine more months of bone-searing temperatures.

Against my will I began to restructure my life around the Valley heat. I exercised at night or in the early mornings, avoiding the full blast of hot air and humidity whenever possible. I cursed my air-conditionless MG and talked to three different mechanics about the feasibility of installing a two-ton unit in its backseat. I cut my hair to military length, even shaved off my six-year-old graduate-school beard. For good measure, and to Morgan's delight, I had the veterinarian cut his long, wavy red fur; although Morgan now resembled a canine marine recruit, he seemed jubilant to be free of his bulky coat.

With some disgust I stuffed clothes prized for fighting off Rochester winters to the back of my closet. I mimicked what I saw others wear. I bought short-sleeved cotton shirts, light-weight slacks in bright colors, socks that weighed no more than a gram, ten tons of t-shirts and shorts, and four pairs of thongs so my toes could breathe deeply in the weighted air. For the first time in my life, I owned more than one swim suit. I started a collection of Hawaiian shirts. I briefly considered a straw cowboy hat, but decided the wind, depending on its direction, would soon blow it to Matamoros or Corpus Christi. I continued to wonder at the sanity of those in Harlingen who drove to the office in dark suit, white shirt, and tie drawn tight against the muscles of the neck.

The shade of a tree took on new importance. I learned more than I wanted to about mini-blinds, their mechanism, their assembly and installation. I fell in love with ceiling fans, floor fans, fans bolted to walls, fans perched in odd corners of the room where you least expected them.

Everything I did to avoid the heat, to contain it, to minimize it, was never enough. I sweated like a pig that first year, walked around with a permanent red face, peeled sticky shirts off my back, dreamed of cold showers. I drank large amounts of cold water, ate light foods, and tried to ignore my new friends like Larry Sauceda and Mayo Martínez, who never sweemed to sweat. I asked Mayo if he ever sweated and he looked at me as if I'd gone crazy.

"Of course I sweat. I'm human. It gets hot around here."

"Not like me you don't," I told him.

"It's not in your blood yet. When the heat is in your blood, then you won't notice it as much," Mayo said.

My father-in-law told me I had "thin blood" because I'd lived in New York, that I would eventually get used to the Valley's tropical climate. I asked him how long it would take. He told me two or three years, maybe more.

As surely as I hid from the Valley heat, thousands upon thousands of old people lemminged into the Valley in November, December, and January to search the heat out, praise it, wallow in it like hogs. They arrived in columns of recreational vehicles, each piled high with lawn chairs, gas grills, bikes and motorscooters, bags of oranges, and enough fishing gear to equip the Japanese fleet.

The temporary Valley residents collected in large trailer courts or filled the mobile homes that covered many neighborhoods in Harlingen and nearby San Benito. In the evenings I saw the heat-worshipers gather around shuffleboard courts, recounting the day's activities. They stood in small groups in the parking lots of H-E-B and other grocery stores, sipping on cans of cola, sporting fresh sunburns, and smelling of coconut oil and fresh fish bait. They looked up at the clear skies, commented on a passing cloud, then reminded each other of the day's temperatures back home in Minnesota, Iowa, and Kansas. They talked of the heights of snowdrifts, grandchildren last seen, canned okra, and the crunching sound that boots make walking across Iowa cornfields in snow.

I emerged from my hiding places in the hours just after dusk, when the broad sky over Harlingen was still aglow. It was then that I could sit outside on the patio of my small apartment or poolside, enjoying the cooling breeze. The wide streets and boulevards of Harlingen, like 77 Sunshine Strip, looked their best in the half-light—dust and particles of cotton, sorghum and, more rarely, charred bits of sugarcane less visible in the air, the lush, subtropical vegetation abloom in oranges, reds, and purples muted by the fading light.

Just after dusk the downtown streets of Harlingen began to cool, the sticky streams of tar in the middle of the pavement once more turning to a solid state. The tamer winds set the palm trees to a slight sway, fronds rubbing one against the other producing an unlikely sound from their rigid edges. The downtown was a ten-block area dominated by three modern ten-story buildings of glass and plaster that looked like they belonged in Miami Beach. Surrounding these newer buildings were a large array of two-story brick storefronts built in the 1920s. Down the middle of downtown Harlingen ran two sets of north-south railroad tracks, splitting the town into distinct sections.

The small retail clothing stores, sewing supply shops, auto parts stores, hardware and office supply stores were devoid of life at dusk. But towards the railroad tracks, and across them on the west side of downtown, there were the sounds of cars braking, an occasional truck horn, and a shout or yell when the doors of the cantinas temporarily swung open to the twilight. The smell of Mexican sweet breads from the nearby bakeries rode high on the breeze, along with a *cumbia* that escaped from a passing car.

Off in the small middle-class suburbs that skirted the city, the streets were quiet. Families sat around dinner tables and television sets completing their evening meals. Men worked the bottled gas or charcoal grills on their patios, barbecuing their chicken, grilling their hamburgers and steaks over coals and briquets. In the Valley back- and front-yard cooking in the cooling evening air was an art form practiced by Mexican Americans and Anglos alike.

The afterglow of dusk still reflected brightly off the car windshields on 77 Sunshine Strip. Car windows were rolled down in deference to the evening breezes, a.c.'s were turned off, and the local radio stations blared from within many vehicles. There were always late-model pickups along this avenue, along with a few ponderous r.v.'s, piloted by the elderly. Much of this traffic was twenty-year-old rusty hulks of cars and pickups, held together by heavy doses of Bond-o under cheap paint jobs. Fumes belched from the tailpipes, mufflers long since rusted to the bone.

On a lark one evening I followed an old car along streets I'd never traveled. It crossed the railroad tracks on the southwest part of town, and drove down F Street. Here, to my surprise, the houses were little boxes, small children played football in the middle of the street, elderly Mexican Americans sat on broken chairs and watched from their front steps. I felt as if many pairs of eyes stared at me as I drove by, looking down into my small white car. I grew nervous, felt for the first time that I was not safe. I turned my car around slowly in the street and drove back to the known territory of 77 Sunshine Strip.

I finally drove to Rio Grande City, heat capital of the world, on an afternoon in June. I headed west on Highway 83, passing by a small town every five miles. A little west of the exit for Edinburg the four lanes abruptly shrunk to two thin lines of sparse traffic. Long expanses of citrus grove and sorghum quickly gave way to mesquite and prickly pear. Past the small community of Alamo the land looked untouched by water, although I knew the Rio Grande flowed ten miles to the south. The wind picked up, the sun beat down and through the roof of my car, and the gearbox burned the side of my leg each time I hit a bump in the road.

Dressed in shorts, t-shirt, and sandals, I ran from the shade of one building to the next in downtown Rio Grande City. A twenty-five-mile-an-hour wind from Mexico City blew hard against the stringy vegetation that clung to the fronts and sides of the shops and stores and grew, against all reason, in the narrow brick alleys. Sweat poured off me, only to be immediately sucked up and dried by the wind, leaving my skin exposed to the dust that blew in sheets down the middle of the street.

I sat alone in a motel bar at the outskirts of Rio Grande City, waiting anxiously for the cooling dusk. I gulped down quarts of ice tea, talking briefly with the bartender. Three residents of Rio Grande City entered the bar, each wearing faded jeans caked in dust, long-sleeved cowboy shirts, and heavy boots. They sat comfortably at the bar, elbows draped causally on its hard wooden surface, drinking their cold cans of beer and discussing the 103-degree June heat. They had spent the day mending fence and soon would hang a gate for a friend. I looked over at them finally, feeling a great distance between them and me, feeling that they could easily be of another species.

I never got hotter than that time in Rio Grande City. As I learned to accommodate the Valley heat, make room for it as was required, I also learned to require it in heavy doses. Trips back to New York in the winter found me huddled by the fire, covered in sweaters and coats, shivering in spite of myself.

The Valley heat permeated my skin, sinking into spaces and cracks I never knew existed. Gradually, ever so gradually, I began to look for this same heat in my foods, in my drink, in the books I read, in the classes I taught, even as it crept like a fat thug into my spoken word and my feelings for others.

Around Town

I was a tourist the first year in the Valley, constantly floundering on the surface of things, rarely understanding the full meanings of situations I confronted or the subtleties of the people I met. My formal sociological training was of little use; I didn't speak border Spanish or know the culture. I was undeniably white, middle-class, and over-educated in a predominantly poor and under-educated Hispanic community which appeared to be run by the Anglo minority. I felt constantly cumbersome, slightly off balance among not only Valley Mexican Americans but Anglos. Somehow the Harlingen Anglos seemed as foreign as anyone, if not more so; they certainly were not like other Texans I had known.

I got to know South Padre Island first. Sitting oblivious to the October heat on the granite rocks of the jetties at the Brownsville ship Channel, walking the long, empty beaches during the mild winter months, gazing out over the breakers at the dolphins romping in the Gulf waves, all these became a part of what I knew best about the Valley.

I ignored the croakings of the elderly winter tourists who gathered at certain spots along the South Padre Island beach, huddled with their backs to the cold wind blowing off the salt water, clothed in heavy Midwestern coats, hats, and gloves. I ignored Harlingen residents when they told me that they seldom went to the beach, that the water was polluted, that if you got your car stuck in the sand you might never get it out.

Instead I haunted the empty spaces of South Padre, the stretches of beach, dock, and water too inconvenient or distant for most. It was in these bays and surfs, wetlands, backwater docks, bulkheads, and salt lines where coyote prints lay lazily fading in the grainy brown sand, that I first felt a wrenching connection to the Valley. The few quirky people who lived off the beaches and the bays – the bait seller, the tour guide, the marine biologist from Texas A&M, the shrimper, the oysterman, the seller of beach art and other ludicrous paraphernalia, the sailor of boats both big and small, the waitress or bartender at sunset — these were the people with whom I felt something commonly held and shared.

Gradually over that first year I extended my awareness of the Valley outward from Harlingen. In addition to my brief visit to Rio Grande City, I toured Reynosa and Matamoros with Andrea and my in-laws. I took the trip west towards McAllen on busy Highway 83, past La Feria, Mercedes, Weslaco, Donna, and San Juan, to the turnoff for Highway 281 South. In the dark we drove the final twelve miles to the two-lane toll bridge that spans the Rio Grande. Several blocks from the bridge we parked at Arturo's Restaurant, a modest two-story building that sat next to other, smaller, pastel-colored concrete structures on the main street of Reynosa. I climbed the outside wooden stairs to the dining room and was greeted by a friendly host who spoke to me in textbook English.

I sat at Arturo's Restaurant in Reynosa, my first time ever in Mexico, and gorged on "game dinners" in a large dark and cool room. Immaculately groomed waiters served plates of frog legs, cabrito, steak, fajitas, and fried shrimp to our hungry table of eaters. The middle-aged men in black tuxedos brought us margaritas and cervezas (beer) with wedges of juicy limes stuck onto the tops of the cans. Young boys dressed in white provided us silverware, glasses of water, fresh bread, and tortillas. When I tried my new Spanish on them, they smiled and patiently answered me back in their language.

I shifted in my heavy wooden chair, uncinched my belt an extra notch, and dug into a healthy portion of the fajitas and guacamole that lay before me; later, after a coffee and Kalhúa, I ordered flan (custard). Groggily coming to in the back seat of the car during the hour ride back to Harlingen, I was a three-hundred-pound blimp fueled by picante, tortilla chips, and cheap Mexican whiskey. I was no ugly, exploitative American; I was simply overweight and spent, returning to my native land of Tums and Tylenol.

More often my in-laws, Andrea, and I found our way to the Drive Inn Restaurant in Matamoros. We drove the twenty-five miles south to Brownsville, exited onto International Boulevard when Highway 77 South abruptly ended, and easily found the new bridge. Unlike the two-laned bridge to Reynosa, this Brownsville bridge sported three toll booths on the American side and four full lanes of traffic. Even so, it often took us twenty minutes or more to traverse the hundred yards of concrete that arched over the brown stream of water just beneath our feet, often a much longer time on the return trip.

At the Drive Inn, Matamoros's best-known restaurant, I danced with Andrea in slow, tight circles and dips, careful to avoid the carousing

Texans who two-stepped roughly through the small crowd on the parquet dance floor, bumping and knocking the less fortunate out of their way. Andrea and I danced to versions of "This Land Is Your Land," "Tenderly," and other American tunes I could not decipher.

At a table for ten next to a glass cage full of molting peacocks and green parrots, my relatives and I consumed the ubiquitous "game dinners," swallowing them down with more margaritas and cervezas. Before dessert the house band took a welcome break; we were quickly surrounded by five violins playing a creaky but recognizable "Somewhere over the Rainbow." Later at García's my in-laws browsed through the tiny, connected rooms of merchandise displayed on long, flat tables. There were leather goods of every description, figurines, chess sets, serapes and *guayaberas*, briefcases and castanets, pots of every size and shape. As is the custom, I carried my quota of someone else's scotch and tequila across the new bridge to Brownsville, waiting while the customs guard stamped the neck of each of the bottles with a special seal.

From these brief trips to Reynosa and Matamoros I could only conclude, although I knew better, that Mexico was a third-class Wal-Mart, a land of black-velvet paintings, professional beggars, and barbecued baby goat. The bright yellow lights of the tourist Matamoros gave me no clues to the real Mexican city that lay beyond my sight.

Again slightly drunk, again in the back seat, I gazed at the streets of Brownsville before we picked up Highway 77 North. Brownsville at first glance appeared to be a city that belonged on the south side of the Rio Grande, not at all similar to the look and feel of Harlingen. Side streets ran at crazy angles this way and that, unlike Harlingen's engineered ninety-degree turns. Down these dark streets, I saw small, gaily painted houses lighted from within by a single, bare bulb. Tiny yards were fenced with rusting chicken wire held up by green, flowering vines. Mexican brown pots were filled with thick, bushy vegetation that bulged out into the streets, narrowing them, creating jungle concrete paths bordered by junker cars jacked up onto cinder blocks. We rushed by couples and families walking along pitted sidewalks, talking loudly to one another, waving, signaling friends in the small houses nearby. It was as if we had never left Matamoros. . . . I saw both bright and somber Mexican faces reflected in the sedan's headlights, but not one Anglo.

When I asked Bob Freede about Brownsville, he painted a gloomy picture.

"Not a place you would want to live, my friend. It's dirty and poor, the worst the Valley has to offer. Unpaved streets, garbage and rats in the alleys, and smog. McAllen is the place for me. Beautiful golf courses, swimming pools, an incredible football team every year, and a mayor who really understands how to run things."

Two weeks later, on a Friday afternoon, I ignored Bob Freede's free advice and returned, alone, to Brownsville. Following the signs, I found the campus of Texas Southmost College, only a few hundred yards distant from the new bridge to Matamoros. I parked in the visitors' parking lot and paid little attention to the heat as I walked down a long sidewalk bordered by tall palms. A few directions later I crossed a large patio between the college library and the student union. At its center was a fountain surrounded by an aquamarine-tiled planter crammed with small bright blue and pink flowers. The patio was completely empty. I crossed through a wrought iron fence, walked down another sidewalk, and entered a large classroom building.

An hour later I left the office of the chairman of the department of behavioral sciences. I had been officially hired to teach a Thursday-night class of urban sociology which began in less than a week. The chairman was both friendly and encouraging; the small department did not have a sociologist but might be hiring one full-time for the fall semester. In the meantime, I would teach the one course with the distinct possibility that I would be hired for the new position in the fall.

I walked across International Boulevard and its three o'clock traffic of pastel Mexican diesel trucks and American tourists lined up at the bridge. Ignoring the heat, I strolled through Brownsville's downtown district, streets filled with jewelry stores, used clothing stores, restaurants, pharmacies, small hotels, and discount and grocery stores. I walked along in the crowds of Mexican and Mexican-American shoppers, stared at the Spanish neon signs, took in the music blaring from the glass storefronts.

On the corner of 12th and Adams I ducked into the La Laredo restaurant and cooled off with several glasses of ice tea with the usual fresh slices of lime wedged onto the lip of the glass. The waitress was pleasant and efficient. No Brownsville gangs were in sight, no waiting desperados. The other customers in the La Laredo were obviously shoppers who, like me, were taking a break from the heat. Conversations at the wooden tables were loud and friendly. Not a single knife fight broke out while I was sipping my tea.

The language of Tex-Mex in the La Laredo restaurant ebbed and flowed, washing out in the clatter of dishes from the kitchen and the scraping of wooden chairs against cheap, plastic-tiled floors. Then it was back again full volume, this time fed by synthesized Mexican Top Forty, a young woman's nasal voice singing of lost love, fidelity, and ultimate regret. Downtown Brownsville reminded me, strangely, of the

beach at South Padre Island, a place overbrimming with highly sea-
soned smells, unpatterned confusions, passions submarined just below
every surface.

Brownsville's cultural circus was oddly comforting. I reluctantly found
my car and drove back north to Harlingen, dogging it along the way,
stopping in San Benito just to prolong the return. As I drove up 77
Sunshine Strip, I felt I was re-entering an Anglo-dominated world of
machine-shop precision and ultimate tourist make-believe, a city which
perpetuated the rigors of the status quo until the grave.

New Year's Eve at the Club

During my initial search for a job in the Valley I had too much time
to spend waiting for the phone to ring and thinking about my empty
bank account. I spent many days at the Harlingen Country Club. A
good workout at the club went a long way towards reducing the increasing stress I felt before I found the job at TSTI; even after I had
a regular job, I found swimming or knocking the stuffing out of a tennis ball to be more than worth the effort.

The modernesque glass-and-brick structure was located five miles
west of Harlingen off Highway 83 on flat-as-a-tabletop land which had
once produced cotton bales for the nearby gin. An eighteen-hole golf
course, an Olympic-size swimming pool, tennis courts, and other ameni-
ties had been carved out of the rich farm land, palm trees planted amid
attractive landscaping.

For a time I became a permanent fixture poolside and, in the early
evenings, I often played tennis. I was careful not to charge food or liquor to my father-in-law's account; I limited my free and uninvited use
of the Harlingen Country Club to the pool, courts, locker room, and
showers. It was not long before I was on pleasant terms with some of
the staff whom I saw on a regular basis. I soon convinced José López
that he should give me a key to the six-foot wooden gate that guarded
the swimming pool. Key in hand, I unlocked the wooden door that
bordered the west side of the pool to swim whenever I pleased . . . during the late hours on a particularly hot night, or before the club opened
in the morning.

While the official members of the Harlingen Country Club aban-
doned the pool waters in late September, I found it still refreshing my
first year in the Valley to swim up to the chill of the Christmas holidays. However, as much as I enjoyed the outdoor facilites, within the
walls of the club I seldom ventured far from the men's locker room,

where I showered and changed clothes. Outside, on the pool deck I felt at home, but I had little desire to explore the inside of the rambling, air-cooled building, where I presumed members sat in leather chairs in the club bar quietly extolling their past exploits on the fairways and greens.

It was with some reluctance, then, that I agreed to join my in-laws at the Harlingen Country Club for a New Year's Eve celebration. But Tom, my father-in-law, was very persuasive when he described the good times that would be shared by all the family at the club's annual party. Besides the live band, the Harlingen Country Club prided itself on its Midnight Buffet.

Andrea and I arrived at the Harlingen Country Club at about ten o'clock New Year's Eve and were soon enjoying ourselves in the main dining room with all the other revelers. The large room was jammed with party-goers and special year-end decorations. Besides Tom and my mother-in-law Betty, there were Andrea's brothers and their wives: John, the oldest, was seated with Dahlia at his side, along with Bill and Luly at the end of the table. A few minutes later George and Sally showed up, completing our party. As the band played a diverse selection of country and western, rock, and Big Band–era tunes, I caroused with the rest, downing my share of scotch, tortilla chips, and guacamole. Family chit-chat at our table ranged from discussion of various plans for travel to world events, complaints about jobs, and the trivial chatter that cements members of a family so firmly to each other.

In turn I took a succession of tours around the dance floor with Andrea, Betty, and each of Andrea's sisters-in-law. There were many winter tourists in the crowd of perhaps one hundred and fifty, each polyestered to the chin. Sprinkled among them and keeping to themselves was, as well, a contingent of Harlingen's uppercrust, appropriately gowned and tuxedoed. There were only a few other groups dressed in the more casual party garb worn by my relatives. As I gazed around the room I noticed that Andrea's sisters-in-law were the only Hispanics in sight.

The evening sped with dogged determination towards the new year and the Midnight Buffet. To my slight surprise, I found the liquor, finger food, smoke, and conversation to be clearing, rather than fouling, my head. Following the tradition of my wife's family, I accepted one of the cigars my brothers-in-law offered me, soon creating smoke rings that blew lazily in the direction of the table behind us.

Around eleven-thirty I sought some privacy at the bar that ran the length of one side of the room, staking out a small space not far from the silent cash register which was busily totaling up the end-of-the-year business. Sipping scotch from a thick glass tumbler, sucking on my big cigar, I managed an on-again, off-again conversation with one of the bartenders. Joe García was a distant cousin, but a cousin nevertheless, to José López, the groundskeeper who had given me the key to the pool. Under the circumstances, Joe and I had enough in common to talk earnestly, oblivious to the human chaos that surrounded us as the clock approached midnight. We bought each other drinks or, more exactly, I charged a round of drinks to Tom's club account for the first time. A few minutes later Joe poured yet another round of doubles, this one "on the house." We toasted, him saying "salud," me saying "to your health."

Still engrossed in the conversation with Joe García, words I realized I forgot five minutes later, I looked across the width of the bar and, at least momentarily, through the swinging double kitchen doors into the heart of food production at the Harlingen Country Club. Seven or eight middle-aged Mexican-American men and women, all dressed in starched whites, stood over gas stoves or at stainless steel preparation counters cooking the food and assembling it for the Midnight Buffet. Then the kitchen doors swung shut and life in the kitchen, from my vantage point at the bar, ceased.

My chemically stimulated brain began, however lazily, to put a few random facts together. There were no Anglos in the kitchen of the Harlingen Country Club, and no Mexican Americans, except those at my own table, among the revelers. A quick check of the other bar help, waitresses, and every other club employee who was in view turned up no additional Anglos, with the major exception of the club manager. In silence I toasted my observation, took another puff on my cigar, then returned to my table.

The ten-piece band took up the traditional refrains at five until midnight as we tooted horns, popped corks, and hugged and kissed each other. After the hugs I realized I had reached my limit of alcohol and tobacco, resigning myself to cups of black coffee for the rest of the evening. The crowd's enthusiasm for music and dance waned as the Midnight Buffet was officially opened. Andrea and I joined the rest of my relatives in the line that was forming at the long, low tables that had been set up in the adjoining room and large entryway.

The Midnight Buffet at the Harlingen Country Club was bountiful. There were piles of hot biscuits and mounds of gravy, scrambled eggs, migas, stacks of steaming flour tortillas, blueberry pancakes, bacon, spicy chorizo, and assorted tropical fruits. I piled my plate high, grabbed yet another cup of black coffee, and carried my booty carefully back to our table. Clearing a place among the empty glasses, paper hats, champagne bottles, overflowing ashtrays, and party streamers, I began to unabashedly attack my plateful of food.

As the other party goers returned from the buffet, a contented hush and hum took over the large room. The band began to disassemble, several members grabbing plates of food at the buffet, others preferring to drink their midnight breakfast. Recorded Christmas tunes filled the hidden speakers in the ceiling and panelled walls. On the other side of the tinted plate glass windows warm winds swayed the palms, rustled the acacia, gently swept over the acres of tended fairways, roughs, and greens. Inside, the a.c. kept the temperature at a frosty sixty-eight.

My brother-in-law George, with Sally leaning heavily against his arm, joined us at the table ten minutes later. I noticed that Sally fell heavily into her chair as George offered it to her, then pulled herself up quickly to her food. She began to pile her food into her mouth as if she were starving and someone, stopwatch in hand, might soon take it from her. There was no conversation among the ten of us as we consumed the Midnight Buffet, heads bent earnestly over mounds of biscuits and gravy, pancakes with butter and syrup, chorizo, scrambled eggs, hash browns, tortillas, picante, and papaya. In this interim I drank two more cups of coffee and swallowed down two extra-strength Tums.

There was a sudden commotion at the end of our table. I looked up from my food to see George saying something to Sally in a firm, but slightly panicked, voice. Then Sally pushed back her chair, stood, wrists propped firmly on either side of her empty plate. She looked ready, in her party dress and new Mexican shawl from García's in Matamoros, to give an impromptu speech.

But when Sally opened her small mouth, her intended words were replaced by a thick stream of regurgitated Midnight Buffet that arched across our table, splattered hard against Bill's shoulder, then ricocheted off to land beside Luly in a thick swamp. Sally did not seem one bit surprised. She straightened herself, then raised her right hand carefully as if to clarify a previous remark. The arch of the flow was more pronounced this time, longer, clearing Bill's shoulder to final Splash Down on a table of four behind us.

No one of us immediately spoke, or could speak. The party goers around us at the Midnight Buffet continued their feast. Then slowly, surely the contented buzz of the crowd rose two octaves as the toilet-breathed stench made its inevitable rounds from one numbed nose to another.

I heard someone behind me say, "My God!" There were other more muted mutterings, but no yells or curses. In the next few minutes a

few individuals quietly excused themselves and hurried off to assess
their personal damage.

Luly, Dahlia, and Andrea eventually swung into action, grabbing
their fellow sister-in-law by the elbows, escorting her to the lady's room.
Tom ordered another round of drinks and relit his cigar. Betty did a
perfunctory rearranging of the damaged tablecloth, then finished her
meal with vigor.

Sally threw up once more in the lady's room at the Harlingen Country Club, this time with less aplomb. Later, on her way home in the
backseat of John's new green Saab, she lost yet another version of the
Midnight Buffet. John parked his new car carefully in the alley behind
his parents' house, choosing to ignore the damage until the next day.
Around three the next afternoon he returned to his new car to find,
to his regret, that the Midnight Buffet had been reheated yet a final
time, gratis, by the rays of the January sun streaming through the closed
car windows.

I awoke that same afternoon of January 1, 1976, with a serious hangover and equally serious misgivings about living one more hour in Harlingen, Texas. I had talked the week before to Michael McDonald about
staying on another year at TSTI. He was neither encouraging, nor did
he say no. With a steady push in the right direction, I knew I could
easily become a fixture at the school, one year smoothly gliding into
the next, until I rose through the ranks from department head, to program supervisor to the Great Administrative Beyond.

As John Boy I knew that as my paycheck increased I could get accustomed to the way things were done at TSTI and in Harlingen, to
the Freds and Olivias, the Gueros, the Pablo Calderóns, the Michael
McDonalds, the Bob Freedes, all of whom were situated in a community based upon rigid notions of skin color and the importance of
money. I knew I was not destined to swim forever in the Olympic-sized
pool at the Harlingen Country Club; I could eventually claim a legitimate piece of turf, however small, within the inner confines of the club.
But like my wife's sister-in-law Sally at the Harlingen Country Club's
Midnight Buffet, I had already consumed far more than I could stomach.

PART TWO

The Brown Pit

The Enchilada Gang

At its beginnings Palm Boulevard was a stodgy old street, lined with seventy-year-old mansions from a much grander era in Brownsville's history. Spindly palm trees filled the dirt traffic island that separated the four lanes of busy concrete. Acacia, poinsettia, and a crop of shoulder-high young palm trees took up the rest of the ground between lanes, wooden and metal stakes protecting the trees' trunks from passers-by. Small brick and plaster apartment buildings, long since past their prime, were sprinkled in among the mansions. A few of these buildings had been renovated top to bottom, but the majority bore the scars of cheap repairs atop decaying foundations.

Andrea and I made the move from Harlingen to Brownsville, the city that Bob Freede called the "Brown Pit," quickly and without regret. We left behind the sterile "adult apartment community" for a building and a neighborhood with "character." Our apartment, just a few feet from the traffic of Palm Boulevard, backed onto a large *resaca*, a small lake, one of many throughout the city that fed directly into the Rio Grande. We were less than two miles from the river and a very short walk from the Brownsville Zoo. Mornings, with the kitchen window open to the muggy breeze off the *resaca*, the roars of the big cats along with the screechings of the gibbons rolled into our small apartment.

After a year we saved enough money from my new job at Texas Southmost College and Andrea's as a social worker to make a small down payment on a house around the corner from our apartment on Palm Boulevard. For twelve years we lived at 24 Poinsettia Place, a one and one-half–story brick home covered by more acacia, poinsettia, and the incredible effluvia of three ebony trees. The backyard was filled with a tall sour orange tree covered with heavy vines along with young grapefruit and orange trees which provided the neighborhood possums with midnight snacks.

During our first four months at 24 Poinsettia Place life went by in a slow, almost drugged pace as we worked to turn our neglected house into a comfortable home. Two years spent in small apartments made the ordinary features of our new house seem luxurious. There was no landlord looking over my shoulder with a set of arbitrary rules and, for the first time, I had room for my own office. I painted walls until my wrists ached and built what seemed like thousands of bookshelves to hold our books.

But what pleased me most was, with the exception of the echo of animals from the Brownsville Zoo, the quiet of our new home, a quiet of a secure and peaceful neighborhood. Outside the walls of our new home the winter rains subsided and the strong winds from south of the Rio Grande brought with them the stultifying heat of a new spring. Inside there was a pleasant respite from the noise of apartment neighbors on the other side of the wall playing their stereos, or tuning their engines in the parking lot at eight o'clock on a Sunday morning.

Without warning the Rodríquez family moved into the rent house next door. The Rodríquez family brought with them, without fanfare, a mongrel chihuahua-dachshund cross, a long multicolored tube of brown, black, and white spots, stomach precariously slung a slight inch above the ground. When the canine enchilada barked, a high, piercing sound was emitted from its throat which immediately set my molars to aching the first time I heard it.

The half-breed lost no time in staking out her territory. That first day she laid claim, like some crazed Spanish conquistador, to all of the Rodríquez yard, the neighbor's yard immediately to the east, and all the concrete of Poinsettia Place. With ritual ceremony she marked out the boundaries of her domain in the dust; it was very clear from the beginning that there would be no limits to her territorial lust.

The next day I drove home to find the enchilada sprawled in the middle of the street. I revved up the engine of my car, assuming that the noises would wake her from her siesta. She didn't move an inch. I thought she had died right there in the middle of the street, a victim of the heat. I honked my horn, concern growing. Then the sausage beast rose slowly to her feet, looked up at me out of surprisingly big, brown eyes, and walked carefully and precisely to the curb. I drove by, only to hear the shriek of those mutant vocal chords as she chased my car into my own driveway.

Irate, I jumped out of the car and made threatening gestures at her. A genetic coward, she quickly dashed into the safety of the Rodríguezes' yard, from which she continued to yelp curses at me. The die was cast that day, the gauntlet thrown; nothing good would come of this first showdown on the hot, dusty streets of the Brown Pit.

In my folly I soon thought I had won. The enchilada grew fatter and fatter, more lethargic every day. It was obvious even from a distance that pregnancy was overtaking her, sapping a little more of her strength with every sunset. I reasoned that she would soon withdraw from the field of battle; it takes more energy to drag a weenie carcass across the yard than it does to haul it on four stumpy legs.

The laws of physics were on my side. Nevertheless, the enchilada found enough calories to regularly urinate on my new white car each night. There was soon a permanent discoloration on the rear tires from her determined efforts. She also stole a pair of my favorite shoes from the front doorsteps. And, using her yard as a staging area, the enchilada took to random attacks as I rode around the neighborhood each evening on my bike. My pleasant after-dinner thoughts were jarred by her buzz-saw yelps as she tried to ram her razor-thin teeth into the heel of my curbside foot. She was so low to the ground that it was impossible to reach her with a healthy kick.

Still, I began to dream of the time when she would be nagged to death by her multiple offspring. Tiny mouths, paws, and furry, low-slung stomachs would drain the enchilada of the vitriol necessary to keep my white car yellow.

I seriously underestimated the enchilada; as soon as her infant quarter-breeds could waddle in a straight line, she set her pack against me. When I went in search of the evening paper, it was to the yelpettes of miniature sausages following their mother's lead. The stains on my tires multiplied, the sources of pollution increased by a factor of five. From my bicycle I was now attacked from all sides at once. This enchilada gang struck in disciplined formation, tubette after tubette rushing forth to attack with demonic fury. It was no longer a fair fight.

Then, as if by conference call, they began howling at night. All night. Every night. I am not a light sleeper by nature, but I found myself wakened from my deepest dreams by their piercing night-time yodels. That first night I shut all the bedroom windows, switched the floor fan to high, and stuck my head under two pillows. By 3:00 A.M. sleep finally overcame me, but I was soon reawakened by a new set of ungodly shrieks that sounded as if the Boston Strangler were slowly, one by one, slitting the throats of the enchilada gang.

I rushed outside my house in the predawn to shake the hand of the Boston Strangler. I found instead two of the weenies madly jumping up and down as if they had treed the last unicorn. But instead of a pony with a lone horn sticking from his forehead, I saw in the predawn light a cat across the street gingerly walk from under a bush to the front steps of the González house. Thinking back on it, I now realize that the baby enchiladas were only practicing, honing their skills for the next phase of the war.

Two nights later the mother and her chorus began their floor show a little after one in the morning. I got dressed and walked across my front lawn, still barefoot, to the Rodríguez house. Along the way my feet managed to find three of the ebony branches recently blown down. So I was not in the best of moods, still picking the tiny thorns out of both feet, when I began pounding on the Rodrígueses' front door.

After about five minutes, someone finally turned on the porch light.

"What's the matter?" asked Mr. Rodríguez between yawns, still in his boxer shorts and t-shirt.

"Your dogs are keeping my wife and me from sleeping. I'm sick of it."

"So?" he asked, puzzled by my problem.

"So do something about it," I said, trying to control my anger.

"Like what? What can I do about it? If they want to bark, I can't stop them."

It was clear enough to him, but the logic of his thinking stopped me cold for the moment.

"Keep them inside your house," I said, trying to remain calm. It was becoming obvious that the man, along with his chattel, needed a group brain transplant.

"I can't do that. They'd keep everyone up all night with their barking," he said, looking at me as if I were learning disabled.

I walked slowly back to my house, trying to think how to best reason with a man who was less intelligent than his dogs. That night I tried sleeping everywhere in my house to avoid the cascade of piercing howls. I finally settled on the floor of my new office. I put a fan on either side of my head, each turned to high, shut all the windows, then stuck my head under the pillow to avoid the machine-made hurricane. Deep within the folds of the pillow I couldn't hear a thing . . . but I also couldn't breathe and the heat soon covered me in a heavy sweat.

Even my wife, normally patient with pets, changed her attitude towards the meat-on-stumps. Andrea was in her seventh month of pregnancy with our first child and sleep was very important to her. She was a heavy sleeper, but found it increasingly difficult to ignore the pandemonium next door. And from me, lying next to her.

I dug out my old b.b. gun which was busy gathering dust in the hall closet. From my second-story bedroom I began taking wild potshots at the canine dwarfs, a form of harassment designed to make their lives a little bit less satisfying. Soon, however, as the stakes escalated, as I began to drift towards the edge, I took serious aim, hoping to ping a juvenile offender into the next world. I got lucky once or twice, nipping a tubette in the hindquarters. But such actions only seemed to enrage the pack which then, depending on the time of day, resumed its pillaging or group song.

As the sleepless nights rolled by, I began to consider other alternatives to the invasion of my quiet, including my twenty-two rifle. I knew I could end it all in a bloodbath of dusty fur and sticky tongues; no jury in Texas, if they but knew the facts, would convict me of the gore.

Twice more I pounded on the Rodríguezes' door in the dead of night, twice more I conversed with the head of the household. I decided, finally, to simply threaten the man.

"The next time your goddam dogs wake me up," I yelled at him one early morning, "I'm going to call the police!"

"Okay," he said with some confidence as he shut the door in my red-eyed face.

I talked to my lawyer brother-in-law the next day. I was informed that by the time the Brownsville police got around to arresting the herd of enchiladas for disturbing my peace and quiet, I would have long since turned old and gray. My brother-in-law John suggested, jokingly, that I poison the critters. I smiled.

I mentally designed a series of enchilada traps. The weenie wench and her crew would begin their nightly search-and-destroy missions only to sniff in the air the rich aroma of a rotting can of Alpo. Marching confidently into my yard under cover of darkness, they would fall into an eight-foot-deep pit I had dug the night before. At the bottom of the pit they would impale themselves on razor-sharp bamboo stakes. But how to dispose of the bodies? The Rio Grande, the Mekong Delta, the local butcher?

Or lobster traps, with a few minor adaptations. Alpo would again be the bait. The micro-howlers would weenie in, then find themselves unable to weenie out with the tide. But again there was the problem of disposal. Perhaps a trash compactor; let the Sears Customer Service Department bear the brunt of any complaints about former pets reduced to the size of salad croutons.

In the end Andrea brought peace to the neighborhood. I was away on business, and sleeping to my heart's content, when at 3:00 A.M. she stomped across our lawn to the Rodríguez house. Mr. Rodríguez appeared at the door, as was his custom. Tired to the bone, my pregnant wife told Mr. Rodríguez that if he didn't do something about his howling enchiladas, she was going to miscarry our first child. Mr. Rodríguez humbly apologized right then and there on his front steps, quickly rounding up his weenies-on-wheels. Silence broke out on Poinsettia Place.

Of course that didn't stop the chief weenette from foraging in our yard during the day, or the herd's habit of keeping my white car yellow. Or the bicycle attacks, missing property, or enchilada outrage whenever I appeared on my own front lawn.

Or the unsanctioned union between the head enchilada and her mongrel companion down the street. The built-for-greed tubettes were produced with amazing speed and redundancy.

But perhaps the gravest injustice was betrayal by my first-born. Shortly after reaching three years of age, my son Travis approached me with the most irrational request of his short life. Pointing across our lawn towards the Rodríguez house, where the newest brood of elongated forms howled and wriggled in the mid-day dust, he said, "Dad, can I have one of those puppies?"

The Wild Man

Each semester at Texas Southmost College I always looked forward to the robust enthusiasm among the students, faculty, and staff, a certain loud and joyful chaos when classes began that usually lasted at least through midterm. Every third week in August and second week in January unwieldly lines of students formed at registration and at the College Book Store, the parking lots filled to overflowing, and students rushed down the halls of the classroom buildings, intent on reaching their classes before the loud ring of the electric fire bells that began and ended each class period.

Students in droves, and with the help of their counselors, waded through the rhetoric of financial forms they filled out. A majority of TSC students received their tuition and books free from federal Basic Opportunity Grants, grants designed to benefit students who came from low-income families. All this activity was fueled by continual talk and shouts, greetings and taunts, blares from ghetto blasters hidden underneath coats and jackets, and by the world-weary angst of faculty and staff who ran about on the last days of registration trying, in vain, to maintain some semblance of academic order.

Each semester I held out little hope that my first meeting with my five different classes would, in the context of this festive atmosphere, accomplish much. My only objective at these first close encounters was to provide some basic information and to help set the tone for the rest of the semester. Students filtered into the door, a few lost, others late because they couldn't find a parking space. I passed out course syllabi the first day, discussed the course briefly, then sent the students off to buy their books at the Campus Book Store so they could read their first assignment.

This particular first day was different.

"Are there any questions?" I asked, looking out over the heads of the forty-five students, ready to dismiss them.

"Yeah," came a voice at the back of the room. "What do you think you're doing?"

He was wearing a fatigue jacket, this despite the ninety-five-degree temperature in the streets outside the building, a brown t-shirt with no logo, old cowboy boots, and faded blue jeans. I didn't see the glazed-over eyes and slack jaw until I casually walked up the aisle between the desks.

I thought it was some kind of joke, like the ones that were played on me my first weeks at TSTI.

"Would you please repeat the question," I stammered, not sure how to continue.

"I mean all this stuff. It just keeps going on and on, you know. It doesn't fit that good."

"I'm sorry, but I'm not following you," I said, starting to get very worried, realizing that the student was not joking.

"I mean, well, see you got this piece of paper here and you're telling us all this crap and, well, what the shit, man?"

Two students who sat next to the man in the fatigue jacket suddenly rose from their desks and left the classroom, not looking back.

"This class is dismissed," I said, deciding that the best thing to do was evacuate the room. "I'll see you on Wednesday for the first regular class. Don't forget to buy your books."

Forty or so students walked out of there very rapidly, all sensing the danger. The student in the fatigue jacket placed himself between me and the door.

"So what's the problem?" I asked, trying to keep it light, not really knowing what to do.

"Don't f—— with me, don't f—— with me," he said. He pointed his right arm at my face, made a gun of his hand, then pulled the trigger. Then he stood back a step to laugh.

"I'm not trying to bother you," I said, edging my way around him. The door was less than fifteen feet away. The classroom was completely empty now.

"If you f—— with me, you're dead," he said, again smiling. I looked at him closely for the first time now. He was about five-eight, stocky, with dark long hair covering his forehead and reaching down over his right eye.

"Are you threatening me?" I said, disbelieving. The situation was, for me, becoming dreamlike.

"You're messing with my head, man. With everybody's head in this room. You stop or it's over." Then he stared blankly at and through me.

It was time for action. I rushed between his lifeless stare and a row of desks, out into the noisy hallway. I half-walked, half-ran up to the second floor of the building, in search of the chairman of the Behavioral Sciences Department. I found Henry in the faculty lounge, his heavy gray moustache deep into a coffee mug and a conversation.

"I've got a big problem," I told him in front of three other college staff. I still wasn't even sure of the student's name, but I briefly described what had happened. The chairman listened patiently to me, then said he would call the dean's office immediately. Coffee cup in hand, he strode out the door in search of a private phone.

The chairman never called me back. The next morning I ran into Hector, the coach of TSC's baseball team, at the campus post office. Before I could say hello, Hector told me about a strange student who had physically attacked him in the gym the day before. The student's name was Luís Abelardo Váldez. His description of the student sounded very familiar. I climbed the stairs to my office, checked the class roll, and found the same Váldez was on my class list.

A day later, at five to nine, I walked over to my class, a sense of dread steadily building. I carefully peeked into the near-empty room. Instead of my forty-five students, I saw Luís Abelardo Váldez sitting on the font row, a few feet from the lectern. Three other students were in the room, all on the back row. Each was staring at his or her shoes, anything to avoid eye contact with the man on the front row. I guessed correctly that Luís had already made his presence known to the few students who were brave enough to enter the room.

I waved my hands at the students, silently motioning them to leave. Gratefully they began gathering up their books. I backed slowly out the door, keeping my eye on the back of Luís's neck. In the hallway I recognized several of my students from Monday's class. They weren't going to go to class, they told me, not with that wild man sitting there on the front row, but they wanted to find out if there was a new reading assignment.

One of the students pulled me off to the side, away from the heavy stream of students that now filled the hallway.

"Váldez is nuts, Dr. Maril," he told me, his face grown serious. "He's been in jail and hospitals for a long time. He only lives a few blocks

from my family. I heard they let him out last week. He's shot two people that I know about personally, over drugs or something. He beat
the crap out of more guys than I could count. Váldez is messed up real
bad. Ain't no way I'm going back in there until he's long gone."

I peeked back into my classroom after the late bell rang. The wild
man still sat on the front row, waiting for the class to begin. I thought
I could hear him singing a tune, but I wasn't sure.

Henry was safe and secure in his office. I told him about Luís Abelardo Váldez and my missing roomful of students. Henry said he'd called
the dean, gotten the run around, but then heard there was going to
be a meeting after lunch to discuss "the problem." I was invited to attend.

"But don't expect much," Henry warned me as I shut his office door.

I walked back to my office through the thick August air. I stopped
suddenly, automatically, at the foot of the outside stairs by the empty
courtyard. Looking up the steep stairs to the landing above me, I could
see the open door to the secretary's office, creaking quietly on its heavy
hinges. The secretary always locked the door when she went on an
errand, otherwise the door was shut tight to keep the utility bill low.
I quietly strode up the stairs, not sure what to expect.

The secretary was not at her desk. My office door, always locked
when I was away, was wide open. I heard loud noises coming from
within. I looked carefully around the open door, ready to run for the
slightest reason. The Wild Man sat at my desk, hunched over, sifting
through the papers in my drawers. He would pull a handful out, ex-
amine one or two, mutter something to himself, then throw them aside.
Papers and books were scattered around the floor of my office; it looked
like he'd been there for some time.

I called Campus Security from an office in another part of the administration building. Jaime Ortega came within five minutes. I explained
what I knew.

"Shit, not again," said Jaime.

"What do you mean?" I asked.

"This guy's been tearing up the place everywhere he goes. And he's
real strong. I'm calling for some back-up."

Jaime talked in code on his C.B., explaining the situation to the dispatcher. Ten minutes later the back-up arrived in the form of two other
campus security men, and the four of us cautiously climbed the stairs,
me coming a distant last. Clubs drawn, the three campus cops rushed
through the secretary's office and into mine. The Wild Man was not
there.

Jaime stuck his stick back into his belt and one of the other men
replaced his can of mace in its sheath. Then we heard noises from one

of the other offices. It sounded like a man was singing, but off-key and in a low whisper.

Jaime crept down the hallway, stuck his head into the other office, then silently reversed his steps.

"He's in there," he whispered to his fellow officers.

Jaime and his two friends were big men. They got the Wild Man from either side and from behind and carried him down the stairs. Luís did not resist. He stared straight ahead as they carried him away, one hand still clutching a fistful of papers.

By the time I straightened up my office, the dean's meeting had already begun. There were six people sitting around the conference table in his large office. I recognized Hector the baseball coach, the new English teacher, and one of the math teachers, although I couldn't remember his name. The dean sat at the head of the table, flanked by the director of institutional research.

"What we have here is a Vietnam vet who needs our fullest cooperation," the dean said, motioning me with one hand to take a seat in an empty chair.

"The guy's a nutcase," said Hector in a disgusted voice. "He threatens to kill me two different times in one day. He attacks me in the gym, for chrissakes, right in front of my players. I thought they were going to beat him to death. The guy's a nut and, on top of that, stupid. Nobody threatens a baseball coach in front of his goddamn team." Hector's face began to turn red, his anger overwhelming him.

"Easy, Coach," said the dean, interrupting. "We've got to realize that this student needs our fullest attention and understanding. Maybe he's got some problems, but who doesn't these days? We'll work with him towards solving them, help him find where he belongs. We can't kick the man out into the cold. The mission of this college is to serve the entire community and Váldez is part of the community."

The director of institutional research shifted his considerable bulk, nodding his head as the dean spoke. The director fancied himself a psychologist and often served in that capacity at TSC but, in fact, lacked the appropriate degree and state license to practice.

"The guy is out of his bloody mind," I said, jumping in. "My students are afraid to come to class. I'm not stepping foot in that classroom till the man is gone."

"Are you now a psychologist, Dr. Maril?" the dean asked me.

"No," I said, beginning to lose control. "But as far as I know, there are no real psychologists sitting at this table. This guy is really dangerous. You don't have to be an expert to see the obvious. Have you even talked to this guy?" I asked the dean, knowing that he hadn't.

Hector the baseball coach had turned an apple-red. The English teacher, when asked, said she hadn't been threatened by the Wild Man, but that she was concerned because only three out of twenty-five students had come to her class. The math teacher, perhaps seeing the writing on the wall, didn't say a word.

The dean ignored us. He read a few sentences from a paper in front of him. Luís Abelardo Váldez would be asked to see a TSC career counselor and if, in the judgment of the career counselor, it was warranted, then Luís would be referred to a private psychologist for preliminary tests.

The dean really had very few options. TSC has no on-campus professional psychological services either for students, faculty, or staff. In fact, TSC for many, many years did not have any professional medical care facilities or professional medical staff on campus. Heart attack victims, attempted suicides, any and all problems fell in the lap of the TSC security officers. Passers-by did the best they could when a student went into a seizure or threatened suicide in the library. Since Brownsville's ambulances were few and very slow in response, a number of avoidable tragedies had occurred within the walls of the junior college.

"This guy is going to kill someone in the next couple of days," Hector told me after the meeting. "Two of my players told me that this Váldez is for real. They know him from before. The man is not fooling around."

As soon as I got back to my office, after first checking that the Wild Man was nowhere in the vicinity, I called up the vice-president of TSC. I explained the situation to him. He'd already heard about it, he told me, from the dean.

"We've got to go through the usual channels on this," the vice-president told me with confidence.

"Have you seen this guy yet?" I asked him, curious.

"No. But these vets are a lot alike, especially the ones who saw some action." The vice-president was career air force and had retired at the rank of colonel before joining the college.

"This guy is different, Sir," I said. "If you haven't seen him, you haven't got the full impression of the man. He's completely off his rocker. I'm not going back into my classroom until you get this guy out of here."

"Well, I'm sorry to hear that, Dr. Maril. I really am."

I went on, even though I knew I was making a permanent enemy. "I'm starting a lawsuit against you and the college as soon as I can contact my attorney. In the meantime I'm calling the *Brownsville Herald* to tell them about the situation."

"I wouldn't do that if I were you," he started. I hung up the phone, disgusted.

I never followed up on my threats but, three days later, Luíz Abelardo Váldez still made the front page of the *Brownsville Herald*. The Wild Man was arrested on felony charges for assaulting two Brownsville police officers who had been called to a downtown movie theater. The police arrived, according to the paper, to find Luís beating one of the theater ushers. Luís then assaulted both officers, sending one to the emergency room. Luís, in the process, broke his arm and, after a trip to the same hospital, was booked at the city jail.

The Wild Man made bail over the weekend and was back on the TSC campus on Monday morning. Broken arm in sling, he paced the hallway of the classroom building, eyes glazed, talking incoherently, sometimes singing his nameless tune. As he made his way through the crowded hallway, students jumped out of his path.

A campus cop, compliments of the dean, stood guard at the entrance to my classroom. His job was to keep Luís Abelardo Váldez out of my class. Meanwhile, according to the dean's fabulous plan, Luís was to be interviewed by a TSC career counselor and referred, if necessary, to a private psychologist. But Luís refused to see the career counselor. The dean held tight to his original plan, staunchly refusing to "disenroll" the Wild Man or even temporarily suspend him. I found out much later that the TSC administration was afraid Luís would sue them.

And so for a week of classes I watched the Wild Man cruise up and down the hallway just outside my classroom door, the campus security officer tensing his body every time Luís passed by. Finally, the cop told me later, Luís would visit another class just down the hall from mine. While I had dodged the bullet, at least for the moment, one of my colleagues was meeting the Wild Man for the first time.

After a week of this routine, my sociology class slowly began to return to normal. The campus cop disappeared from my classroom doorway. The Wild Man, however, still roamed the campus. Luís began hanging around the TSC Vocational School on the south side of the campus, three blocks from my office. Wherever the Wild Man went, he left a trail of havoc in his wake.

I remained very scared of the Wild Man, convinced that he would, if given the chance, do grave harm to me and my students. I began to carry a loaded gun in my briefcase to my classes, to the Student Center, to department meetings, and to the restroom. I was not alone. Several TSC teachers who still had the Wild Man on their class rolls, or had seen him on campus, also armed themselves.

Luís Abelardo Váldez never did make his appointment with the TSC career counselor. But two months after I had confronted him in my classroom, they held a sanity hearing for the Wild Man at the Cameron County Courthouse in Brownsville. Before the proceedings could officially begin, Luís Abelardo Váldez jumped up on the defense council's table and, in the words of a friend of mine who was there, "howled like a wolf." The court bailiffs struggled with Luís and eventually were able to return him to his holding cell. One of them received a minor injury and was taken to the emergency room.

The Wild Man was placed in a Valley mental institution for six months. On August 23, the first day of the fall semester, I saw him in the TSC Student Center. At first I couldn't believe my eyes. But it was Luís. His broken arm had healed, his hair was cut shorter, but it was him.

I ran back to the chairman's office to tell him the news. Henry called the registrar's office. The secretary there told us Váldez had registered and paid his full tuition. She told us that Váldez was on academic probation.

During the first week of classes three of Luís's teachers called me. They had heard that I knew something about him and, sounding relatively desperate on the phone, they each wanted quick answers. When I told them what I knew, each at first thought I was joking.

Luís the Wild Man was soon back to his usual tricks. The dean called another meeting, but I declined to attend. I didn't want to hear the same excuses made for a student who simply didn't belong on any college campus.

Luís Abelardo Váldez was not the only student who did not belong at TSC. My classes at TSC, and those of my colleagues, were the dumping grounds for young men and women who had nowhere else to go. Often they were the products of a Valley institution which had not done its job. At a time long before the "deinstitutionalization" of the mentally ill and others, TSC and the other Valley colleges were being used, however ineffectively, as holding tanks for those with severe problems.

I will not soon forget Gloria, for example, who talked constantly and in a loud voice from the first day of class. I asked her to be quiet. For about a minute she did not talk. Then she resumed her conversation with herself. I was never able to get her to stop talking although, after a week of my repeated requests, I was able to convince her to talk in a quieter voice. I lectured to my students who filled the first eight rows of the classroom, while from the twelfth row, at the very back, came the steady, but quieter, drone of the woman who could not stop talking.

Perhaps one of the saddest cases was a blind student who, the first day, barely found his way to the front row of my class, just next to the lectern. I began my normal first-day routine. Before I had gotten through a sentence, the blind student raised his hand.

"I can't hear you," he said.

"I'm talking as loud as I can," I said, surprised.

"What?" he said. Then, "I can't hear you."

The blind and deaf student had just been released from an institution and had been immediately enrolled at TSC. His new hearing aid awaited a check from the government which was "in the mail" but hadn't arrived. Nevertheless, blind and deaf, they had sent him to TSC in a cab.

There were others, some serious, some who just sat absolutely silent in class week after week, eyes forward, comprehending little in their institutionally drugged state. Then one day they would not come and I would never see them again.

Luís Abelardo Váldez made the front page of the *Brownsville Herald* one last time. A year and a half after his first classes at TSC, he drove his car into a palm tree that stood to the side of State Highway 48, just outside the Brownsville city limits. He was driving at a high rate of speed, according to the newspaper. The Wild Man was slammed against the steering column of the vehicle, while his passenger was thrown through the windshield of the car. Both were instantly killed.

La Boca

Rubén Manuel Hidalgo, Jr., had a mouth, *la boca*, that would not quit. Often La Boca began talking even before I had a chance to unload my briefcase at the podium.

"Okay," he said, clearing the air, "what you're saying in so many words is that poor people in this country are always getting messed around with just because of the fact they are poor." He waved his hands about, awkwardly emphasizing his point.

"Right," I said. "That results in what is called 'blaming the victim,' what we talked about last class." I looked around the room at the twenty other faces, some listening, some not. A large portion of the class was composed of TSC's baseball team, currently on a twelve-game winning streak.

"So, that's got to be happening right here in the Valley, now, right under our noses?" he asked.

"Yes."

"So why isn't anyone doing something about these injustices? If it's as bad as you say it is, then why don't the people in Austin or Washington, D.C., help us?" Rubén shrugged his shoulders into a question mark, unconsciously passed his left hand through his dark, wavy hair, and waited for an answer.

"That's a big part of the problem," I said, noticing that the starting left fielder and the catcher, both of whom regularly camped out on the back row, were beginning to look interested. The catcher was the key. If I could get him involved, usually the rest of the line-up followed. The catcher's hand shot into the air.

The bell rang fifty minutes later. By then Rubén was reaching full stride, his passion vacuuming in the attention of the baseball team and the non-jocks, too. No one in the room had kept silent, some joining Rubén's side, others more cautious, a few derisive.

As I stuffed my notes and books back into my briefcase, already late for the next class down the hall, Rubén walked over to the TSC baseball team which was informally huddled around their catcher. La Boca high-fived it all around, then went at them a final time in rapid-fire Spanish, his finger pointing at the sociology text between pauses in his verbal assault. Still smiling, talking, he left the classroom, giving me a big wink as he passed by.

Ten seconds later he was back again.

"I think I've about got them convinced," he said triumphantly; then he was out the door a final time, down the hall, into his next class.

Not surprisingly, Rubén Manuel Hidalgo, Jr., became involved in campus politics. He regularly attended TSC Board of Trustee meetings, meetings usually crowded with TSC administrators, faculty, staff, and sales reps seeking vendor contracts with the college. He kept a tight eye on the budget and soon noticed several disturbing trends. He remarked, in front of a hushed room, that TSC administrators seemed to be very well-paid when compared with the state average, while faculty and staff were far below those of other similar insititutions.

A short time later La Boca zoomed in on TSC's president, questioning the wisdom of granting him a five-thousand-dollar annual car allowance on top of his hefty salary. Before the usually complacent crowd, La Boca noted that the president of TSC received more in one year to operate his car than many in the Valley took home to feed, clothe, and house their families.

When the vice-president of TSC roundly criticized Rubén for what he characterized as Rubén's "inappropriate remarks," Rubén questioned the necessity of the vice-president's own annual thirty-five-hundred-dollar car allowance. The reporter for the *Brownsville Herald* recorded the exchange, which appeared in the next day's paper. Rubén became mini-famous in Brownsville.

Rubén left that summer for Austin and the University of Texas. He planned to finish his undergraduate degree in sociology, then get a master's degree there. He promised me that he would return to the Valley to "raise some hell." In passing, he mentioned that his marriage was rocky and that a change of scenery would do his family some good. La Boca had never lived outside the Valley and was anxious to experience the rest of the world. Austin, he told me, would be just the right place.

Rubén was back again in Brownsville by Christmas of that same year. He hated Austin, missed his Valley family and friends. His wife had divorced him that fall. Rubén was happy about the divorce, but he deeply regretted that his wife would not let him see his young son.

A few weeks later La Boca stopped by my office to talk. I asked him about his grades at the University of Texas.

"Straight D's and F's," he said.

"Were the courses really that hard?" I asked.

"No. But the competition was incredible. And I wasn't able to keep up with all the reading they assigned. There were research papers for each course and the tests were difficult. But I'm not making excuses for myself. It's a different world there in Austin. It's an Anglo world. I never could seem to get my head into it. Most of the people were very cold, like you didn't exist or something."

Rubén's story did not surprise me. Few of even my best students managed to last more than a year at a college or university outside the Valley. There were exceptions, but only a handful. Most who tried soon returned to the Valley discouraged, often having lost their self-confidence. They frequently complained about feeling alone and isolated in the Anglo culture.

Hunched over in my office chair, Rubén looked as if he had hit rock bottom. In less than four months he had flunked out of college, lost his wife and child, and had his self-confidence severely challenged. He was also out of work.

I seriously underestimated Rubén's resilience. He soon re-enrolled at TSC and graduated in the spring with an associate's degree. Wasting no time, he enrolled for six summer courses at Pan American University–Brownsville (PAUB). He found a part-time job at one of the convenience stores, putting in thirty-five hours a week. During the times between rushes, he pulled out his textbooks and read his assignments.

Rubén also started using *la boca* again, with increasing success. He appeared at a public hearing to discuss raises in Brownsville's utility rates. He eloquently defended the interests of the elderly poor and, for his efforts, got thirty seconds of air time on the six o'clock news. Again his name appeared in the Valley newspapers, this time in recognition of his fight to get indigent patients better treatment in Valley emergency rooms.

Rubén's oratorical skills continued to improve as did his knowledge of political strategies. Not infrequently he tried them out on his PAUB professors.

". . . then the prof stands there and says that Mexican Americans always test in the lowest percentile because the tests are culturally biased. Right?"

I nodded my head and ate another chunk off my flour tortilla.

"So I raise my hand. He ignores me for a few more minutes. He knows I'm going to challenge what he's been talking about. See, I know what he's trying to do is find excuses for the public schools by blaming the tests. Everyone around here is always looking for excuses for the schools. But I keep my hand in the air there, and finally he has to call on me or it makes him look bad. I ask him why Brownsville students are still testing badly when Princeton Educational Testing Service has spent millions of dollars to make the tests culturally unbiased. I mean, are those guys complete jerks or what? Of course they're not, no way. So I had him."

"What did he say?" I asked.

"He didn't say anything. Just looked at me funny, like I was intentionally making things hard for him. But then I could see he was thinking about it my way, maybe for the first time. The prof isn't dumb. I mean, we'd just got through talking about how bad the schools' test scores were last year, so he couldn't deny the facts. I asked him how come the Brownsville public schools spend one hundred million dollars a year and still our kids can't read or write."

"And?" I said, actually feeling a little sorry for his professor.

"He says, 'Rubén, you ought to run for the School Board.' That's what he said."

La Boca learned how to pressure welfare supervisors to cut through red tape. He learned how to urge Valley politicians to make the right decisions, decisions which made them look good to their voters, but decisions which they would never have made without Rubén's phone calls, letters to the editor of the newspaper, and frequent speeches at hearings and public meetings.

La Boca gradually developed his own style of public speaking and political strategies, a style which worked best for him. His delivery and presence were confrontational, streetwise, but filled with facts that others could understand. What he said often made sense to many of the poor who had grown tired of the same old political promises at election time.

Rubén also developed a patience that served him well. He became known by those who ran the Valley political machines as a legitimate rival, one who was rational, willing to make compromises, carried weight with the voting public.

Even so, Rubén did not get away scot-free. He paid a price for rocking the political boat in the Valley. No one would hire him when he graduated from PAUB with a master's degree in history and certification to teach in the public schools. At a time when Valley schools were forced, because of a local shortage of teachers, to conduct national searches to find qualified teachers, Rubén was systematically ignored. There was no official blacklist, but the word was out about Rubén.

After months of searching Rubén eventually found part-time work at a state-run poverty agency. In a year's time he worked himself into a full-time position as a counselor in the program. He again began speaking his mind, airing his political agenda at public hearings, often making the six and ten o'clock news.

Rubén married a woman from Matamoros and started a new family. He was a fourth-generation American. His great-grandfather had fought in the Mexican Revolution and, when only seventeen, crossed the Rio Grande to escape the chaos of that violent political upheaval.

At twenty-six years of age Rubén Manual Hidalgo, Jr., recrossed the Rio Grande, moving into a small house that his father-in-law owned in a Matamoros neighborhood three miles from the New Bridge. He joined the many Mexican nationals who crossed the bridge each morning to work in Brownsville and the surrounding area, then struggled back across the stream at the end of the day.

Rubén bought his clothes in Matamoros stores and began sporting a new mustache, which his Mexican barber trimmed twice a week. He openly bragged about how much money he was saving by living in Matamoros; he was paid in dollars and, as inflation continued to sky-rocket in Matamoros, his slim American wages increased in value relative to the Mexican peso. He became more fluent in Spanish, which he now used more frequently. His views on Valley politics deepened as he continued to live and raise a family in Matamoros.

After two years, Rubén again crossed the Rio Grande, this time with his new wife and two babies. He settled in a modest middle-class apartment complex on the north side of Brownsville. I asked him why he moved back to the United States.

"It was time," he told me. "I learned what it was like to be Mexican, and it was time to remember who I really am. I'm a Chicano. Besides, I got damn tired of the traffic on that bridge."

Rubén was now the assistant director of the poverty agency. He was thinking hard about going to law school in San Antonio, but wanted to wait another year or two until his youngest child started school. He worried that his wife, who was having difficulty adjusting to life in the Valley, would find it hard to live in a large American city like San Antonio. Rubén believed, however, that family sacrifices would, in the long run, be worth the effort.

"What will you do when you get your law degree?" I asked Rubén when I unexpectedly ran into him and his family in a Harlingen restaurant. Rubén Manuel Hidalgo, Jr., leaned back in his chair, carefully balancing his toddler on his right knee. For once he was strangely quiet. No words came, no well-rehearsed rhetoric, nothing. La Boca just smiled.

Humberto and His Rocks

"Rocks," said Humberto Guadalupe Valdez, president of Texas Southmost College. He gestured grandly around his large desk.

"Rocks?" I answered back, puzzled.

"They can tell you everything. You just have to listen to what they say," he continued.

President Humberto leaned back in his large leather executive's chair. He was short, overweight, balding, and liked to dress in cheap suits. Despite a well-publicized five-thousand-dollar-a-year car allowance, soundly critiqued by La Boca and duly trumpeted by the local media, Humberto drove a fifteen-year-old, rusted-out Chevy Nova. Humberto, as many called him at TSC, was fond of pointing to his trash heap on wheels, which he carefully parked each morning in his reserved parking space, to remind his companions of the moment of his humble Brownsville roots. His wife, however, drove a forty-thousand-dollar Mercedes. Humberto was no one's fool.

I stood forewarned of Humberto's tendency to hand out tirades on the nature and meaning of compressed dirt. I was determined to indulge Humberto, then to escape at the soonest possible chance.

"You know the García family?" Humberto asked me, shifting his considerable bulk in his president's chair.

"Which one?" I asked. There were thousands of Garcías in Brownsville.

"The ones that live over next to the zoo. You know, in that big white house that sits just back from Boca Chica. The one with the pillars. It's got burglar bars on it and a new sprinkler system. They had to dig up the whole yard to put the thing in. I hear it works real good. Steve García and I were roommates at Texas A&M after the War. World War Two. Shoot, I think we were about the first Mexican Americans those Aggies ever set their eyes on."

"Sir," I hestitated, "I wanted to tell you about the grant that I got." I knew that there was no stopping Humberto once he warmed to one of his stories.

"Right. Well, Steve and I had some good times our freshman year at College Station. You used to have to take the train to get there. We were just green kids from the Valley, didn't know a hoot about anything. And here we were with all these Anglos who were smart as whips. I mean, those guys knew their stuff. But there was never any question in my mind. It was always geology, from the very beginning. I've never regretted it, not one day. I wouldn't have seen most of Mexico and a good part of South America without my degrees in geology."

Humberto palmed the nearest chunk of hard earth from the pile of small boulders that covered his desk, appraising it carefully, fondly. With his other hand he unconsciously straightened his tie around his thick neck, then shifted once more in his high-backed chair.

I felt helpless before the avalanche.

"Do you know what this is?" he asked in a friendly way.

"No, sir, I don't." The rocks looked all the same to me, although some were obviously of different colors, shapes, and sizes. I had been told that for every rock on his desk there was at least one, maybe more, story that accompanied it. I settled back into my chair, waiting like Indiana Jones for the first boulder to roll down the trail.

"I picked this one up right off the ground, in plain view if a person knew what to look for. Right there on the jungle floor, between this little vine and the roots of a tree. Couldn't be more than ten hours by car from where we sit right here. A real jungle down there, tropical rain forest. Me and Tommy LeFont. You know Tommy? Old Brownsville family. His father was a lawyer for a long time with White and Whitney. Tommy walked right by it, but it caught my eye as soon as I saw it. It's chalcopyrite. Fool's gold to the common man. Very obvious that it's not the real thing, but only to the trained eye. The average guy, he might think he'd discovered a lost gold mine right smack in the middle of that Mexican jungle." Humberto chuckled to himself, remembering.

I waited, assuming that a moral to the story, or at least a metaphor, was just around the corner. Neither emerged.

"But you don't want to talk about rocks, Lee. I know that. Rocks are boring to the average person unless they've studied them like I have." Humberto paused. Sensing perhaps my only chance, I seized the moment as best I could.

"Sir, I'm going to be starting a research project in three weeks about Valley shrimpers. With money from Texas A&M University. I should get the official word in writing in another week or so."

"Wonderfull, Lee, just great. Keep up the work. Great institution. I'm proud to have my degrees from them. See here on the wall. A B.S. and a master's, both in geology. I made a good living from those pieces of paper. You get used to the Aggie jokes. They're all in fun, no harm to them."

Humberto told me three Aggie jokes in quick succession. Then he discoursed on two more rocks he pulled from the pile on his desk. Finally, close to an hour having passed slowly by, I excused myself and returned to my office to recover. I didn't care one iota about chunks of granite, chalcopyrite, sandstone, and all the other pieces of earth. It was all just dirt to me, pieces of very old dirt.

Humberto felt more at home with his rocks than he did discussing the management of a junior college like TSC. After working many years as a professional geologist, Humberto had taught math in the Brownsville high schools and, on a part time basis, at TSC. Rumor had it that he was a first-rate math teacher. Then he became a supervisor for a federally funded poverty program in the mid–nineteen seventies.

Humberto had strong ties to the Valley's political patronage system. He was the first cousin of the superintendent of the Brownsville public school system, arguably the most influential person in town because of the budget and personnel he commanded. Humberto's roommate at Texas A&M was a prominent member of TSC's board of trustees. Humberto, despite his reputation as a mediocre administrator and without a terminal degree in his field, was, nevertheless, selected from a large pool of more qualified candidates. That's how it had always been in Brownsville, and that's how it had always been at TSC.

To the surprise of his detractors, Humberto turned out to be a reasonable head administrator at TSC. He was smart enough to surround himself with competent people in whom he put his trust. He left the daily operation of TSC to his hirelings, while he worked at what he did best. Humberto knew Brownsville and Valley politics inside and out. For eight years he wheeled and dealed from his office and his old car, in the best tradition of the streetwise politico.

Humberto hired a grant writer who began churning out a large number of state and federal grant proposals. Proposals in hand, Humberto pounded the pavement in Austin and Washington, D.C., often returning with fistfuls of dollars from agencies and programs happy to invest in a poor Mexican-American college on the Border. With these monies Humberto started new programs in TSC's vocational and academic divisions. He raised faculty and staff salaries for the first time in many years, bringing faculty salaries more into line with other state junior colleges. Humberto encouraged local business leaders to participate in the decision making at the vocational school. He hired consultants to analyze the strengths and weaknesses of the institution.

Humberto had his enemies, and for good reason. State and federal monies were thrown at programs that, realistically, could never be expected to work. Staff were hired based upon personal friendship rather than professional merit. One of Humberto's first administrative decisions, in fact, was to hire five of his best Brownsville friends as deans at TSC. In order to accomplish this feat, Humberto had to create several new deanships. Humberto's critics referred to this action as Humberto's deanorama.

In the meantime, high-profile functionaries from Austin and Washington beat their way to Humberto's office door. Humberto toured them around Brownsville and the Valley. They were lodged at a condo on South Padre Island, shopped at the *mercado* in Matamoros, and fed in Brownsville's and Matamoros's best restaurants. When the visitors left, they carried with them armfuls of colorful Mexican curios for the folks back home.

One of Humberto's undeniable liabilities was his temper. He could explode, dumping his invective on whoever happened to be in the vicinity. When a reporter from the *Brownsville Herald* irked Humberto with the wrong question, Humberto cursed her and had her unceremoniously escorted from his office. To be sure, Humberto stuck his foot in his mouth on more than a few times. He couldn't give a coherent speech if his life depended on it, even though he had an articulate assistant write his speeches. Humberto never stuck to the text before him, preferring to tell little stories, jokes, or other tales that led nowhere.

Several months after my first "talk" with Humberto, I made, with some hesitancy, another appointment with his secretary to see him.

"I got this in the mail last week and thought you might like it," I said modestly, taking a seat in front of the rock pile in his office. I handed him the package.

"It was taken from the old Aggie geology building just before it was torn down," I went on.

Humberto removed the brown wrapping paper from the piece of concrete and hefted the rock fondly in his hand. He smiled at it, no doubt awash in old memories of years gone by. I excused myself thirty minutes later, after several Aggie jokes and a long, extended remembrance of his senior year at Texas A&M. My hope was that I had given him back a small piece of what he had given me. At TSC Humberto was constantly supportive of my research efforts, even though I knew what I was doing was completely foreign to him.

Humberto gradually fell out of favor in Brownsville. For eight years, each fall semester was rumored to be his last as president. Finally, however, Humberto lost his control over the majority of the TSC trustees when a disgruntled former employee successfully ran and won with a slate of anti-Humberto candidates. Humberto gamely clung to his position as president, despite the increasing criticism from various quarters. He finessed his way around disputes that would have sunk lesser men. Wiley as an old fox, he secured a long-term contract from the old TSC board just before the elections for new board members.

The new board quickly decided to demand Humberto's resignation at its next monthly meeting. Public opinion was heavily on their side. No amount of outside grant monies or other achievements could hide some of the flaws of Humberto's administration at TSC. Humberto's deans kept getting into trouble. The college's physical plant showed years of benign neglect; roofs leaked, the air conditioning in the library didn't work properly, and the paint peeled off classroom walls. Faculty morale was low. The list of problems was a long one.

Humberto got wind of the planned coup by the trustees. He alerted his supporters in the community, who flooded the usually tranquil board meeting with a sea of signs depicting President Humberto's achievements. The media showed up, eager to capture the bloodbath on film. No fools, the new trustees, unwilling to make Humberto a martyr, insisted on a private session with President Humberto. Their plan, since revealed, was to listen to Humberto's plea for mercy, then fire him.

The ambulance was called only a few minutes after the private session got underway. Humberto, in the midst of his own defense to save his honor, dramatically collapsed in a heap upon the tile floor. Amid the chaos which soon followed, he was carried on a stretcher through the stunned crowd of his supporters who were awaiting the outcome of the private session. Oxygen mask covering his worn face, television cameras rolling, sirens at full blast, the ambulance whisked Humberto away to the hospital.

The new TSC trustees were left to face the angry crowd who blamed them for their president's heart attack. The unfounded criticism from the new trustees, it was said by Humberto's supporters, had been too much for their president to handle. New-found sympathy miraculously arose from the ashes of Humberto's heart attack and spread throughout the city.

In one very timely swoon Humberto sealed his financial future. Common decency compelled the new trustees to buy out the remainder of Humberto's long-term contract with no attempt to negotiate the price tag. Humberto, who made a quick recovery from his heart attack, walked away with $350,000 in cash from his job as president of TSC.

One year later Humberto was back on campus to register for a real estate course. Ex-President Humberto made his traditional rounds of the faculty who were busy working registration. He fondly embraced his old friends and former employees, ignored his enemies, smiled constantly. He looked tan and very fit as he shook my hand warmly, asked me how my research was progressing, then patted me on the shoulder as he passed on to greet another teacher.

Humberto earned a realtor's license and began selling condos on South Padre Island. Not long ago, with little public fanfare, he ran for a position on the TSC board of trustees, the same board that had witnessed his swoon into permanent financial security. Humberto lost the community-wide election, but by less than two hundred votes.

I have little doubt that Humberto Guadalupe Valdez, or one of his close associates who speaks for him, will soon be back in the political spotlight. Beneath the buffoonish exterior Humberto was, like many Valley politicos, as hard as his beloved rocks.

Arnoldo

My Korean thongs made a sucking, mushy sound as I plodded through the muddy salt flat. Already an eleven o'clock sun was marking the back of my neck, just below my gimme cap. I took another bite of the Milky Way for some instant energy, then gazed at Arnoldo's rusted-out car, now glowing in the distant shimmer between the beach and the Laguna Madre. I thought of the pleasures of a big glass of ice tea or a cold beer, then took a swallow of tepid canteen water from my belt.

Arnoldo, twenty feet to my left, crouched low again on his thin haunches, collecting bottle in one hand, homemade butterfly net in the other. His dark eyes, set deep into his long face, showed little as he unwrapped the folds of the white net to reveal a fragile black fly.

With a practiced hand he maneuvered the insect into his glass collecting bottle and plugged it with a rubber stopper. He carefully replaced the bottle in his green knapsack, then asked me for a drink from my canteen. His words floated lazily over the empty mud flats, breaking a thirty-minute silent pursuit.

Arnoldo and I had spent most of the morning fly hunting on South Padre Island. Since the sun had risen over the waves of the Gulf of Mexico at six after six, Arnoldo had added twenty-four specimens to his bottles. Every hour or so he would stop in his muddy tracks, pour a pinch of liquid ether onto a cotton swatch, cram the cotton into his killing jar, then resume the stalk.

I was glad to be out on the mud flats when the sun rose. I didn't regret rising in the dark from my bed at 4:45 to stumble over to Arnoldo's house. We drank hot coffee from his plastic thermos as we drove through the quiet streets of Brownsville, then caught State Highway 48, the Wild Man's final road, to South Padre Island. The two lanes wove past the silent rusting hulks of the freighters permanently docked at Port Brownsville, past the tank farms, the fleet of shrimp boats, and the grain silos.

I had made fun, again, of Arnoldo's car, what he called his "fishing machine."

"Did you remember to wind up the ducks?" I asked him, referring to his rebuilt engine. In response, Arnoldo floored the accelerator of his green 1962 Plymouth Valiant and we slowly reached maximum cruising speed of forty-two miles an hour. Solitary cars came speeding out of the shadows behind us, zooming by in micro-seconds. Arnoldo finally steered his rusting Plymouth to the shoulder, where we motored along at our stately speed.

But now, as twelve noon approached, my baked neck, shoulders, and back demanded a break. All the tiny creatures that Arnoldo so intensely sought had, for me, long since lost their uniqueness. Indistinguishable minutiae of wings, legs, and bulging eyes, they fell onto their backs at the first whiff of gas, exposing a predictable brownish underbelly. They dropped like flies.

"I need lunch," I told Arnoldo, "and a cold drink and a soft chair."

"No problem," he said, eyes to the mud.

"This is not meant as a criticism," I said, "but catching flies is really boring."

"Most people find it boring. But don't worry about it, that's just what you have to do if you're an entomologist. For me, it's very relaxing, takes my mind off things."

We slowly circled back towards the fishing machine, Arnoldo frequently pausing to check on the flies that grazed the mud under our feet. He had a pattern that he was following, but I had long since given up trying to determine his method. If he found a certain subspecies of fly within a certain space, then he got excited and tried to capture it. When successful, he shouted out a victory yell, but when an insect escaped, his frustrated curses hounded it across the mud and shallow bay waters.

No one heard Arnoldo's yells of victory or my pleas to stop for lunch. We were three miles north of where Highway 100 turns into sand dunes, sea oats, and stretches of vista that extend all the way to Corpus Christi, one hundred and twenty miles to the north. Far from the sunbathers and the fishermen, we had the cracked mud, large sky, and flies all to ourselves. Or practically ourselves; we'd already spotted three coyotes that, seeing us, quickly disappeared into the dunes.

"Tell me one more time why you are doing this," I said as we finally stood once more in front of Arnoldo's fishing machine. I was busy climbing out of my gear and searching for the Solarcaine. I was looking for a rational explanation for spending six hours walking in large mud and salt circles.

"You've gotta remember that these flies are a special kind. They appear only during certain times of the year. If they don't appear every year at about the same time, then something is wrong in the food chain. Something is getting screwed up so that the flies didn't develop the right way. Think of the flies like canaries in a coal mine. If there is a significant decline in their number, then bad things are happening."

"Like what?" I asked, spraying my neck and shoulders with the Solarcaine, reveling in the temporary relief it gave. My knowledge of basic biology went as far as my freshman class in college. I thought hard to remember the professor's name, but all that came to mind was a frayed image of her stained lab coat.

"Probably pesticides, but that will take a lot more work to determine. See, the Valley farmers and growers spray their crops and groves with the stuff. Then rain washes it off into the Arroyo Colorado. Eventually it all ends up here in the Laguna Madre in the water and the mud, in the flora and the fauna. It kills the fly larvae. At least that's what I think is happening. Two more years of data and I'll be able to prove it one way or the other."

Arnoldo pulled a small notebook from his pack as soon as we reached Highway 100. He explained to me how he had divided South Padre Island into sections. At exactly the same time each year he collected flies in each of his sections.

"Next week I'm going to cover the area down by the Coast Guard

Station. I haven't collected there for six months," he said as we finally reached the restaurant. I could already feel the ice tea as it made its way down my parched throat.

Arnoldo Luna was a good friend and someone whose company I enjoyed, even if it meant hunting flies. Arnoldo was also the best teacher at Texas Southmost College, possessing a rare blend of professional competence and compassion for those around him.

The next Tuesday I ran into Arnoldo in the college cafeteria. By then my sunburn was under control and the back of my legs had stopped aching at night. I was halfway into a plate-sized flour tortilla when he sat down beside me. Wordless, we chewed silently on our lunches. When the student approached, Arnoldo nodded a greeting.

"Dr. Luna," she began without hestitation, "I had to take my mother to the hospital yesterday and that's why I missed your test. Should I take a make-up on it, or what?"

For a brief moment Arnoldo eyed her closely over his flour tortilla, using the delay to make her uncomfortable. She expected Arnoldo to make a special set of arrangements for her because of her sick mother, something Arnoldo would usually do. The student began to fidget.

Arnoldo put down his lunch, carefully wiped his face with a paper napkin, then sighed heavily.

"You know, Isabela," he said firmly but with no trace of harshness in his voice, "I just saw your mother at the K-Mart yesterday. I had a nice long conversation with her. She didn't look very sick to me. Of course, I could be mistaken. If you want me to, I'll give your father a call and we can clear all this up in a minute."

Isabela blushed deeply, stammered an apologetic answer, then disappeared into the cafeteria crowd.

"I think Isabela's mother is going to make a quick recovery," Arnoldo said, returning to his lunch.

Arnoldo had a reputation at TSC as a tough, no-nonsense teacher who taught the most difficult courses. Two semesters of biology were required and, if you didn't pass them, you didn't graduate from TSC. Biology was very foreign to TSC students, the majority of whom were trained in Brownsville and Valley public high schools. These students entered TSC with very little preparation to do well in a college-level biology course. But while other sections during TSC registration were slow to fill, Arnoldo's biology classes were usually closed by noon of the first day. The word about Arnoldo got around fast: he was tough, but fair in his teaching and, even more importantly, he had a way of making the material interesting.

Arnoldo had done it the hard way. He made it through the Brownsville system of public education, his pride and confidence intact. There'd been one science teacher who spotted Arnoldo's talent, befriended him, guided him through high school. The Brownsville schools, Arnoldo told me, were easy to get through, in fact were in many ways too easy. The real trick was to learn something, to not waste time in the endless activities, including classes, that were often little more than daily entertainments.

With the encouragement of his mother, Arnoldo worked hard in high school. He took the few college-prep courses that were offered, spent one summer at a special program at the University of Texas.

When Arnoldo finally entered TSC in 1967, he was one of the rare students who was prepared for the college curriculum. At that time TSC was still run by Anglos. In the pre-Humberto days, there was an all-Anglo administration, and there were very few Mexican-American teachers. There were strict entrance requirements which eliminated many Mexican Americans; those who survived freshman biology, British lit, and a stiff math course were few and far between. Even though Brownsville was ninety percent Mexican American, the majority of TSC's student body in the late 1960s was Anglo.

Arnoldo made himself an exception. He graduated with honors from TSC and earned a full scholarship to the University of Texas. In Austin he majored in biology, again graduating with honors. He was offered scholarships from several different universities and, upon the recommendation of his TSC biology teacher, finally selected the University of Pennsylvania.

Ph.D. in hand, Arnoldo had his pick of employers. He was actively recruited, finally settling on a major university in the Southeast. But he soon grew dissatisfied.

"The students were so spoiled there. Not as bad as the ones at Penn, but still very spoiled, real brats. They were all affluent and had everything they could want. But they still bitched all the time like a bunch of cry babies. My parents worked hard, but we never had much to go around. But you wouldn't hear us complaining about it. You wouldn't hear my brothers or sisters saying they didn't have this or didn't have that. For one thing, my mother would have slapped us on the head for complaining.

"Every one of us has gone to college and every one of us owes it to my parents. They were the ones that stood by us, saw us through the hard times. I owe them and I also owe my chemistry teacher from high school."

"Have you told your teacher?" I asked, curious.

"Damn right I have. The man is unique. Besides me, there are at least five others I know of that he's helped. Two went to Harvard."

In 1978 Arnoldo and his new wife moved back to Brownsville.

"I sat there one day in my office at this other university and realized that here I was earning a big salary, looking soon at a promotion, maybe eventually chair of the department, and I was the only Mexican American in sight. Me and this other guy in the history department. Two out of four hundred and eight. Can you believe that? I was just a token. So why should I sit there taking their money and satisfying their Affirmative Action Program when I missed my parents, my brothers and sisters, cousins, all of them. I wanted to raise my own kids here, not in some Anglo culture in the middle of a university community. Brownsville may not be heaven, but it's the real world, not artificial, not a Disneyland."

It was a long, long way from a big-time university to a small junior college on the Texas border. I asked Arnoldo if he missed the university life.

"What's to miss? The students here need me. It's that simple. I know them, know what they are feeling. I know they are afraid of failing. I know that if they fail, like they've been programmed to do, then they have to go back to their parents and explain it. Their parents know that if their children don't make it in college, they'll be pushing a broom the rest of their lives. There's pressure on these kids, lots of pressure.

"I use that pressure. I tell them to stop making excuses for themselves. I tell them that if they fail a course, then they take it again, and again. Whatever is necessary. Sometimes I yell at them. But they don't walk away from me because they know why I'm yelling at them."

Arnoldo made the best of a bad situation. His biology students couldn't read their lab manual so he rewrote it to their level. He scavenged materials for his classes, begged and borrowed equipment, wrote grants to improve the curriculum, developed new experiments with specimens he dragged in from the beach. Arnoldo had the patience to fight through the institutional red tape to get what he wanted. Year after year he worked small wonders. He had his big successes, his bright students who eventually graduated from Harvard and Yale, but it was the small successes in whom he took the most pride. It was the student who learned enough biology to keep from flunking out of TSC, or the surfer who took a new interest in the ecology of the beach, or the housewife who learned basic principles of nutrition.

At the same time, Arnoldo was plagued with a number of minor faults, inconsistencies. He secretly detested one of the TSC administrators. Arnoldo also could not tolerate any signs of recalcitrance in his biology students. He was particularly driven to distraction by students who ignored scholarships and other educational opportunities that were offered them.

"Jesus H. Christ," he yelled at his office wall one afternoon. "You should have seen what Lupita Medrono just turned down. I mean, it was a total free ride to Texas A&M, no strings attached. She wouldn't have to spend one cent of her own money for two years. But no, she has the hots for some Pedro and she won't leave the Valley without him. Pedro stays so Lupita stays. So she'll wind up working as a checkout girl at the grocery store for the rest of her life . . . if she's lucky. And Pedro, he'll promise her the moon, but leave her in three months. Shit, sometimes Mexican Americans are just plain stupid!"

He then listed for me the scholarships and other incentives that his best students had recently ignored. The situation infuriated him.

"Sometimes I think that it's too easy for them these days, too easy for the really bright ones. They think that because of the color of the skin the recruiters owe them something. They don't know that getting the money is the easy part. The hard part is doing the work, trying to live in an Anglo culture that doesn't really care if you succeed or fail. I tell them, but they have to experience it for themselves, even the smartest ones."

"You're going to get an ulcer worrying about it," I cautioned my friend.

"I've already got one," Arnoldo admitted for the first time.

Several years later, I developed my own stomach problems.

However, I still felt that I was always twenty steps behind Arnoldo. Whether we were hunting flies, drinking beers in a cantina in Matamoros, fishing for speckled trout in the surf off Padre Island, teaching reluctant college students, or comparing notes on our upper-tract gastrointestinal X rays, I was always just getting to a new place, only to find that Arnoldo had been there for some time.

Arnoldo was in fine tune with the Valley, with its insects, its sweaty heat. He knew the fibers at the deep core of the mesquite as well as he knew the hearts of the people whose rhythms beat under a steaming Valley sun.

Berta

Much of Texas Southmost College sits on the parade grounds of Fort Brown, a former frontier bastion erected by Zachary Taylor in the 1840s to keep Mexicans on the south side of the Rio Grande. Its twenty acres of land lay directly adjacent to the banks of the river, a stone's throw from Matamoros. Each day I looked out the window of my new office on the second story of the TSC Administration Building, formerly the infirmary for the officers stationed at Fort Brown, and enjoyed my view of the bridge which spanned the Rio Grande, its wide steel arches fronting the skyline of Matamoros.

When I first moved into my TSC office, I spent an afternoon hammering picture nails into the painted brick walls, the pitted baked rock more than a foot thick in many places. I hung a small watercolor of a Valley shrimp boat on the east wall of my office, next to the large wood-framed window that looked directly down into the shaded brick courtyard below. Students often sat on one of the three cement benches in the courtyard where they held hands, talked softly to each other, kissed. The courtyard was bordered on one side by Fort Brown's morgue, now converted to a small campus post office. Fifteen feet from the young lovers, behind a red poinsettia on the south side of the stone-walled morgue, a metal plaque pronounced the modest building as the site of the first experiments to cure malaria.

I pushed and shoved two large wooden bookcases into place to cover the two office walls that were made of cheap paneled siding. The officer's infirmary, originally one large open room with windows on all sides to catch the breeze, had been unceremoniously chopped into three offices, a wide hallway, and an entry area and small office for the secretary.

During my lunch break I often walked across International Boulevard to eat at one of the many small downtown Brownsville restaurants. When I needed a change, I met friends or family for lunch at García's or the Drive Inn Restaurant in Matamoros. Sometimes I drove the mile to the restaurant "*en el otro lado,*" but soon I took to walking, enjoying the sights as I crossed the Rio Grande to lunch in another country.

Teaching at TSC, a community junior college then with an enrollment of about five thousand, was a new and challenging experience. I taught five, sometimes six, sociology courses each semester for more than ten years. In practice that meant I spent much of my time at TSC in the classroom, most of the balance grading papers. For several years I also moonlighted at Pan American University–Brownsville (PAUB), a small upper-division university which shared the campus with TSC.

I met Berta in the summer of 1977, my second year at TSC. She was eighteen, a recent graduate from Pace High School in Brownsville. That summer I had developed a renewed interest in research, and a colleague, Antonio Zaveleta, and I designed a preliminary project to gather information about the health needs of Brownsville's low-income Mexican-American population. We sorely needed interviewers to complete our project, interviewers who were from Brownsville and who could gain the trust of the people with whom they talked.

Antonio came up with the idea to use incoming TSC freshmen to help us do the survey work; we planned to interview more than eight hundred people, a task that would take us much time if we did all the interviewing ourselves. Thanks to Antonio, we received some minimal funds for our project from a state agency. More importantly, the agency staff helped us to identify, hire, and pay graduates from Brownsville's three high schools to serve as interviewers in our research.

For reasons I don't remember, Antonio and I interviewed the first group of potential research assistants at an elementary school for the children of migrant farm workers. The school was located in the Southmost area of Brownsville. Antonio and I sat behind a small desk in a trailer propped up on concrete blocks on the dirt playground to the side of the school. The air conditioner rattled mightily as we talked with each potential interviewer. Each would enter, hesitantly scan us and the bleak inside of the trailer, then sit uncomfortably on the wooden chair we had provided them.

We'd been interviewing different students for about two hours when Berta opened the trailer door, cautiously stuck her head inside the room, then quietly took her seat in front of us. Sitting there before the two of us, Antonio and me, she was not very impressive. Her English was rudimentary and difficult to understand. She responded quickly to our questions, but in a reserved voice. Our project called for aggressive interviewers who could knock unannounced on barrio doors, state their business, conduct a thirty-minute interview in Spanish in a professional manner, then report back to us with the data in hand. We needed confident individuals who were streetwise, willing to take on a considerable responsibility. Berta didn't seem to fit any of our requirements.

At the end of the short job interview, I asked Berta if there was anything else we should know about her before we made our decision.

She thought a minute, then said carefully, "You don't know me, but I will work very hard and learn very fast. You should hire me."

Berta's bold words surprised me. I looked more closely at the person who sat before us in the wooden chair. Berta was several inches under five feet tall, slight of frame, dressed in starched jeans and a checked shirt. Her long black hair sat carefully fixed atop her head in a tight bun; except for the fact that she was shorter than the rest, she looked little different at first glance than many of the other students we had already interviewed. But on closer inspection, one noticed the oval, dark eyes, hidden in a wide and handsome face.

Berta's high school transcript lay on the desk before us. She had graduated in the top ten percent of her class, this despite her obvious difficulty with the English language. She had good references from her teachers. But could she handle herself in the situations she might confront in the Southmost barrios? I looked to Antonio for advice.

"She could be a diamond in the rough," Antonio said after Berta had left the trailer, but he said it with little conviction or force. There were other students who spoke better English and who exuded the tangible self-confidence necessary for the research project. Along with seven of these individuals, we also hired Berta.

Berta was a diamond in the rough. At the time I first met her, her English wasn't very good because she'd been in the United States less than two years. Berta had lived most of her life in Matamoros. First her oldest brother crossed the Rio Grande to find work in Brownsville, then the next oldest, then the next. Each in turn married, built his house with his own hands, and raised a family. At sixteen Berta, her mother, and her father finally crossed the river to live with her oldest brother until the family built a small house about six blocks from the TSC campus. Berta told me she knew only a few words of English when she settled in Brownsville.

With no one's help Berta enrolled herself at Pace High School. I asked her what the first semester in an American high school had been like for her. She threw up her hands for lack of the proper words to express the frustration she had felt.

"I knew most of the time what the teachers were saying, at least after three or four months. My friends helped me a lot, translating for me when I didn't understand. But I couldn't speak or write in English for a long time. I was very embarrassed."

"What about a program for non-English speakers?" I asked, surprised.

"They didn't have one. But I learned real fast. It was hard at first."

Before six weeks had passed, Berta was administering our research project on a day-by-day basis. She quickly became indispensable. She was our best and most reliable interviewer. She plodded on from one house to the next, completing twice as many interviews as anyone else did. On very hot, dull July days she rallied the other research assistants around her, serving as group cheerleader and motivator.

The summer crept along, day by day, as Antonio and I pushed towards the completion of the data collection stage of our research. Berta informed me in late July that she was enrolling in the computer tech-

nology program at TSC. She also told me that she was going to be the
work-study assistant during the fall semester for Antonio and me. She
had already arranged all the paperwork for the job; all that I had to
do was sign a few forms she had collected.

That fall Berta proved to be a good work-study assistant, but I frequently had to tell her to take a break from her work. Unlike Olivia
at TSC, Berta was constantly on the move, constantly demanding to
do work for us. If Antonio or I didn't have work for her to do, she
would make some up. Berta eagerly tried out a new filing system on
my filing cabinet mess. She went on constant missions around campus
to collect necessary office supplies; TSC put very little money in its
budgets for pens, pencils, paperclips, envelopes, typing paper, and all
the other usual office necessities. When Berta had nothing to do she
paced the hallway just outside my door, hands in jean pockets, bored
to the edge of her tolerance.

Berta's English improved tenfold, yet she clung tightly to her Mexican heritage. She made frequent weekend trips to see family and friends
in Matamoros and she always vacationed in Mexico City or Guada-
lajara, where she had more relatives. She told me she was very proud
she was Mexican by birth and she was always very quick to criticize
those who had become totally assimilated into American culture. Berta
and others in the Valley referred to these individuals as *bolillas*, white
breads.

Berta thrived in the computer department at TSC. Her initial language problems did not keep her from learning about computers faster
and better than the rest of the students. She finished the two-year program in a year and a half, graduating at Christmas time from TSC with
an associate's degree in computer science.

Upon Berta's graduation, TSC immediately hired her as a staff assistant in the computer lab. I watched Berta through the glass windows which separated the large gray room that houses the college's
mainframe computer from the brown carpeted hallway that runs the
length of the building. Students came to Berta in droves. I could see,
from my vantage point at the large window that looked into the mainframe room, the sympathy and caring she held for the students, ex-
pressed in her silent gestures towards them and by the bright light in
her oval eyes. Berta soon became the most popular staff member in
her department.

Berta knocked on my office door one day with an engraved invitation to her wedding. She told me she wanted me to be one of the *padrinos*. It was the duty of the *padrino* to help with the cost of the
wedding. A *padrino* also made a personal commitment to the general

welfare of the new couple, helping out whenever he could. The role of *padrino* was relatively flexible in Brownsville; one could take it seriously or not. I was very flattered by Berta's request, but cautious at first. I didn't know anything about being a *padrino* and I was afraid I would let her down. On the other hand, I knew Berta would always tell me or show me what she expected. After talking it over with Andrea, I accepted the honor.

I wasn't surprised that Berta's wedding, and the party afterwards, big by Brownsville standards, came off like clockwork. Berta was particularly good at organizing people and making arrangements for events. She'd learned the TSC bureaucracy very quickly and could get things done that I couldn't. Berta could find the best copier on campus when ours broke down and she could cajole office supplies out of the clerk in the mailroom, whom she called "the snail."

The wedding reception was held under a large public picnic pavilion across the street from the Brownsville Zoo. Wedding guests sat on metal folding chairs at concrete tables covered with paper towels. Andrea and I, along with one other couple, were the only Anglos among the one hundred fifty guests at the party. The people we were introduced to were Brownsville poor, as was Berta's family, but she had stretched her limited financial resources and staged a party she and her new husband Carlos could be proud of. All the *padrinos* had given a small sum, along with the bride's family. There was plenty of good food, the record player blasted *cumbias* from the corner of the pavilion, and everyone seemed to have a good time as they ate, danced, and talked.

With her marriage to Carlos, who had been born in Brownsville, Berta officially became an American citizen. Since she had first crossed the Rio Grande to live in Brownsville with her mother, father, and brothers, she had been an undocumented worker, or, as many Texans said, a "wetback." At a time before the INS's Amnesty Program, Berta's family did not have the money to pay an American lawyer to initiate the citizenship process. The INS forms and regulations, in spite of what the INS often argued, were so complex that many Mexicans had a difficult time filling them out. Even when they were completed correctly, a Mexican national often still required an American lawyer to help him through the INS red tape.

So Berta lied to the officials at Pace High School in order to gain admission, then lied again to gain entrance to TSC; she could not afford the extra tuition charged to Mexican nationals. Given the ways in which the INS laws were formulated, and the ways in which the laws were arbitrarily enforced in the Valley on a day-by-day basis, I knew that, in a similar situation, I would have done the same as Berta.

After three years of married life Berta and Carlos decided to have children. Berta was very happy about their decision and hinted for several months, without actually saying it, that she was trying to get pregnant. Berta's slight frame ballooned out during her first two trimesters as she shuffled around the computer lab assisting students with their questions. She was frightened of the changes that were taking place in her body. I told her that she should talk openly with her doctor, but she came from a culture and a class in which one was expected to follow the orders that the doctor gave and ask no questions.

Berta worked up her nerve and, one afternoon, told the doctor there was something wrong with her. The doctor, dubious, nevertheless ran a few tests on her. The tests showed that she had high blood pressure and was borderline diabetic. Although shocked at the results, Berta was proud she had taken control of her life. The confrontation with her physician was an important victory for Berta, one to which she continually referred.

After the birth of baby Marta, Berta decided she and Carlos needed a larger income. Keeping her job at TSC, she took other part-time jobs at night. Five days a week she worked from nine to five at TSC, then grabbed dinner and saw her baby for an hour before she began work as a computer operator from seven to ten at a Valley bank. Saturdays she worked from eight to five at a second bank. After a year of this grueling schedule, she quit one of the part-time jobs so she could re-enroll at Pan American University–Brownsville to complete a bachelor's degree in science. She also convinced Carlos that he should return to college; together the two of them spent four nights a week at PAUB.

In spite of her many accomplishments, Berta's life did not get better from one year to the next until, at last, she and Carlos could lay claim to the American dream of a cozy home in the suburbs, two cars, an Irish setter, and all the rest. Over the years I saw no logical progression in the material status of Berta's life. Berta's father died at fifty-eight from a heart attack. Berta said that he had complained frequently of chest pains, but her parents could not afford the cost of a visit to a hospital emergency room. Berta's mother was fired from her job as a school janitor soon after her husband's death. Unable to find work in Brownsville, Berta's mother moved with one of her sons to Houston. There her failing health was finally attributed to diabetes. She refused to follow the strict prescribed diet and spent many days sick in her bed. Berta regularly sent money to help support her mother, just as she had always helped her parents. Then one of Carlos's brothers lost his job, so Berta and Carlos dug into their meager savings to help him until he found work again. Berta and her husband were never able to save much of their earnings.

Berta soon joined the Brownsville Junior Chamber of Commerce. She invited me to be a guest speaker at one of their monthly meetings. She presided at the meeting, introduced me to the small crowd in attendance, then coordinated the social event after my talk. She told me a year later that she was soon going to quit the J.C.s . . . she'd learned from them all she could and, she said, it was time to move on.

One morning in the middle of final exams Berta knocked on my office door. She flew into the room, threw herself onto a nearby chair, began violently sobbing. I quickly ushered out the door the student I'd been talking with, then sat at my desk while Berta continued to cry. She needed a good five minutes of tears before she could say anything.

"I flunked the goddamn course," she finally said. "Can you believe it? I've never flunked a course in my life. British literature. I'm so embarrassed."

Then she cried some more.

"How about Carlos?" I asked.

"He flunked too. But he was expecting to flunk. It's not fair. It's really not fair. Mrs. Robinson told me the last day of class that I had made more progress this semester than any student in her classes. Screw her. Why the hell do I have to take British literature in the first place? Is this London or something?"

I listened to her for a few minutes more, then went down the hall to get her more Kleenex. The truth was Mrs. Robinson had a reputation as a rotten teacher. And I couldn't think of a single reason why Berta should have to take a course in British literature. Mexican, or Spanish, or Chicano yes, but British?

"How many passed the course?" I asked when the time was right.

"Four out of twenty-eight."

"Doesn't that tell you something?" I offered.

"I have never, ever, flunked a course. Not British literature, not anything. Never. I can't believe it happened."

Berta shed a few more tears of frustration and then returned to the computer lab. I hadn't seen her so mad since the baby contest.

Berta had entered Marta, age three, in a Brownsville beauty pageant. Marta won second place. Berta stood waving the pictures of Marta before my eyes, then in disgust showed me the pictures of the winner. The winner, it seemed, was determined by the number of pageant tickets each mother sold. Berta sold more tickets at one dollar a shot than all but one woman. The winner, according to Berta, was a woman who'd never put in an honest day's work in her entire life.

"She was so fat she could barely get through the door. She had nothing to do all day but bug her friends on the telephone to buy tickets. And look at her baby. Can you honestly say that she is more beautiful than Marta?"

I knew Berta when she was eighteen. I watched her sit on one of the benches in the shade of the courtyard below my office window, holding hands with Carlos during her lunch break. I'd known her as a research assistant, student, wife, mother, teacher, in dozens of situations and circumstances—most noble, some not. If Berta differed at all from other Americans, it was in but this: she was better.

Graduation

Arnoldo molded his big-eyed, long face into a living caricature of President Humberto Guadalupe Valdez. Giggling like a five year old, I buried my head in my copy of *People Magazine*, shielding myself with the sleeve of my black academic gown. As President Humberto droned on, oblivious to the one hundred fifty faculty who sat zombie-like before him in three tight rows of folding chairs, I read, on pages ninety-one and ninety-two, about the lives and loves of yet another Hollywood starlet. This one, like all the rest, had finally found fulfillment as a "serious actress," sharing an idyllic life with her two poodles and her second husband in a ten-room house in the hills overlooking the Pacific Ocean.

President Humberto at last came to the conclusion of his speech, catching everyone by surprise. Having regained control of my surface emotions once more, I looked over my left shoulder at the five thousand eager faces that filled the seats of the Brownsville Civic Center. Studiously ignoring Arnoldo's antics, knowing well that to laugh out loud during TSC's commencement exercises would bring instant disapproval, I scanned the rows of soon-to-be graduates, looking for someone I knew.

The three hundred graduates of two years of TSC education sat fidgeting in their uncomfortable chairs, anxiously awaiting their signal to march to the stage to receive their diplomas. Far behind them, in the cavernous reaches of the large public hall, babies cried, mothers comforted, small children moved restlessly about the aisles, and grandmothers struggled to identify the robed backs of their grandsons and granddaughters. Six- and seven-year-old children squirmed on their parents' laps, and infants (it seemed as if there were hundreds of them), all wrapped in elaborate blankets and capped with intricate bonnets of blue and pink, sung out in chorus.

In the streets outside the blond-brick building, the heavy bridge traffic rumbled by on International Boulevard: eighteen-wheelers from Kansas City and Chicago bound for the industrial parks of Matamoros, brightly painted produce trucks from Mexico headed north with their loads of fruits, peanuts, sorghum, and bricks of marijuana and cocaine. Every few weeks, with unending regularity, a trucker was stopped at the INS checkpoint just south of Kingsville. Despite his protests, a sniffer dog would do his duty, soon smelling out a cache of thousands of pounds of illegal drugs.

One of the TSC graduates, adjusting her square white hat, waved quickly to a small face in the balcony. It was a fleeting exchange, but an important one. For many of the husbands, wives, brothers, sisters, mothers, fathers, grandparents, and cousins in the audience, this graduation day was very special. Those lucky enough to attend (there were never enough tickets for all those who wanted to join in the celebration) greedily soaked up the pomp and circumstance, applauding wildly when awards were announced. The applause and cheering always re-awoke the infants. They took up a common song once more, their chorus a background to the microphoned mumblings that emanated from the stage.

President Humberto introduced one of his many Deans of Something who began reading a prepared statement from the podium. The graduation ceremonies staggered along at a sluggish pace, the heat of so many bodies crammed into one space, however large, already outpacing the huge compressor units in the alley. The large crowd ignored the heat and the other inconveniences as incidental to a momentous occasion. Few of the parents of TSC's graduates had survived junior high school, far fewer had graduated with a high school diploma. Many in the audience had been forced to go to work full time to support their families, to drop out before they reached eighth or ninth grade.

While for many white, middle-class families a college graduation was certainly a time of importance, for these Mexican Americans assembled in the Brownsville Civic Center the ceremony taking place before them was a time to be remembered for the rest of their lives. It seemed as if there were more cameras than people, all metered to record the big event. There were hundreds of instamatics with built-in flashes, even some expensive thirty-five millimeters with auto-focus and other high-tech doodads. The crowd was restless, yet patient. From the back reaches of the upper balcony, for no discernible reason, a flash went off, then another, then another, and another. The Dean of Something paused in his remarks, looked up from the podium and out towards the small exploding lights, then continued, unperturbed, with his prepared comments.

The TSC college chorus sang another medley of Broadway show tunes. Then President Humberto took the podium again, reading a fifteen-minute biography of the commencement speaker. Finally, at last, President Humberto introduced his long-time friend and colleague from Princeton, New Jersey. My heart sank as the TSC president's esteemed friend reached deeply into his rented robe to bring out his speech. In the brief glimpse I had of it, it looked to be a sixty-minuter. The first paragraphs of the speech were deadly, coated with educational jargon, pronounced in an Eastern accent that few in the audience could understand. Arnoldo, one row behind me, two seats to the left, clasped his right hand to his throat which lay exposed just above his gown, then silently mimicked a victim seriously in need of the Heimlich maneuver.

In self-defense I read another story in *People Magazine*, snuck a peek at my watch, and caught a few glib sentences from the Princetonian. I gazed once again at the rows of graduates behind me. I grew sullenly angry, frustrated at TSC's annual Grand Charade.

Of the three hundred twenty students, males in black robes, females in white, I counted twenty-three whom I had taught in at least one of my sociology courses. Of those I knew, two could not write a coherent paragraph, fifteen could not read a college-level textbook. Two students of the twenty-three could, I judged, successfully compete with other college students in Texas; they had the educational background and skills to do well whether they chose to continue their education or look for a job.

The rest, the other twenty-one, would not fare so well. They would soon join Guero, Olivia, Fred, and the majority of students I had known at both TSTI and TSC, trading their rented graduation gowns to work in Valley discount houses, sell Big Macs, cut clothes for piece rate in the plants run by Haggar and Levi's, or join their parents in the fields as migrant farm workers. For every Berta, there were twenty more at TSC who had her ambition but had never honestly been given the opportunity to get a solid education, one that would prepare them for a good job.

Most of TSC's faculty were diligent in their work, took their jobs seriously, did not shirk their duties; their attitudes were very different from those of the instructors at TSTI in Harlingen. The few at TSC who were just there for the paycheck never lasted very long; they soon grew bored, developed other interests, often quit their jobs and moved away. There was, except for retirements and ill health, very little turn-over in the TSC faculty.

But in spite of the dedicated faculty, it was very difficult to work with graduates of Valley high schools who could barely read or write, who could perform only rudimentary math operations, who were at a loss when asked to analyze a page out of the sociology text. Each year the cream of the Valley's high school crop walked through the doors of TSC and each year they brought with them the skills of sixth and seventh graders. Dropouts were a national problem, but at TSC the numbers were numbing. By the end of the first year, three thousand TSC students were reduced to six hundred, only half of whom sur-vived to graduate the following spring. Less than one out of ten fresh-men graduated from TSC in the normal two-year time period, and these graduates, I well knew, were very poorly educated.

The Princetonian at the podium firmly believed that if these TSC graduates would but "try ever harder, never accepting defeat, always reaching higher and higher . . ." their futures would be bright, their lives secure. After his commencement address, this same gentleman would get on a jet to return to his position as director of the nation's most prestigious testing service. I doubted that during his brief visit to the Valley, during which time he had been pampered by President Humberto at a condo on South Padre Island, toured through the *mer-cado* in Matamoros, and dined with members of TSC's board of trustees, this man had learned very much about the real educational needs of the students who patiently waited for him to finish his long speech. I did not doubt, however, that he would get considerable mileage back home in Princeton from his short trip to the borderlands.

In truth, all these TSC graduates had to do to assure themselves of better jobs was to learn to read, write, think analytically, and learn basic math skills. Then, skills in hand, they could retake all their courses at TSC. Of course I knew that was not going to happen. I knew, too, that it was a national problem. But it was worse at TSC, in spite of the institution's denials. Incoming freshmen regularly scored in the bot-tom one percent on the Princetonian's standardized test.

President Humberto pumped the Princetonian's hand several times, gave the commencement speaker a warm embrace, hugging his short, stout body against the taller, angular fellow as the audience politely, with little real enthusiasm, applauded. Then, but a moment later, a genuine wave of excitement swept through the crowd, a sweep of energy that quieted my pre-ulcerous stomach, that woke yet another time the sleeping infants, that stirred the great-grandmothers as well as the young children.

Cameras popping, another Dean of Something began reading the list of TSC graduates. The students crossed the wide stage to receive their diplomas from the president of the Board of Trustees, the microphone at the podium amplifying the staccato clickings of the women's long, black high heels, replicating the sounds of leather against wood to the farthest corners of the auditorium. The fusillade of camera flashes continued until the very last student had grasped in his hand the roll of paper bound with red ribbon and, once again, returned to his row of folding chairs.

After a night of celebration, the graduates would wake up the next morning to a more somber day. As the Princetonian winged his way back to the largess of Princeton, New Jersey, the home of more than a few celebs who regularly appeared in the pages of *People Magazine*, TSC graduates, degrees in hand, would, in the weeks to come, take to the streets of Brownsville, Harlingen, San Benito, Edinburg, and the other Valley communities, all in search of a good job.

With my fellow faculty I marched out, on cue, to the prerecorded music that now blared out over the speaker system. Cameras continued to click as the long line of faculty paraded, two by two, out of the large auditorium.

Angry, despondent, I saw myself as no better than the Princetonian, perhaps twice as ignorant. While I knew much about the academic games played in the Valley, I knew very little about life on the street, about the real world that began where the college campus ended. I saw part of the problem, but felt helpless; if anything, all I was doing at TSC was simply perpetuating the Grand Charade. I marched along with the rest of the robed TSC faculty, out of the hall and down the corridor, but no longer in step.

Under a Heated Moon

Unable to sleep, I dragged a faded canvas chair through the thick grass of my backyard, careful to avoid the mesquite branches that littered the ground. I placed the chair on the cracked cement sidewalk that led from the back door of my house to the crumbling garage. In the hot night air I moved as quietly as possible, careful not to awake the Enchilada Gang.

It was one-thirty in the morning and the temperature was ninety-two degrees. A sluggish breeeze from south of the Rio Grande rustled the big sour orange tree that hugged the eastern corner of my house, then stirred the branches of the mesquite tree that overpowered the backyard with its constant sloughing off of buds, thorns, branches, beans, and other tree paraphernalia.

My eyes focused on the moon. It was a heated moon, heated in the dusty Brownsville streets, turned from its normal white to an orange-hot glow that lit up the sky over my crumbling garage. It was a heated moon, heated by the sun that had battered Brownsville all that day, cooking the people, the vegetation, the buildings, the glass and metal cars, cooking them far beyond their tolerances.

When the moon finally rose, it came out of all that baked heat, struggled through the thick truck fumes on International Boulevard, wafted up over Brownsville roofs where the tar stood about in vast, smoking puddles, up past the power lines and telephone poles caked with dry dust in the back alleyways.

I sat down stiffly in my chair, stared up at that heated moon, then noticed the tricks that the shadows from its light played upon my crumbling garage, the wooden fence, and the sour orange and mesquite trees. The aroma reached me of unripened, steaming citrus, thousands of them cooking on tree branches in Brownsville backyards.

A fat, wobbling possum suddenly appeared on top of the back fence, careless in its noise. It stumbled onto a tin can, knocking it to the pavement of the alley below. The possum stopped in its tracks, waited silently beneath the heated moon for several minutes, then proceeded quickly along its path. Ignoring me, it crossed from the back fence to the rotting timbers that bordered Enchilada Gang Territory. In the shadows the possum seemed to hesitate, taking each step more carefully, even daintily. Reaching the big sour orange tree, the animal flung itself into the thick vegetation that covered the trunk, rustled its way up to the roof of my house, crossed the patio outside my second-story bedroom door, then stood there in the moonlight sniffing at the doorway that led to the room where Andrea still slept soundly. I hurled an unripened sour orange at the intruder, the foul animal disappearing at a gallop over the peak of the roof.

I stood there, sweat beginning to pour off my body, caught in a heat warp, now smelling the possum's funk as it slowly filled the night air.

It was the heat that made me see the possum for the first time. It was the Brownsville heat that stopped everything in its tracks, slowed time to a standstill, reduced the familiar to the unknown, then back again.

It was impossible to live in Brownsville in any way that I had ever been accustomed to, impossible not to see the persons around me crawl about in counter-time, slowed to their very essences like the possum. It was impossible not to see myself revealed under the heat lamp which injected every living thing with a fusion of steams and boils.

Brownsville was no pit. Bob Freede was wrong about this city, just as he had been wrong about many other things. In Brownsville nothing was disguised, all was raw, open, festering in the heat or lolling about under the dark cover of the mesquite. There was also a lushness of life here, a brimming over of unretarded human expression and action F-stopped down to a sleepy, sometimes deceptive pace.

I squirmed in my canvas chair. The moment was stretched like taffy at a Christmas pull, like a Brownsville afternoon in August. At the end of State Highway 77, where the Rio Grande calls America to a halt, I could finally stop. Under a heated moon, there was no reason to hide.

PART THREE

In the Streets

Ignacio and His Pride

I heard the roar of the motorcycle in the driveway and immediately looked out my front window. Ignacio sat proudly perched on his machine under a ten o'clock sun, waiting impatiently for me to greet him. One more time he revved the unmuffled Japanese engine, the high-pitched reverberations scattering into the thick vegetation of the neighborhood like bilious cockroaches, rousing the dope-eyed gang of thieves next door. I heard one give a half-hearted threat, then return to the dust beneath the acacia. Ignacio revved the engine a final time, then sat back on the motorcycle seat.

I was not ready for him. On my desk before me were two sets of papers to be graded. To my right, on the book shelves which I had grafted onto the pine boards that lined my office, was a beginning to a manuscript on the Valley's shrimp industry. It was a Saturday morning, a free morning when I had no scheduled TSC classes, no regular obligations to meet. All week long I had looked forward to the time I would have; now Ignacio, unannounced, was here.

I shook Ignacio's hand, mustering the enthusiasm I knew he required. I asked him where he'd been the last six months.

"Been working on them Louisiana oyster boats. Make pretty good money. It's good work. Nobody is getting on you, not like it was when I was at the Boys' Home. Except for the captain, I can be my own boss."

Ignacio pulled back the sleeve of his worn, blue t-shirt and, as was our custom, I felt his right bicep.

I had time, now, to take a closer look at him. The earring was back in place. It had gotten him into several fights at the Boys' Home. We'd argued over whether or not the earring was worth the fights. The small loop of gold shone against the luminescent brown of Ignacio's skin. His coarse black hair was cut in a miniature Afro, partially covering his ears. He'd put on at least ten pounds to his wiry frame since I'd last seen him, most of it in his arms and chest. He looked beat up, but good.

"Got me a bike," he said, pointing to his machine.

It was a Honda 350, ten years old, maybe older. In its most recent rebirth it had received thick coats of dark purple paint that covered the metal, all the plastic, the rubber, and even the spokes of the worn tires. I knew, without having to be shown, that there was a ton of rust beneath all that purple.

With considerable pride, Ignacio showed me how he had managed to mount the large rectangular stereo speakers on each handle bar, how he had molded the metal brackets to hold the tape cassette, its face also a dark purple, which rode atop the dented gas tank.

"You wanna hear what it can do?" he asked me. I nodded. Ignacio popped a cassette into his purple unit, turned the volume knob to the far right, then stood back, arms folded to guage my reaction. The music blared forth, but not as loudly as I had expected. The gang next door sent a scout to investigate. Ignacio laughed at the poor excuse for a dog, showed him the back side of his cheap black leather boot, and watched as the spy returned to his own yard.

"Still got them darn old dogs?" he asked, knowing the answer.

"Yeah. Can't seem to get rid of them." I held my hands out in front of me, palms up. Whenever I talked to Ignacio, I always seemed to do half the speaking with my hands.

Ignacio stood there waiting for me to invite him in. I tried not to think about the papers and the manuscript. Or Ignacio's earring, half-hidden under his Afro. Ignacio was almost nineteen. He was, legally speaking, an adult who was supporting himself the best way he could. If he had his earring, a motorcycle, and a job he could go back to, then, by his standards, he was doing very well. I slapped him hard across the shoulders, told him that Andrea and I had missed him, which we had, then motioned him towards the front door.

"How's Andrea doing?" he asked me, sitting on the wrought iron chair at the kitchen table. He placed his two elbows on the round glass top, then gazed down through the table at his two feet. Andrea and I bought the set at a store on Boca Chica, then I hauled them carefully back. The glass was less than a quarter-inch thick, but weighed a ton as I rolled it across the living room rug, through the small dining room, and onto the thick kitchen linoleum, gilded with the images of tropical flowers.

"She's still working at the Boys' Home. This'll be her second year with them. She likes it better than working for Child Welfare. She got burned out working with the kids, epecially the small ones who were treated badly by their parents."

Ignacio nodded his head in agreement. He'd spent thirteen years in foster homes before being sent by his mother at age sixteen to the Boys' Home. She hadn't wanted him in Laredo with her and her two daughters, in fact was embarrassed by him. She was Mexican American and his father had been black. Ignacio was the color of coffee with two creams, a blend of cultures and races that had landed him, by no fault of his own, into much trouble before he came to Brownsville.

Andrea brought him home with her one Saturday afternoon. I found them sitting at the glass table in the kitchen drinking Cokes and talking. Ignacio wouldn't look up at me as we shook hands. He mumbled something that I couldn't understand as he grasped my hand; it was a firm, dry handshake, stronger than I had expected from so shy a boy.

Ignacio stayed for another hour or so. At Andrea's prodding, he drew us several pictures. I don't remember what the pictures were of, but the colors he used were bright, imaginative, and he took great enjoyment in presenting them to us. Andrea put them up on the refrigerator; Ignacio rearranged the frig magnets several different ways until he had them just the way he wanted.

Ignacio told me goodbye, again avoiding any eye contact, shook my hand with the same surprising strength, then followed Andrea out the front door to her car. I stood in the kitchen after they were gone, wondering where this new relationship was going to lead.

At our invitation Ignacio began to visit us almost every weekend, usually on a Saturday afternoon, but sometimes on a Sunday. He brought presents for us, presents he had made in his room at the Boys' Home. He brought us pieces of wire twisted together in special ways, a paper plate painted with a bright design, pictures of sailboats and sunsets, lowriders, fish in the sea.

Ignacio liked to do small things for us, to repay us in part for our interest in him. At Andrea's instigation, I gave him small things to do around our house. He was very creative. He took electric appliances that were old or broken and fixed them, at least most of the time. He took speakers out of an old radio and jammed them into his radio. He liked to work with electric things, with sockets and wires and fuses. His cassette tape recorder and five tapes—his hero was Michael Jackson —were his most important possessions.

We took Ignacio to the beach with us, to the movies, to visit Andrea's family in Harlingen. I did not know how to be around a teenage boy, so I faked it the best I knew how. I had a hard time reading Ignacio, and I frequently felt as if I was making a fool of myself with him. But he didn't seem to mind.

Christmas came and Ignacio's mother called the Boys' Home to tell the head counselor that she didn't want Ignacio to come to Laredo for the holidays. Usually everyone was sent home for five days, virtually closing down the institution. In theory the time that the boys spent with their families over Christmas was supposed to help resolve their problems; in reality, the boys always came back after Christmas in a deep blue gloom, their worst doubts about their families having been proved.

Ignacio had nowhere to go. With some apprehension I agreed with Andrea to take Ignacio in, but I wondered if we were doing the right thing by him. The honeymoon with Ignacio had ended two weeks before Christmas. He'd gotten mad for some reason, stormed out the front door, walked around the neighborhood for an hour, then spent the rest of the evening in silence.

"What's wrong?" I asked him.

"Nothing's wrong," he said. Andrea tried, but with the same results.

"If you don't tell us, we can't help you," I said, growing impatient. He sat lost in the big couch that fronted our tiny black and white TV, acting as if he were engrossed in the program.

Ignacio was having a tough time at school. For the third year in a row he was flunking ninth grade. He'd already flunked it twice in Laredo before he came to Brownsville. His teachers said that he was not a problem in class like some of the other students. He sat at his desk quietly, although he could be easily distracted. He was not a good reader, but he could still read and, in a class of nonreaders, he had much to be proud of. He worked hardest in his art class, and took great enjoyment from his projects. But still, for reasons that seemed mysterious to the majority of his teachers, Ignacio was again flunking most of his courses.

Andrea read through his records again and again, searching for a clue. At first I thought it was drugs. Quite a few of the kids at the Boys' Home had regularly used grass, sniffed glue from empty cola cans, or become addicted to other cheap street drugs. Because of some of his actions, I reasoned that Ignacio suffered from some kind of brain damage, perhaps brought on by drug use.

At first Ignacio had seemed quite normal. But gradually, as Andrea and I spent longer periods with him, it became obvious that something was very wrong. Ignacio was always several steps behind, not quite sharp enough to keep up with the other boys at the Boys' Home. He took offense when no offense was meant, in part because he could not always interpret the intentions of others, however well-meaning they really were. The Boys' Home was no Boy Scout Jubilee; Ignacio got into his share of trouble with the counselors and the other boys. At times it seemed to me that he just wasn't tracking. Then, suddenly, Ignacio would explode in a rage, storming about our house or the Boys' Home, out of control, unseen demons tearing his insides into little pieces.

Still, at bottom, there was Ignacio's pride, a pride that drove him to a rigid personal code of conduct. When Ignacio's upbringing was taken into account, there seemed little reason for the pride. His mother had never wanted him, his father was never around, he'd been kicked from one foster home to another for most of his life, and his biracial roots had made him the victim of much hatred.

One aspect of the pride was that Ignacio refused to have anything to do with drugs. While his friends at school and at the Boys' Home played with a variety of drugs that were all around them, Ignacio avoided them with a single-minded diligence. He knew they were bad for him, had watched others around him, including his mother, sink into their grasp, and had learned from it. Long before Andrea or I ever knew him, Ignacio had made a personal decision, then he'd stuck to it, no matter what.

Ignacio also spread the word about drugs to his friends at the Boys' Home and at school. He seemed unfazed that they usually ignored them.

"Jeff is just about as stupid as they come," he told me one Saturday afternoon.

"What do you mean?" I asked, knowing Jeff was one of his best friends, lived just across the hall from him.

"He be always taking some shit, smoking it or whatever, acting like he's the biggest thing that was created."

"Did you talk to him about it?" I said.

"I tried, but he don't listen. Thinks he knows it all, but he don't know what he's getting into. I seen what it can do to a person."

Andrea and I talked over the possibility of Ignacio moving in with us after he turned eighteen. His mother had already sent word that he was not welcome in Laredo. I respected Ignacio's pride and his other positive characteristics, but was afraid of his darker side, afraid of the rage he barely held in check. Andrea thought that Ignacio might have some partial brain damage, perhaps from birth, that was undiagnosed. There were a number of possibilities to explain his behavior, but none of them, of course, helped to resolve it. Given the unknowns, I didn't think I, or Andrea, was ready yet for the responsibilities of raising Ignacio.

We tried talking to Ignacio about the situation, but it was difficult to do. Andrea asked him if he liked spending time with the two of us.

"On a scale of one to ten, one being very miserable, ten being very happy, how do you feel with us?" she asked him.

"Ten," Ignacio quickly said. "It's the best I ever been."

I thought about what Ignacio said for a long time. We had given him very little over the course of the year, a few weekends of attention, some caring and support, not enough, in sum, to merit anything close to his response. Yet I had no doubt that Ignacio felt we had given him much.

There came a time when Andrea and I had to tell Ignacio that we couldn't take him in after he left the Boys' Home. By then he had come to the same recognition, although that didn't keep him from wanting what might have been. Ignacio was very hurt by it, couldn't understand it. He left town without really saying goodbye, returned to Laredo to try to make peace with his mother and the rest of his family. That was the last we heard from him.

Ignacio now sat at the table in front of me, eyes cast down again, talking in brief sentences about his work on the oyster boat and the money he was making. He was proud of being able to make it on his own. But at the same time I knew that he would, at the drop of a hat, move in with Andrea and me, be our foster son.

"Come back around dinner time," I finally told him. "Andrea will be back home by then and we can talk some more."

"Okay," he said, losing heart. He wanted badly to hear some other words.

I walked him back out the front door, down the sidewalk to the driveway where his Honda 350 sat roasting in the heat. He climbed on the machine, fired it up with his key, then took off loudly down Poinsettia Place.

I couldn't be a father to Ignacio, and he was too old, had experienced too much, to live with us as a son. I know now, because I know him, that Ignacio's still mad at me, thinks I don't care about him, thinks that if Andrea and I had made a home for him all his problems would have been resolved. They wouldn't have.

Ignacio never came back. His pride wouldn't let him. If he's got food on the table, a place to sleep, and some work that pays, then by his standards he's sitting pretty. I hope he's got those things. I hope that his pride and his other good qualities have been enough to keep him going, that he hasn't seriously hurt himself or anyone else, that he's stayed out of jail.

I still do care for Ignacio. A part of that caring is contained in a respect I have for his character, Ignacio's resistance to forces, both in ternal and external, which he cannot control, his refusal, against all odds, to ever give up.

The Cowboy Son

Laurio was a cowboy of sorts. During the summer he'd been raised by his grandfather and grandmother near the King Ranch, out with the mesquite, buffle grass, and prickly pear, out in the big, open spaces that stretched as far as the eye imagined. Laurio could ride and rope and herd cattle, mend fence, and talk cowboy talk. Laurio grew tall and lean, a full head taller than his friends, his long, jet-black hair combed back over his ears and stuffed under his wide-brimmed straw cowboy hat, one of three that he owned.

During the other nine months Laurio lived with his mother and three half-sisters in a one-bedroom apartment in a housing project in Kingsville. He didn't have a horse of his own, or a saddle, or rope. He found small animals and brought them home. He raised snakes, lizards and geckos, toads, and baby birds. He did poorly at school, but was very popular with the girls. He coveted his cousin's Camaro, but was too young to buy a car even if he'd had the money.

One summer his grandfather helped Laurio build a rabbit hutch and he found himself breeding and selling rabbits. Back in school that fall, Laurio quickly fell back into his routine of daily fights. After school and evenings Laurio rode shotgun in his cousin's Camaro while they cruised the three-mile strip of State Highway 77 that ran through the center of their town.

Laurio's mother drank too much on Saturday nights. She angrily chased him around the small apartment, cursing and threatening him, swearing that Laurio was no good, that he was just like his father. Laurio's father, who also drank too much, left the family and moved to California. He called Laurio on his birthdays and at Christmas and always promised to send money so Laurio could buy a plane ticket to visit him. But he never sent the money. One of Laurio's dreams was to buy a new Camaro, drive to the West Coast, find a good job, and live with his father and his father's new California family.

When Laurio was twelve he set up his first serious business. He stole bicycles from school, then took them to a friend's garage. He tore the bikes down with a screwdriver and vise grips, reassembled the parts into different bikes, then sold them to his friends and their friends. He bought beer with his profits. Some of the beer he drank himself, but most of it he gave away. As his business and his expertise grew, he hired his friends to steal more bikes and to help him at his chop shop.

Laurio made more money. He bought grass with his profits, smoking some, but giving most of it away. One of his cousins told him he was stupid to give away dope when he could sell it for big money. Laurio ignored his cousin. He gave some of his money to his mother and he bought himself two motorcycles. He rode his motorcycles at night through the back alleys of the town, careful to avoid the police because he had no license. By the time Laurio was finally caught by the police, he had, he told me, stolen more than three hundred bikes. Business was booming, but he still was always short of cash because he spent his money as fast as it accumulated, on himself, his friends, and his mother.

Laurio knew he had a big problem long before his arrest; the town was less than twenty thousand people and Laurio soon ran out of bikes to steal. So he had to steal bikes he'd already stolen. Laurio didn't want to do this, but he didn't see what else he could do.

It was one of his best customers who tipped off the police. One day after school Laurio looked out the front window of his apartment to see two policemen walking up the sidewalk. He squeezed out the bathroom window, jumped on his favorite motorcycle, and made his getaway in the best cowboy tradition. But in the excitement he'd forgotten to grab his cash and, after three boring days of hiding out, he'd gone to school to borrow money from one of his friends. The police found him there, in English class, and arrested him on the spot. Laurio never forgot the indignity of it, of being handcuffed in front of his friends and roughly led away to the waiting police car.

Laurio was sent to the Brownsville Boys' Home. He hated it because he felt as though he was constantly being watched by someone, a counselor, another boy. He hated the smallness of the building, its dark and narrow corridors, and he hated the noise of downtown Brownsville that came through the windows. He hated being confined to an inside place, where he couldn't see the sun set or ride the streets on his motorcycle or cruise in his cousin's Camaro.

Laurio couldn't cowboy and he couldn't practice his business skills, but he could still fight, fight driven by a ferocity of spirit, bent emotions, and frustrated hormones that earned him a big reputation in Brownsville. He had little use for school, but school was where the fights took place, as well as the audience and the glory that went along with the fights.

Laurio was a cowboy charmer. He looked good in his jeans, checkered shirt, boots, and hat. His eyes sparkled with intensity; his smile, which came quickly, could be disarming. Laurio, for those few whom he trusted, also wore his heart on his sleeve. He was open with his emotions, articulate, a loving young man who'd already led a hard and fast life.

Laurio was as accepting of Andrea and me as we were of him. We set out the rules before he moved in with us, discussed them around the dinner table, reached agreements and compromises. Laurio couldn't go back to his mother and sisters—they didn't want him—and he couldn't stay any longer at the Brownsville Boys' Home. Laurio seemed to be everything that Ignacio was not; I willingly, and naively, took the plunge into adult responsibility, into foster fatherhood.

Laurio moved his few things into the extra bedroom, the same room in which he'd spent weekends with us, the same room that Ignacio had coveted.

"Would you guys mind if I painted my room?" he asked one evening, about a week after he'd moved in with us.

"No, of course not," I said. "What color?"

"Black. Black looks real good with silver. I could cover the windows with that foil you got in the kitchen. It'll only take me twenty minutes or so to cover all the windows in my room with it."

I grimaced and looked across the table at Andrea, who was doing her best not to laugh. Laurio put on his best smile, but he knew it wasn't going to work, so he backed off from his request, at least temporarily.

For the next six months life with Laurio went, relatively speaking, rather smoothly. I made huge adjustments to our first foster child, and I know Laurio, in return, did too. The way Andrea and I lived, our routines, expectations, style of life, were very different from Laurio's. Besides the obvious material differences between a middle- and lower-class family with which Laurio was forced to contend, Andrea and I were Anglos attempting to foster a troubled Mexican-American teenager. We had, in fact, everything going against the relationship with Laurio, from differences in ethnicity and class, to differences in important values and definitions of acceptable private and public behavior.

Laurio, even more importantly, was not used to parental supervision, although he badly wanted it. In Kingsville he'd spent as little time at school as possible, then hung out with his friends until hunger or tiredness drew him back to his mother's apartment. In contrast, Andrea and I ate our meals at the same hour each day, drank little, and went to bed early. We made numerous demands on Laurio, starting with wanting to know where he was at all times day and night. I know that our life and our expectations of him must have seemed very strange to Laurio.

To his credit, Laurio adjusted to our new demands on him and his time, often working to conform to rules that he found meaningless, stupid, or counterproductive. The three of us managed to hold together, live as a family, for more than a year. There were many good times during that year, and there were times I wanted to slit Laurio's throat.

Laurio badly craved the use of one of our cars for Saturday night dates. After taking out his share of the garbage and doing other chores around the house, he earned the right to drive Andrea's new Honda. But the following Sunday morning, after his big Saturday night car date, I noticed that the Honda looked strange as it sat in the front driveway. The inside of the driver's seat was covered with mesquite leaves and pods, the same kind of roughage that covered the front lawn.

I unlocked the front door of the car and swung it open, noticing for the first time that the window had not been rolled up. Laurio, in all his anxiety to get back home on time, had jumped out of the car, locked both car doors, but forgotten to close the window. I reached inside the door, cranked the handle, and stood in amazement as nothing happened.

It was then that I noticed the small fragments of glass on the car floor and the seat on the passenger's side. Laurio hadn't bothered to roll up the window of Andrea's new Honda because there wasn't any window.

I stormed back into the house, my anger growing when I thought about the fact that Andrea's car wasn't even paid off yet.

"Laurio!" I yelled, ready to hang him from the big mesquite in the backyard.

"What's the matter, Pop?" he asked me, innocence oozing from him like water off a duck.

"What happened to the car?" I said, trying to lower my voice. For a second there I heard myself sounding just like my father the time I drove the family station wagon into a ditch.

"You mean the window?" Laurio asked, rubbing his eyes awake.

"Yeah, I mean the window," I said, remaining unsoothed.

"I was going to tell you about it last night, but I didn't want to wake you up. See, I was driving under the bridge at the corner of eleventh and the railroad tracks, when somebody threw a brick through the window."

"A brick?" I said, half incredulous, but beginning to believe the story because it sounded so unlikely.

"Yeah, a brick. I kept it, figured the cops might want to see it or something."

So Laurio and I had gone back outside, stood and looked at the brick he showed me. Andrea came out then, protective of her car, but more concerned about the safety of Laurio and his new girlfriend Amy. We called the police about the incident. They came out several hours later, took down the information, looked at Laurio's brick and silently filled out their forms.

Andrea and I were naive foster parents then. Eight years later Laurio, in a burst of honesty, confessed the truth to us.

"I'd done something that really pissed Amy off, I can't even remember what it was, and when we got out of the car at her house, she slammed the door real hard. I mean, it was really hard the way she slammed that door. The window completely cracked like in a wreck or something. I knew you guys would have my hide for it, so on the way home I found a brick. I stopped under a tree and knocked all the rest of the glass out of the window with the brick. Then I made up the story about how it happened. I didn't think you'd go for it, but you did. Then I felt worse about it, especially when I told it to the cops."

Or there was the time he called from a pay phone one Saturday night to say he had a "minor" car problem. The minor car problem was the result of wanting to find a quiet place to park with his girlfriend. In order to get to the quiet place, he'd driven the car through a hundred yards of knee-deep mud. By the time I slogged my way to the car at one-thirty on a Sunday morning, the mud was up over the car axle. I called a tow truck, but even the tow truck couldn't reach it. We left the car there in the mud and the dark. For the first time since I'd known him, Laurio remained speechless on the ride back to town.

These events were more or less to be expected of a teenager, although not ones I figured on when I envisioned being Laurio's foster father. I thought that Andrea and I could provide the economic and social stability that Laurio's family had never had. Laurio would thrive in this kind of situation, his best characteristics shining forth, his worst shriveling because they were no longer necessary. These expectations of Laurio were unfair and not very realistic. I had also, of course, neglected to consider that Laurio's growing up might in some very specific ways resemble the familiar, that his blunders and tricks might be a South Texas version of my own youth.

Laurio's fights became more and more serious, a fact of his life that Laurio could no longer hide.

"It's simple," I told him. "You go to school, attend your classes, do your homework, and stay out of trouble. Someone wants to fight, you look the other way."

Laurio looked at me across the kitchen table like I was from Mars.

"I can't do that, Pop. I just can't. Somebody looks at you real hard, then you can't walk away. It gets around you have no *huevos* and everybody starts hitting on you."

"Ignore them. Shit, ignore them."

"You don't understand," Laurio said. "What kind of person am I if I walk away from trouble? You got to stand up for yourself because nobody will do it for you."

"Lee doesn't get into fights," Andrea told Laurio, trying to reason with him.

"Pop's an old man. He don't have to fight. He's got nothing to prove. He's got education, a good job, nobody's going to mess with him. But everybody is always messing with me, trying to put me down."

Two weeks later, Saturday night around eleven, Laurio came hobbling in on one leg, blood on his shirt. He limped over the chair in the living room, fell down, then crawled up on it, out of breath.

"What happened?" I said, scared for him.

"I was talking to this guy in an alley and all of a sudden some other guy came at me with an ax. I was real lucky, Pop. He swung that sucker at me but missed and I hit him twice and kicked him in the stomach. Gave him a real good shot."

"What's wrong with your leg?" I said, not knowing whether to be angry, or thankful that Laurio was still alive.

"I banged it on the car door trying to get out of there fast. They chased me down the street, but never got close."

Andrea and I gave an annual Halloween costume party in Brownsville. We started the tradition because we wanted an excuse to give a big party and because not very many of our friends in Brownsville dressed up for the holiday. Laurio got very excited about the party. He spent several hours working on his costume before he went to pick up Amy.

The two of them walked through the front door about an hour after the party had started. Amy was dressed as a cowgirl, red and white checkered shirt, blue jeans, boots, and hat. Laurio, by her side, was Zorro. He wore a black cape that he had borrowed from Andrea, black pants and shirt, and had penciled in a thin mustache underneath his black mask. He wore a toy gun at his side, and carried an old whip he had borrowed from one of his friends.

Laurio was Zorro for the evening and loved it. He could play out his fantasy for a few hours, a dashing young man who lived life intensely from one day to the next, who had a romantic flash to him that was more suited to the open range than to the urban barrios. When he left our home after one year, something he said he had to do, it tore him up. But despite his tears, and ours, he was ready to go, ready to prove himself back in his hometown.

Laurio was no longer just a successful bike thief. His plan was to find a job, set himself up in his own apartment, stay away from his family and their problems, make a life of his own. The first thing he wanted to do was buy his own Camaro, not a new one, one that had a few miles on it but still was in good condition.

I drove him down to the Brownsville bus station. We embraced, I said a few words of encouragement, and we put his things on the bus.

"Don't you and Mom worry," Laurio told me, then he swung up the steps of the bus and disappeared down the aisle of seats.

Mando's Karate Academy

Mando's Karate Academy stood on the corner of Elizabeth and Seventh in downtown Brownsville, not far from Our Lady of the Sacred Heart Cathedral and directly adjacent to a large *ropa usada*, one of many used clothing stores where customers from across the river combed and sifted through large mounds of garments scattered about the cement floors. To ensure privacy within, Mando had covered the large plate glass window which faced the busy street with old copies of the *Brownsville Herald*. Both the curious and potential students of the karate academy were forced to peek through the slits in the *Brownsville Herald*, the sheets of newsprint already molding in the heat and humidity. The bolder ones ventured in the entrance on the side street where they stood patiently, waiting for someone to attend to them.

Mando usually ignored these unwanted visitors, letting them stand with hands in pockets or at their sides, looking uncomfortable in their street clothes, while the roomful of students paraded about in their white karate uniforms. Some of the kids, after twenty minutes or so of inattention, would drift outside again onto the sidewalk, just as they had drifted in, but the more determined ones, the ones who wanted to learn the secrets of the East, stayed, asked questions of the students who lay prone on the floor stretching their limbs. In this fashion the newcomers usually made enough noise so that Mando finally was forced to stop teaching. He strutted over to them briskly, asked them their business, then either pointed to them to join in the training, or waved them out the door.

This was Mando's first business and Mando was no businessman. He had never really intended to start a karate academy, but his mother had finally kicked him and his friends out of her garage, sick of the commotion, the yells and shouts, the rock and roll that escaped into the neighborhood, her neighbors' complaints, and the frequent visits from the police.

Having nowhere else to go, Mando and his friends went to Enrique's house, but Enrique's mother ran them out within the hour. Mando opened up his karate school three weeks later. He told me that he regretted it from the very first day. Mando hated meeting new people, like the ones who constantly drifted in off the street to see what the karate school was all about. He hated having to tell them over and over how much the lessons cost per month, how much a *ghi* would set them back, and what the other rules were, rules he often made up as he went along.

On the other hand, Mando and his friends now had a place they could go every afternoon, a place where they could play their music as loud as they wanted, a place where they could punch the heavy bag, and shout their karate yells. Now no one bothered them, no one called the police, or yelled at them, or gave them a hard time. Mando picked the building because he was from the neighborhood, had in fact been born in a house just four blocks down the street, a two-room, shotgun house like all the other houses which filled the side streets just to the north of the downtown stores and shops. Some of the small lots had two or three houses squeezed onto them, the newest always facing the back alley.

Mando knew he would be left alone as well as he knew anything in his life. He'd quit the gang at twenty-three. It was not a real gang anyway, not a gang like in the barrios of East Los Angeles, more just a group of guys who had grown up together on the same streets, hung around each other after work or on the weekends. Mando still had friends who were in the gang, but they weren't into crime or heavy drugs; they just sat on the front porches of each other's houses drinking beer, talking big, commenting on the people who passed by them on the sidewalk or in the street. Mando knew that the plate glass window would be left intact, that no one would punch a hole in the tar paper roof of his rented building to steal his equipment, that the storefront brick would not be sprayed with luminescent paint.

Laurio had spotted Mando's Karate Academy his second week in Brownsville. Three weeks after Laurio moved in with us, we again drove by Mando's place of business on the way to the TSC campus.

"Pop, look over there, on the corner. See it. Do you think I could take lessons there sometime?"

"Sure," I'd said, and Laurio reminded me of the promise every time we'd passed by.

I reasoned, however incorrectly, that the discipline of karate would do Laurio some good. In spite of Laurio's superficial good health, I knew he was in poor shape; he rarely exercised and he had been forced to subsist off the starchy food at the Brownsville Boys' Home. Laurio breathed hard even after carrying in the groceries from the Honda. I gently kidded him about his poor physical condition, hoping to jar him into some action, but he ignored me. I also reasoned, at least initially, that some of the philosophy of the martial arts would rub off on Laurio. I badly wanted him to gain some self-confidence, to be able to ignore the taunts at school, to avoid the fights.

A few days later we both stood at the entrance to Mando's Karate Academy, ready to learn the martial arts. We waited for at least fifteen minutes at the doorway before Mando strided over, dressed in a black *ghi*, a patch of a red fist sewn over his heart.

"Do you mind if we just watch?" I asked him, wanting to check out the place before I spent my money.

"Sure, go ahead," Mando mumbled, grateful to be released so quickly. He rejoined his class of ten students, barking out orders in a demanding voice.

An hour later Laurio and I were out on the street where I'd parked my car. The sun had set, the street was dark, street lights long since disabled, and I was glad to see my car was still in one piece.

I was very sure that I had just visited the Karate-Academy-from-Hell. If there was discipline to be learned from Mando, I didn't yet see it. If there was good sportsmanship to be shared, it remained hidden by the assumption that the winner of the fight was always in the right. If there was any vestige of Eastern philosophy to be gleaned from Mando's few words or his moustached countenance, I never captured it.

"I'll do anything you say, Pop, just tell me you'll let me take lessons," said Laurio, climbing into my car. "I'll do any chores you want me to do. I'll even clean the garage. You name it. I've just got to take lessons. You name the price and I'll pay it. Shoot, Pop, I might even get into shape if I work as hard as Mando does." Laurio sat there in my car as I pulled away from the Karate-Academy-from-Hell, waiting for an answer.

I thought about pot bellied Mando and his karate lessons. I thought about Mando's unruly hair that rode atop his head. I thought about the tattoos on Mando's right arm and fist, the ones that started on his fingers and continued until they disappeared under the sleeve of his *ghi*. I knew one of them was a gang sign.

"On one condition," I finally told Laurio, after talking the situation over with Andrea.

"Name it. It doesn't matter what it is, I'll do it. I've got to go back to that place again. Just name it and I'll do it."

"I'm going with you," I told him.

"Great, Pop, we'll be the Dynamic Duo."

I told myself, as Laurio and I hung his green army duffle bag from the ceiling of the family room by a long, thick rope, that I had made the right decision. As father and son, Laurio and I would share the same experiences, ones we could talk about on a common ground. I told myself, as I saw Laurio awkwardly kicking the bag with the force of an adult mule, that there was some wisdom in attending the Karate-Academy-from-Hell, that some good would come of it. Meanwhile Laurio continued to kick at the bag with his bare feet until he hit a metal grommet, let out a howl, and limped away to recuperate.

The following Monday evening, at six-thirty, Laurio and I again presented ourselves at Mando's Karate Academy. We were dressed in shorts, t-shirts, and bare feet. Laurio had confided to me in the car on the way over that he wanted to be the best kickboxer in Brownsville. I was determined, more than ever, that Laurio learn something more than how to connect the bottom of his left foot with the thorax of one of his lunchtime enemies.

We lined up with the small group of five initiates, and Mando, looking us over with a glance, began the drills, stopping only to ignore or rebuff newcomers at the door or to change the cassette on the tape recorder. Most of the music that blared forth in the small room lined with cracked wall mirrors was heavy metal. With the beat jarring the glass of the plate window and rattling the moldings of the wall mirrors, Laurio and I jumped, hopped, kicked, and punched our way through the first hour.

"Hit the stretching machine," Mando told us around eight, dismissing us with a wave of his hand. He joined two of his buddies on the sidewalk outside the door, smoking cigarettes, talking quietly now that the cassette had been turned off for the night.

Laurio and I watched as one of the brown belts, Gus, forced his legs into clamps, then twisted and worked the screws on the steel braces until his legs were artificially stretched into a full split. He grimaced as he worked at it, one of the more experienced students giving him encouragement.

When Gus was through, he motioned Laurio to give it a try. Laurio immediately sat down behind the machine, propped his back against the wall, and began the process of ever widening the gap between his two legs. After a few minutes of composure, sweat popped out on Laurio's forehead.

"You don't have to do it all the way," I told him.

Laurio ignored me, worked at it for another few minutes, then gave up. Pulling himself stiffly up from the sitting position that the leg-stretching machine required, he gingerly hobbled over to the other side of the room. Soon he was punching at the heavy bag, making it buckle and sway, enjoying himself as he worked at it.

I gave the machine a try. But I didn't get very far with it, refusing to rupture the muscle tissue that kept one of my legs attached to the other.

Three weeks later the *ghis* arrived UPS from Dallas, and Laurio and I began to look, if not feel, like real students of Mando's Karate Academy. Three nights a week Laurio and I took our place in line with Gus, Noe, Carmen, Fred, Tony, Angel, and one or two others. Mando stood in front of us, acted out the motions he wanted us to go through, then stood at the side of the room as we went through the drills and *katas*. Occasionally Mando would, in a heavy Brownsville accent, shout to us in Korean, or what I took to be Korean because that's what Gus told me it was. Gus told me that Mando had studied with a sixth-degree black belt in Dallas who only spoke Korean and that, in four more months, the Korean master was coming to Brownsville to give tests to Mando's students (he never did come).

Gus was sixteen and was a junior in high school. He was five foot two, very stocky and strong, and his hair was cut like a marine's. Gus told me he was in the high school ROTC and was going to enlist as soon as he graduated. He'd been learning from Mando for a year and a half, first at Mando's house in his bedroom, then at the karate academy. I introduced Laurio to Gus, Laurio said hello to him, then didn't talk to him ever again.

Laurio took to sparring with Noe, learning his tricks, following his moves, sharing from the same pack of Marlboros as we all stood outside on the sidewalk after the workout, watching the traffic go by in the streets, making comments about the females who ventured by in the dark. Noe went to one of the other Brownsville high schools, the one on the poorest side of town. He looked in his twenties, but I knew he was only fifteen. Noe told me he boxed at the Boys Club Gym and he had the nose to prove it. He was taller than Gus, wiry tough, and in excellent condition from the boxing and the karate. He had a big, homemade tattoo of a heart and an arrow on his left forearm. He inhaled his cigarette smoke deeply, held it dramatically for five seconds, then let it out slowly through his nose. Noe always used his thumb and index finger to squeeze out the red hot tip of the kitchen matches he lit his cigarettes with.

Carmen, in contrast, was round and plump, her long, black hair tied tightly in a bun which rested squarely on top of her head. Her mother had made her come to Mando's Karate Academy to lose weight, which she had done, but she had stayed on for two more years, enjoying the exercise and the companionship of the other students. Carmen was very talkative, willing to discuss her plans to graduate in the spring from the same high school as Laurio, anxious to ask questions about TSC when she learned I taught there. Carmen was also Gus's sister, and she worried that when Gus stopped comimg to karate her mother would make her stop coming too.

"What does your mother think about karate?" I asked her.

"She thinks it's crazy. But she's proud of me too. And she likes that she doesn't have to worry about me on the street all the time. People leave me alone because they know better than to personally mess with me. And they know Gus."

Laurio and I usually got home between eight and eight-thirty. Many evenings he stood at the homemade punching bag in the family room jabbing away, dancing back and forth in his imitation of the moves he'd seen Gus make, hitting the green canvas awkwardly but hard. I often joined him, taking turns holding the bag, practicing the new kicks we'd learned.

We sparred. Laurio was wild and free with his kicks, while I was slow and careful. We jumped around the family room, landing harmless blows on each other's arms and elbows. It was fun. Laurio got in a good kick to my stomach, knocking my breath away. I pretended I was angry at him, chased him around the house and out onto the front lawn. He taunted me to come after him and I chased him down Poinsettia Place in the dark, in my bare feet.

I caught Laurio, still out of shape, at the corner of Acacia, threw him over my shoulder and carried him back to our house. Hiding my heavy breathing from him, I tossed him on the sofa next to where Andrea sat reading.

"I got something for you," I told her, before throwing him in her direction. Laurio landed safely with a loud thump.

"I give up, Pop," he laughed.

About the fourth month of lessons Laurio told me he didn't want to go anymore. I was surprised, and told him so.

"Look, Pop, I just don't need it anymore. I'm not learning any new kicks and its getting boring."

"You're just starting to get good at it," I told him, disappointed. Laurio was quick, and his long legs gave him a big advantage when he sparred with Noe or the other boys.

I could have quit too, but I decided to keep going to Mando's Karate Academy. I liked the foreignness of the place, the fact that Mando was so totally nonverbal, that he was the worst businessman I had ever known. Mando often forgot to collect our monthly fees, drove customers away by the truckload, seldom cleaned the room . . . the thin rug that covered the cement floor had a life of its own. I liked practicing *kata* forms to the tunes of Led Zeppelin. I liked talking to the kids before and after the workout, walking out to my car in bare feet, the insides of my legs still burning from the strains of the stretching machine.

On the fifteenth of May, a sultry Wednesday evening cooled by a stiff breeze from across the river, I parked my car on the street a half block down Mando's Karate Academy. I grabbed my gym bag full of karate *ghi* and belt as I swung out of the car, and walked slowly down the sidewalk, stopping in front of store windows to stare at the display cases.

I walked right by Mando's Karate Academy before I noticed it. The lights were off inside and the door was padlocked. I peeked through the slits in the newsprint, shading my eyes from the glare of the street. The room inside was completely empty, even the wall mirrors were gone. There were no stretching machine, no posters announcing karate contests in Houston and New Orleans, just a naked, and ugly, room.

I waited for an hour. Gus showed up, seemed surprised that Mando and his karate academy were no longer there, smoked three Marlboros, shook hands elaborately with me, clenching wrists and bumping elbows the way Laurio had showed me, then left, walking slowly down the street, karate *ghi* wrapped in a tight bundle by the belt, swinging it from his shoulder gracefully and casually.

I left after another thirty minutes of waiting. Carmen had come by briefly, looking for Gus. And Tony's mother had circled the block twice; each time Tony, in the front seat, nodded at me, looking uncomfortable, unsmiling.

A year later, several months after Laurio had left our home, I ran into Mando at a pool hall on Central Boulevard. His potbelly was a little bigger and his curly hair looked wilder, in total disarray. His left wrist and elbow were encased in a heavy cast, but the injury didn't seem to bother his stroke.

"What happened to your place?" I asked him as soon as he'd run a few balls.

"The landlord was being unreasonable. So I closed it down. You remember Gus? He's still coming over, or was until I got this." He looked down at his cast.

"How'd you do it?" I asked, expecting him to tell me that he'd single-handedly put five men in the hospital. After all, he was a black belt.

"Got into a fight with my mother. She kept nagging at me and I finally got enough of it. I gave her a good punch, but damn if it didn't bust my wrist up. Doctor says it'll be another six weeks until I can take the cast off."

I went home later, turned the lights on in the family room, took my shoes and socks off silently, unbuttoned my shirt. I began hitting Laurio's bag, systematically. I worked at it hard, raising a sweat fast, jabbing and punching, trying a few fancy spin kicks, even throwing an elbow or two at the hard canvas. When I finished, I felt better.

Evangelina

The Brownsville Jail is on 12th Street, just four blocks south of the zoo. It is a new building of brown brick and concrete, windowless except for the ground-floor reception area. I parked my car between the two yellow lines on the hot asphalt, then walked across the parking lot to the glass entrance.

"Juvenile detention," I said to the face behind the window in the wall. The desk sergeant told me to wait a minute, motioning me to some black plastic chairs against the far wall. I sat down, waited for ten minutes, then the sergeant called me over to the window. The glass in the window looked two inches thick, pieces of thin wire woven through it like thread in a quilt.

"Who was it you wanted to see?" the sergeant, Pedro Malina, asked me.

"Evangelina Baptista. I'm her legal guardian. She's a runaway, been here since last night."

The sergeant looked at a three-ringed notebook before him, asked to see my driver's license, then pushed a button which opened the steel door to my left.

I walked through the doorway — the door closed stiffly behind me — and down a short hall. A few minutes later Pedro Malina came down the hallway, walking quickly, smoking in practiced inhalations as he talked to me.

"Sit right in there. Make yourself comfortable. I called the jailer and he'll have her here in awhile. Sometimes he's busy and sometimes he can get right to it, but it being Saturday afternoon and quiet like it is, it won't take him too long to get her."

I sat down in a chair in the small room, got claustrophobic, then stood in the hallway, leaning against the gray wall.

The jailer took his time about it. Twenty-five minutes later there were footsteps, then the steel door at the other end of the hallway opened on smooth hinges and I saw Evangelina coming towards me. She didn't look scared, not like I thought she would, but she looked very small in that jail hallway, very frail and out-of-place.

"Call me when you're through," the jailer told me. I thought I recognized his face, but couldn't be sure. I think he'd been a student of mine at TSC. I had many criminal justice majors take my courses and, as a result, I knew several Brownsville cops.

I nodded agreement to the jailer, then stood embracing Evangelina, not sure what to say. She started crying, wordless.

"You want a cigarette?" I finally said to her when we sat down in the small room.

"God, I sure do," she said, wiping away the tears with her hand.

We went through the cigarette ritual. I'd grabbed a pack from her room along with her propane lighter, the kind that is made of clear plastic so you can see how much fluid remains.

Evangelina sat distractedly drawing on her cigarette. I still didn't know what to say so I sat there, too, wordless.

"Do you want to come back?" I finally got out. I knew that, given the situation, I should be more demanding of her, show her my anger at her actions, recut our emotional pact so that it would be stronger than before. But all I wanted to do was get her out of that place, take her home from the Brownsville Jail.

"Sure," she said. Evangelina looked down at the floor, the smoke from her cigarette drifting up towards the ceiling. She combed back her pitch black hair from her plain, young face, wiped a stray tear from her wide-set, dark eyes.

"How bad?" I asked, beginning to remember what she'd done.

"Bad," she said, looking up at me now, again fighting back some tears.

"If you come back," I said, the brief words sticking in my throat, "if you come back, then it's still on our terms. You've hurt Andrea and me a lot. I don't trust you anymore. I was very worried. When you didn't come back last night, we didn't know what had happened to you. When you case worker phoned us, we were just about to start calling the hospitals."

"I know, I know it was stupid. I just couldn't control myself. I got so angry at your telling me what to do. So I went down the street, smoked a cigarette, but I was still angry. I was going to come back right then, but one thing led to another and then, when I was walking down this other street later on, the cops saw me and picked me up. Shit."

"Are you okay?"

"I'm real tired. And I feel real dirty. God, I'd just like to take a shower and sleep for a few days."

We talked a little more, me asking her again if she was really ready to come back, Evangelina swearing that she would do anything Andrea and I asked of her. I had to get her out of there, even as I realized, despite what she said, that she could not live with us much longer, that between us a fundamental tie had been severed.

I signed for Evangelina at the wire window, Sergeant Pedro Malina shoving various forms in triplicate in front of me. I drove my foster daughter the short mile home. She walked quickly up the sidewalk and disappeared into her room, shutting the door noiselessly behind her.

Evangelina had lived with us for more than a year, during a good portion of which Laurio had also shared our household. Laurio left two months earlier, and now it looked like it was Evangelina's time to go. She'd run away from us twice before, although never overnight. Each time she'd called up a few hours later and, through many tears, asked to come back. She was showing us—she couldn't force herself to say it out loud—that she felt ready to try it out on her own, away from adult supervision.

A few times I felt as if I was simply acting out a minor part in a play Evangelina had written, one in which I never was told my lines. I know that I was supposed to be a villain, one who drank too much, beat her mother, and abused her. Since I didn't do any of those things, Evangelina often seemed unsure of how to act around me; she could vacillate from being a good daughter to being a terror, invective rolling off her tongue as if it had been pre-programmed.

Like Laurio, Evangelina had come to us with much hope. She was sixteen, extremely articulate, and very bright, always a good student in school in spite of her family problems. Her real father had left her family when she was twelve and her mother had raised her, her sister, and her three brothers the best she could. At thirteen, Evangelina left her family to live with her aunt who had recently remarried. Evangelina respected her aunt, looked up to her in a way she never had to her own mother. Her aunt had a good job in a small Valley town near Mercedes. But much to the aunt's dismay, Evangelina soon began running away from her, absent for up to a week before she would call and, tearfully, ask to be taken back. Often Evangelina stayed with her girl friends from school, but sometimes she stayed with older boys and men until they kicked her out. Evangelina's aunt became worried that her niece was a bad influence on her own daughter. She realized, slowly at first, that she had totally lost control of Evangelina.

Evangelina ran away again and again. Several times the police found her and brought her back to her aunt. She was interviewed once by a social worker and admitted, for the first time, that her father had sexually abused her. Evangelina blamed herself. Again she ran away, but this time when she was caught, her aunt, at the suggestion of the social worker, sent her to the Brownsville Girls' Home. Like many of the other girls there, she had committed no crime, but was herself a victim.

Laurio and Evangelina got along well enough together, although Laurio was, at first, very jealous of her and protective of us. Several times he tried to tell us about Evangelina.

"She's not what she acts like," he told me cryptically one evening.

"You lost me," I said. Laurio wanted to tell me, but could not, that Evangelina was sexually promiscuous, at least by his definition; he would not consider his own behavior, more or less identical, as falling into that same category. Laurio believed in the traditional role of the Mexican-American female, one which Evangelina ignored.

"Pop, she's pretending to be something she's not," he tried again, attempting to save us from what he thought we didn't know.

Andrea and I had talked about the sexual abuse Evangelina had suffered. I thought it would be easy not to get caught up in a teenager's acting-out of her emotional problems; I felt I had learned much from living with Laurio. Still, it was really very hard at times. Evangelina had a way of successfully starting arguments over nothing, of getting Andrea and me mad at each other before we knew what happened, of making the whole household miserable.

She could be very manipulative. More than a few times I got so furious at her that I wanted to hit her, but always, with Andrea's help, I regained control, saw Evangelina's emotional machinations for what they were.

Evangelina, as one might expect, was very unsure of her sexuality and identity, much more so than other teenagers her age. From the beginning, with mixed success, Andrea and I tried by example to show her that we were comfortable in our marriage, that we enjoyed and loved each other, that Evangelina was living in a secure and stable family. In turn, at her worst, Evangelina would run the gamut from ideal daughter to street urchin. It was impossible at times to really know which daughter would show up at the dinner table.

"I'm being treated like a six year old," she stormed at us one evening. "You're always watching everything I do. I have no privileges here at all. I feel like a prisoner. I want to go back home."

Evangelina was also an intelligent young woman who was warm, loving, grateful to be a part of our family. Cigarettes in hand, she studied her schoolwork at night, worked the phones like any teenager, agonized over her appearance, pretended that she didn't care that her intellectual abilities seemed to drive away the Brownsville teenage males. She loved to curl up around a novel and, like Laurio, played her records at ear-splitting levels.

Evangelina was a closet high school jock. She was, unfortunately, ahead of her time. She was much more coordinated than Laurio, who often in his teenage gawkiness bumped into inanimate, immoveable objects. Evangelina had a competitiveness of heart, a strong determination of will that would have made her a first-rate high school athlete if she'd been given the same opportunities as the high school boys.

Two months after I brought Evangelina home from the Brownsville Jail, she moved to Houston to live with her sister and her sister's husband and two children. She called us every few months, telling us proudly of her job as a secretary in a large geological firm, of the money she was saving, and her plans to go back to school at night. She eventually earned her GED and attended two years of junior college in Houston.

She moved in with Jaime, a friend of her brother's, and Jaime's mother. She didn't like living with Jaime's mother because she always tried to tell Evangelina what to do, how she should be living her life. Evangelina called us late at night, often drunk, almost incomprehensible, and complained of her life. Then we wouldn't hear from her for months. One night she called, crying, to tell of Jaime's beating her. She was going to leave him, find her own apartment, start over again in Houston.

Evangelina got pregnant and married Jaime. Jaime stopped hitting her while she was pregnant, and Evangelina cut back on her drinking. Jaime's mother watched little Jaime, Jr., while Evangelina worked during the days. Evangelina, Jaime, and his mother loved Jaime, Jr., very much and unashamedly spoiled him. Because of the downturn in the

Houston economy, Jaime lost his job; he began to spend his days drinking beer, watching the tube, and getting into small kinds of trouble.

Evangelina still drinks too much, and Jaime, when he gets drunk, beats her. But Jaime doesn't beat her like he used to before Jaime, Jr., was born. Jaime found work again with one of his brothers-in-law and his mother again watches Jaime, Jr., during the days.

Evangelina, at twenty-seven has been married to Jaime for four years, she has a healthy young son, she is educated, and she's worked for the same employer for seven years. While Evangelina remains less than satisfied with her life, and complains about it regularly, she's got much more than she ever thought she'd get, much more than she ever thought she deserved.

The Zoo

Evangelina thought the Brownsville Zoo was a waste of her time, and she preferred to read one of her books or to run laps around the neighborhood. Laurio, in contrast, would spend, if given the chance, every afternoon at the zoo. He loved all the animals, from the tree sloths to the polar bears swimming in their crystal clear pool. He was curious about even the ones he couldn't pet, ride, or groom, like the three ugly camels, which spat at you if you so much as looked in their direction.

Our house was less than five blocks from the entrance to the zoo; between us were two blocks of houses, the city park where Berta had her wedding, and one of Brownsville's prettiest *resacas*. In the early mornings, you could hear the gibbons screaming their group cheer in anticipation of the sunrise over the Brownsville Zoo. The primates worked their way up through octave after octave, their vibrations carrying clearly over the shallow, muddy waters of the *resaca*, up over the peaks of roofs, through palm, mesquite, and sour orange, and into our bedroom window. I was living in the land of Tarzan until the morning traffic from the overpass on State Highway 77 began to seep in, covering the jungle with hot, liquid cars and trucks.

Between five and six o'clock, at feeding time, more unearthly noises escaped the cages and the confinements of the Brownsville Zoo, noises originating from the stomachs of animals who waited impatiently for their food. Unlike the sunrise gibbons, this feeding frenzy competed against the regular tumult of five o'clock bridge traffic, commuters returning to Matamoros or Brownsville after a hard day's work, or vehicles bound for other points on the compass. The roar of the king of beasts could be submerged in the gear grinding of an eighteen-wheeler loaded down with ten tons of onions freshly harvested from fields outside Raymondville.

The scary noises came in the middle of the night, between the hours of two and four, when most of Brownsville was asleep. Monster sounds escaped the circumference of the six-foot-high barbed wire, bass rumblings from atrophied bowels originally fashioned to soak up the juices of homo sapiens. These prehistoric earthquakes rattled the panes of the windows, sent me struggling up from deep sleep like a madman, instinctively reaching for a club to kill the intruders. I always caught only the last syllables of these past eons, syllables whose profundity temporarily reorganized the molecules of window glass into waves of sand crystals. I felt with my fingers the peaks and valleys of these tremors, waited, catching my breath, to hear again the yawnings of the sabertooth. I never did.

Whatever animal made these night sounds, sounds which were of primal dying and death, disguised itself during the day, hid out in the back caverns of the big cats, in subterranean tunnels beneath the reptile house, or at the bottom of the polar bears' chlorinated swimming hole. Under a subtropical sun the Brownsville Zoo was a paradise of exotic animals in all the fantastic glory of colored feathers, furs, talons, and crowns. Visitors viewed the animals from a maze of pleasant walkways and bridges over narrow canals and ponds filtering lazily into the nearby *resaca*.

The small zoo, not more than six blocks square, was crammed with endangered animals from the tropical jungles around the world, animals who at times seemed to compete for the most outlandish costumes. The large flock of pink flamingos looked mundane when compared with the birds from the other side of the Rio Grande that flew about the eaves of the aviary or walked stiffly, pompously, in pairs between copies of their native plants. In the reptile house the common varieties of indigenous rattlesnakes were but brown fishing worms to the snakes of the Mexican jungle, each ringed in stunning combinations of earth tones and pastels, victims of a shaman's insane brush. I often returned to stare in disbelief at the tropical frogs and toads, some of which, the signs warned, were extremely poisonous.

Large carp teemed in the artificial canals, fed by tourists who could buy ice cream cones jammed with fish food at the concession stands. Outlaw gulls made a good living from zoo visitors, stealing the fish food, begging for popcorn, vacuuming the grounds of the refuse left behind by the thousands of tourists, many of them elderly, who came to the zoo.

The different species of animals were carefully tended, well fed, always under the watchful eye of zoo attendants who sported about in zebra-colored golf carts. Docents were everywhere, ready to answer questions on the animals or the many tropical plants; the zoo had an excellent cactus garden near the entrance. On a Saturday afternoon cameras clicked, families walked the pathways pushing rental baby buggies before them, the smells of wild animal dung covered by the acacia, poinsettia, honeysuckle, and the popcorn and chili peppers from the concession stands. The zoo was a popular stopover for Mexican families from Matamoros and Monterey; in front of the cages designed by the best zoo architects, border Spanish blended with the more unfamiliar accent from the interior of Mexico.

In the chilly months of December and January, when the beach at South Padre was fogged in or a stiff breeze from the Gulf lowered the temperature into the fifties or even forties, I often spent time at the Brownsville Zoo without Andrea, Laurio, or Evangelina by my side. Although I was initially drawn to the more exotic animals, I soon spent all of my time in front of the chimp cage. Hot coffee in one hand, I stood there leaning against a concrete pillar, feeling at times as if I were a primate peeping tom.

I could not take my eyes off of one chimp, whom I named Dale, and Dale's close friends. Dale was deeply into begging, like the rest of the chimps, but when a piece of popcorn fell beyond his immediate reach, outside the electrical wire that circumscribed the cage, he was not afraid to venture after it. With no help from his peers, Dale would spring into action. Dale's Plan A required him to stretch his limbs and trunk to extraordinary length to reach between the wire to capture the popcorn or peanut or piece of bread. If Plan A failed, Dale, with no change in demeanor, moved on to Plan B.

Dale carefully, and slowly, limboed underneath the electric wire, much to the amusement and interest of his friends and family. Edging along the contours of the concrete forms that encircled his cage, Dale deftly reached out with his four fingers and prehensile thumb to capture the errant popcorn, then contorted his way back into the enclosure, carefully avoiding the hot wire. I usually applauded Dale's sortie, for which he nodded, briefly, in my direction.

What Dale had done, in short, was briefly leave the confines of his cage, capture his quarry, then gingerly return with the prize, which he quickly consumed. Only a shallow strip of water separated Dale from complete freedom, that and the six-foot-high fence that surrounds the zoo. Dale could easily have leaped over the ditch and, in an instant, been sharing my coffee. If he had really wanted to.

One of Dale's close family did decide to tour Brownsville. He got as far as the King Mart Grocery on Palm Boulevard, seven city blocks north of the chimp cage. Behind him he left a trail of havoc. No one wanted to give him the snacks he deserved, so he was forced to borrow without permission. By the time he reached the produce section at the King Mart, he was in a rotten mood. But his mood quickly changed when he realized he'd just discovered chimp heaven. There were bananas, of course, hundreds of them right off the truck, along with any other fruit you could want. And, right next to the produce section, were the chips and dips. He helped himself.

They cornered Dale's buddy behind some empty boxes in the stock room. A naive clerk grabbed the intruder by the scruff of the neck, thinking he would send him back to the zoo with a swift kick to the posterior; luckily he was not seriously injured by the chimp who, by then, just wanted to take a quiet siesta.

Dale's buddy was given, free of charge, a gallon of Gallo's best vintage. It was a hot day and the chimp was very thirsty; in less than thirty minutes, the chimp slumped to the floor. He was quickly transported, before he could even give an interview to Eye Witness News, back to his cage in the Brownsville Zoo, suffering only from a wino's hangover.

The story received much attention in the Brownsville and Valley press. Each of the stories stressed the care that was regularly given to all the zoo animals, the efforts made by the zookeepers to provide the different species with a close approximation to their native climate, environment, and food. The Brownsville Zoo was indeed extremely clean, even after a visit from a Saturday afternoon crowd. The cages were cleverly designed to allow the visitor full view of the animal in an unobtrusive way. It was an operation that required skilled management, a trained staff with many years of experience. The Brownsville Zoo was an expensive operation which, the community was often told, attracted thousands of tourists and their dollars to the area every year.

The octave-jumping of the gibbons in the anticipation of sunrise, as well as the errant noises of unknown nighttime beasties, went wafting down the streets of other neighborhoods than mine, poor neighborhoods on the south and southwest sides of the zoo, which were typical of Brownsville. Streets filled with large potholes were bordered by shotgun houses, many in dilapidated condition with patched roofs, torn screens over missing windowpanes, sagging front porches, doors unhinged, paint peeling from the wooden siding. Outhouses faced the narrow alleys that ran in back of the small lots, along with second and third dwellings in which additional families resided. Thick tropical vegetation covered much of the surface of these tiny one- and two-room houses and the boards of the outhouses. Only when a freak freeze had turned the leaves and vines to rotting brown did the shabbiness of these structures become glaringly apparent.

The residents of these two neighborhoods sometimes walked over to the Brownsville Zoo to see the animals. They paid five dollars for an adult to gain admission, two dollars for children; a man with a wife and five children, not unusual in Brownsville, must pay about twenty dollars to see the rare and expensive animals. Admission revenues did not, however, come close to covering the operating costs of the Brownsville Zoo. Every year there was a "Zoofari," a series of fund-raising events designed to raise several hundred thousand dollars to pay the operating costs of the zoo and to raise monies for new acquisitions and projects.

The Zoofari attracted patrons from throughout the Valley and Texas, as well as supporters from California and New York. They flew into the Harlingen airport or the Brownsville airport in their private jets and spent several days helping to raise money for the zoo. Silent auctions, banquets, and special tours of the zoo's facilities kept the visitors busy. The zebra golf carts whizzed along the pathways as patrons were shown the newest animal offspring or most recent exotic acquisition.

One result of this philanthropy was the continual construction of new facilities for the animals. The kangaroos and wallabies now lounged in what looked, to my untrained eye, like an Aspen ski lodge. Wooden beams and glass dominated the imaginative structure, the likes of which have pushed the Brownsville Zoo onto a shortlist of the best American zoos.

As I stood there watching Dale for yet another afternoon, my hands warming to the steam coming off my third cup of coffee, it struck me that in Brownsville the zoo animals received more attention and better care than the majority of the citizens. The animals were better housed and fed, air-conditioned in the summer and warmed during the colder months, free of charge, by the city utility company. When the animals got sick, all of them received excellent medical care from the trained staff. Before the animals gave birth, they were put on special diets and, once in labor, they were tended by skilled physicians concerned for their welfare. I knew more than a handful of citizens in this city who would gladly have traded their dwelling to live in the new cage for the kangaroos and wallabies.

I and others in my family, along with many throughout Brownsville and the Valley, would miss Dale and all the animals, so I certainly didn't want the zoo to close. There was no doubt that the tourists who visited the zoo did pump dollars into the local community, that some revenues and benefits did, in the politicians' quaint terminology, "trickle down."

But not five blocks from the Brownsville Zoo, over on Jackson Street, the Brownsville Boys Club didn't have the ten thousand dollars it required to run a summer swimming program for the disadvantaged youth of the city; they had an old swimming pool, but no money for its upkeep or insurance costs. Not a single individual, program, or business came forward to help the Boys Club.

Maybe a trade was at last in order. Maybe it was finally time to give swimming lessons to the kids of Brownsville and, this one summer, let the polar bears sweat, let the wallabies get wet when it rained, and allow the rhinos to deliver their own offspring.

The H S Words

I finished the lecture in my class on the sociology of marriage and family, then threw my books and notes into my briefcase. I had only a few minutes to get to my next class and I was determined to be on time. Four slips of paper sat in a pile near the lectern. I had asked the students, at the end of the class, to write down any questions they had about the course material, promising to answer the questions during the next class period.

The first one read: "Is it true that you can get V.D. from the door handle of a bathroom?" The second had scrawled on it, "My boyfriend says I can't get pregnant if he takes his boots off. Is he right?" The third one, written in tiny, pinched characters, wanted to know if having intercourse when the moon was not full was as good, or better, than using birth control pills. The last one was blank, the questioner apparently losing his nerve before he could ask the question.

I already knew that the Brownsville high schools, like most of the Valley high schools, did not teach sex education or human reproduction, but I had counted on the fact that TSC freshmen were required to take a year of college biology. I asked my friend Arnoldo what kind of background in human anatomy and reproduction TSC freshmen were getting in the required two semesters of TSC's general biology course.

"None," he said. "They are getting zip and *nada*. Nothing."

"But you have them for two semesters," I told him, surprised.

"They cut out the chapters on human anatomy and human reproduction from the textbook at the College Book Store. They use a razor blade. Been doing it for years, ever since before I graduated from here."

"You must be kidding," I told him, unbelieving. "How could the biology department stand for such a thing?"

"Because, dumbo, the chairperson of the biology department, who has been chair for thirty-three years, requires the College Book Store to do it."

"Personally, I'm all for it," Henry, the chairman of my department, told me, after carefully closing his office door. "But you've got to understand that this is a conservative community. The Catholic church is a big deal in Brownsville. You get my meaning? You'd be rocking the boat and I couldn't do a thing to help you."

I went back to my desk, rewrote my course notes. For the next three weeks I taught my marriage and family class the basics of human anatomy, human reproduction, and birth control. My students showed extreme interest, asking more questions than I'd ever encountered in a TSC classroom. Several brought their girlfriends and boyfriends, the latter sitting at the back of the room, motionless, intent, listening closely to the lectures, but completely silent, eyes to the floor, when the students discussed the issues.

"We badly need a class on the sociology of human sexuality," I told Henry a month later. "It's already recognized as a legitimate course at most of the other state junior colleges. If they are not going to teach basic human anatomy and reproduction in biology, where it belongs, then I could teach it in this course along with basic methods of contraception, family planning, and all the rest of the concerns they want to know about. It would be a very popular course."

"I'm all for this, Lee. It's a great idea. But you're going out on a limb here. You can present it to the dean if you want, but I can tell you beforehand he's not going to be very happy about it. Write up a course syllabus, get hold of a sample text, then go talk to the dean. But I have to warn you, I'm not optimistic about this. You're going to stir up a hornet's nest on this one. And remember, you don't have tenure yet."

Several weeks later I went to the dean. He was not glad to see me.

"Look, Dr. Maril, I agree with you one hundred percent on this. The students should have an opportunity to take a course like the one you have proposed. But let's be realistic. This is a very conservative community. All it would take is one phone call from an irate member of the community who doesn't want his son or daughter learning about this stuff, and you'd be out of here. And with something as controversial as this is, there's sure to be more than one phone call."

"So you're against the course?" I asked him.

"No, not at all. I'm very supportive of it. But I can't just go to the administration with this. They'd never accept it."

"You are the administration," I said.

"I have to tell you, Dr. Maril, that this kind of attitude of yours is not appreciated in this office. It's very unprofessional."

I remembered, after the meeting, that the dean had been very careful to never once utter the words "human sexuality."

I made appointments in the following weeks and months with the vice-president and the president of TSC. The vice-president was sullen when I spoke to him, quickly referring me to the president. Every time I spoke the words "human sexuality" to the vice-president, a retired military man, he visibly winced. The words seemed to possess a power of their own, an ability to strike fear in the hearts of grown men.

President Humberto shook my hand as I entered his office of rocks. "Good to see you, Lee, good to see you."

But before I could get settled in a comfortable chair, prepared for at least a twenty-minute lecture on whatever rock happened to be closest to his hand, President Humberto said, looking not at his beloved desk of rocks but at the floor to my left, "I know why you're here. I'm going to form a special committee on it. You'll get a memo as soon as the committee is ready to go on this."

Then, without another word, he gracefully ushered me from his office, never once having been forced to speak the dreaded H S words.

The special committee met four months later, at twelve noon in the wood-paneled conference room in the administration building. Around the long, polished table sat at least fifteen people, about half of whom I recognized. The federal district judge was seated at the table, flanked by a prominent local attorney who'd spent some years in the Texas legislature. The bishop of the Valley's Catholic diocese sat quietly in his chair. Two other priests, one of whom I knew quite well, were present, along with a nun in full habit. Across from them sat the local supervisor of the Texas Department of Human Services. The public relations director of one of the Valley's two television stations was there. There were also two public school nurses present, my chairperson, my dean, the vice-president, President Humberto, who presided over the meeting, and a handful of people I had never seen before.

President Humberto spoke first and longest, thanking each of the members of this very special committee for taking the time to meet with him. He talked on and on. The federal judge grew impatient, looked at his watch, and finally excused himself, saying that he had to get back to his court. President Humberto, never fazed, continued, outlining the history of the college, its record of achievements, and its close relationship with the community of Brownsville. I was glad there were no rocks in sight, afraid that he would pull one out of his coat pocket, doom us all to thirty minutes of geological trivia.

Finally President Humberto stopped talking, quickly excused himself, mumbling that he had an important prior engagement. He handed the meeting over to the dean. The vice-president scurried out on the coattails of the president, afraid to hear the H S words spoken in a public setting.

The dean passed out the course syllabus I had provided and asked if there were any comments. All the members of the special committee spent several minutes eyeballing the syllabus, a few making notes in the margin. No one said a word.

"Is there any discussion of this course or suggestions for Dr. Maril?" asked the dean.

"It's about time," said the bishop. "We've needed this for as long as I can remember. It's about time we had this at the college."

The dean seemed to deflate then, the anxiety oozing from his face, leaving his features flaccid.

Everyone at the table agreed it was a good idea. Ten minutes later the committee meeting ended.

I got a call from the dean's office a week later. There was going to be a special subcommittee meeting of the special committee on the following Saturday morning at eleven-thirty in President Humberto's office. According to the dean's secretary, representatives of the medical community of Brownsville would be present.

At eleven-thirty I walked into President Humberto's office, not exactly sure what to expect. President Humberto and two prominent Brownsville doctors were huddled around the radio on Humberto's desk listening to the pre-game warm-up chatter for the upcoming Texas A&M football game. All three were alumni.

"We got to do this quick," one of the doctors said to Humberto. "The game starts in thirty minutes."

I was introduced by Humberto to the two doctors, who ignored me, quickly turning back to the radio.

"Dr. Maril here wants to start a new course next semester. I showed you guys the syllabus."

The two doctors nodded their heads.

"Let him do it. If you get stuck on something, need the answer, then just give me a call," one doctor told me, smiling in my direction before he turned again to the radio.

Then the other doctor told two jokes about homosexuals. They laughed. After a round of handshakes, I left President Humberto's office. I knew, from the moment of the handshakes, that the course on H S had received the official support of Brownsville's medical community.

I taught the first class on the sociology of human sexuality the next fall. There were twenty-one students in the course, fifteen of them female. The students seemed to enjoy the class and they told their friends about it. After I'd been teaching the course for two semesters, male college students began signing up in equal proportions to the females. The men always sat at the back of the class for the first several weeks, eyes to the floor, looking very uncomfortable and out of place; only after several class discussions and projects did they begin to feel at home, no longer afraid to discuss human sexuality in public.

Word got around the TSC campus quickly and soon I was teaching two sections of the course during the day, and another section was being taught at night by a colleague. We could have offered more sections and they would have filled. In spite of the administrators' fears, not a single area resident ever protested the course.

The second year I taught the course, I had President Humberto's only daughter as one of my students. Shortly thereafter, I ran into President Humberto in the TSC parking lot. He was just getting into his rusty clunker when he saw me.

"Amelia took your course last semester," he said, shaking my hand, then looking over at my left shoulder.

"She's a good student. I'm sure you're very proud of her."

"We talked about your course at home," President Humberto told me in a matter-of-fact voice. "Sometimes at the dinner table. My daughter's generation is more open about those kinds of things than ours. My mother and father, may God bless them both, would never have allowed that kind of subject talked about in their house. They'd have washed our mouths out with soap. Or worse. But times change. I'm glad Amelia took the course."

President Humberto smiled, still not looking at me directly, then got back into the driver's seat of his beat-up car, shaking his head back and forth in slow rotations, carrying on a silent conversation with himself that I would never hear. But I would bet a ton of money that he was talking to his parents, telling them that Amelia was growing up to be a fine young lady and that the times, even in Brownsville, can never stand still.

Educating Juan

I taught at TSC for almost six years before I felt I reached a dead end. I enjoyed teaching the students—the Wildman and a few others were the rare exception—anticipating the start of each new semester, feeling real regret, a sense of loss, at the end of each sixteen weeks. But from this teaching experience and from TSTI, in addition to working as a consultant with several Valley public school systems and my contact with the Brownsville high schools as a parent of foster kids, I well knew the serious problems inherent in the Valley educational systems, problems that at least in part were created by the systems themselves.

I also knew that these educational bureaucracies were very slow to change and, very often, actively resisted those who suggested new ideas or ways of doing things. Through persistence I had forced TSC to offer courses in human sexuality. But it took this junior college more than two years to relent; along the way I had been told that I might lose my job for pushing too hard. Even though I had won a small victory, the effort and energy required had been disheartening.

As my years at TSC passed quickly by, to my surprise I found I was fast becoming one of the senior faculty, a full-fledged, but unwilling participant in a system that helped to promote educational inferiority. My choices were few at TSC. I could continue to gripe and complain about the situation to those who would listen to me, but fundamental change, a reordering of educational priorities at TSC, was clearly impossible. At bottom, I felt confident that I knew how to educate students better than TSC or the Valley public schools, that I had gained enough insights through my years of experience to do a better job than was being done, or could be done, given the existing systems and their constraints. It was time to put up, or shut up.

In the winter of 1982 I turned thirty-five years old. I had lived seven years in the Valley. It came to me, as it no doubt has to others who reach or exceed this chronological age, that my life was more than half over. I no longer could claim to be either young or dumb. I had come of age in the Valley, despite my own procrastinations and reluctance at involvements. I was determined not to end up a bitter old man at TSC, drinking coffee in the teacher's lounge while muttering slathers of criticism at the administration. I could see myself turning into a tenured, slightly daffy, old grouch at TSC, pained by the situation, yet destined because of the circumstances to achieve only a few Pyrrhic victories. That spring I decided to start a private junior high and high school in Brownsville, a model school that would demonstrate Valley kids could, if but given a reasonable chance, succeed in their education as well as or better than any others.

Under the influence of a hot March wind that whipped across the Rio Grande and blew down a section of my rotting backyard fence, I made my decision and stuck to it. It was not a difficult decision to make, given the alternatives. I could run, as I had in the past, or I could hide, a difficult thing to do in Brownsville, or I could stick my other leg into the hyper-heated swill of life that surrounded me, taking a genuine risk for the first time in a very long while.

With the voice of failure singing its sweet and sweaty tune in one ear, the ghosts of John Dewey and Summerhill dueting in the other, I plodded and stumbled my way through the planning stages of a new school. Architectural designs and educational philosophies were inscribed in earnest on backs of cocktail napkins and check stubs, on fleeting pieces of paper that fell like large flakes of snow from the pockets of my shirts and pants as I tossed them into the laundry basket. Retrieving the bits, I shaped them into small piles on my desk, gleaning through them, deciphering the pearls of thought that lay hidden next to the logos of local restaurants and franchises.

I analyzed the demographics of the community, determined how many kids were between the ages of twelve and eighteen, located the sector of parents who would be most interested in my school. I constructed tables and graphs, wrote elaborate explanations and justifications, and finally gave two presentations at one of the downtown banks. I laid out my grand plan to the loan executives sitting around a long, narrow conference table: the initial costs to open, the annual dollars I would need to operate my school the first year.

Loan promised along with words of encouragement, I searched out potential sites for the new school, interviewed real estate agents, glared through darkened windows of empty burger franchises, pizza parlors, insurance agencies run-amok, and other unlikely buildings in Brownsville. In the end I found a local builder who agreed to construct a building to my specifications and lease the building back to me at a yearly rate. The next month was spent designing a workable set of classrooms, offices, corridors, restrooms, and playgrounds.

Actual construction began in late May and was finished in time for the start of classes in September. Land was leveled in a field one block east of Central Boulevard, in the northeastern part of Brownsville. Each afternoon I drove to the site, walked on the concrete slab through the spaces outlined by two-by-fours, dreamed educator dreams. At dusk one heavy July evening I sat on the floor of the director's office, clearing a place for myself amidst the dirt, nails, and pieces of wall and ceiling insulation. Cars drove by in the street outside, occupants pausing to read the sign announcing the new school. Two boys on bikes rode up, saw me there in the roofless building, and quickly pedaled away. Sitting contentedly on the unfinished floor of my new office, I felt as if I were perched on top of the world. I saw myself as a rare breed of capitalist-educator about to work a real miracle.

I could not be at two places at once, both teach at TSC and run my new school. As plans progressed, Andrea and I shared more and more of the ideas and dreams we had of it. We finally decided we needed the income from my teaching in case the new school bombed, so Andrea quit her job at the Brownsville Boys' Home to help manage the school while I was at TSC in the mornings. "My" school became "our" school. As "co-directors" of the new school, Andrea in theory handled the day-to-day administrative operations of the school and taught English classes, while I continued to handle the money side of it and the advertising and taught physical education in the afternoons. In practice, as it turned out, we both at times did whatever was needed, worked twenty-five hours a day and on the weekends, and constantly, after that first year, wondered out loud how we ever got ourselves involved in such a mess.

We hired our teachers carefully. I put an advertisement in the *Brownsville Herald* and spread the notice of the new positions by word of mouth. Twelve teachers called for interviews for the four positions we had to offer the first year. I had never hired anyone for a job in my life. All the teachers looked virtually the same in their professional vitas, but during the free-swinging job interviews their interest in and commitment to teaching were quickly revealed. We did not offer a salary that competed with the public schools, but we could offer small classes, administrative support, a minimum of bureaucratic paperwork, strict but sensible discipline, and an educational philosophy that stressed treating each student as an individual.

Gloria Montoya was the first teacher we hired and the best we ever had. She was very nervous at the interview, stumbling over her words, refusing to establish eye contact with me. Andrea called up her references and, to a one, they recommended her highly. We invited her over to our house for a second interview. By then Andrea was convinced about her, but I remained unimpressed. I wasn't sure what good teachers looked and sounded like in interviews; I knew that the proof was only in the teaching. Gloria's appearance certainly did not fit my expectations. She was short, considerably overweight, and dressed as though she were on welfare. She had originally come to the Valley from Mexico, working many years as a migrant farm worker with her family. Gloria had done well in school and earned a scholarship to Texas A&I University where she had majored in history. She had ten years of teaching experience in seven different Valley schools; she had excellent teaching evaluations, but had frequently not been rehired by her principals.

Sitting uncomfortably in a straight-backed chair in our living room, her back to the bright afternoon sunshine that came streaming in through the panes of the front windows, Gloria Montoya finally looked me straight in the eye.

"Dr. Maril, teaching is my life. I would do anything for my students. That's what is wrong with the school I teach at. The other teachers don't really care about the welfare of the kids. Neither does the administration. I don't know what I'd do if I weren't a teacher. I'd probably go crazy. With me, my students come first."

Gloria was an immediate, although not unqualified success. The majority of students in her classes grew quickly to respect her and learn from her. We were not afraid to give her the most difficult students. Gloria was especially good with students who had given up on themselves. She pumped them full of her enthusiasm and love of learning, gave them a sense of the importance of education in their lives, worked hard at instilling in each of them a powerful dose of self-esteem.

Like all teachers, Gloria had her blind side. She worked less well with the brighter students, her rigid classroom manner unable to make a space for those who required more intellectual challenges than the average. But Gloria, unlike most teachers, recognized her own limitations and could even talk about them to Andrea and me, especially after she trusted us.

The trust began in earnest when a man came to the school just six weeks after it opened. Maria, our secretary, told me that someone wanted to see the principal immediately. Maria made an ugly face and rolled her eyes at me, letting me know without words what she thought of our gentleman visitor.

The tall, angular fellow walked briskly into my office, then sat down unasked in one of the chairs across from my desk.

"Do you know that one of your teachers is a lesbian?" he said, not wasting any time.

"What are you talking about?" I asked, both surprised and puzzled by the man and his words. He was dressed in khaki shorts and a plaid sports shirt, his tan face unshaven, bloodshot eyes staring out from behind thick-rimmed glasses.

"Do you know that you have a lesbian teaching here? Do your students know their teacher is a homosexual? Do their parents?"

"Who are you?" I asked him, my anger beginning to rise. I was not about to let someone barge in off the street and tell me how to run my school.

"My name is Jack Lloyd. I'm trying to do you a big favor. I live in Port Isabel. Last year Gloria Montoya taught junior high school there. She taught my daughter history. They fired her because she's a lesbian.

Now she's teaching here. There's no telling what she's already done to your students."

"Why do you think she's a lesbian?" I said, finally beginning to understand. I knew Port Isabel was one of the most backward of Valley school systems, a town in which petty politics and patronage ran the schools.

"I have evidence. Several girls were sexually molested by your teacher. What are you going to do about it?" Mr. Lloyd leaned forward in his chair aggressively, grasped the front of my desk with two bony hands.

"I'm not going to do a thing about it, Mr. Lloyd. I've never seen you before. I don't believe a word you've said. Ms. Montoya has excellent references from Port Isabel. She is one of our best teachers. Now get out of my office."

Lloyd rushed out the door as suddenly as he had come. I walked out in his wake, watching as his old truck labored out of the parking lot in a puff of smoke and headed off in the direction of Port Isabel.

Gloria came in thirty minutes later, during the mid-morning break. "Maria told me Lloyd was here," she said, looking very anxious.

"Yeah. The guy must be a real nut case. Do you know him?"

"He bothered me all last year when I taught at Port Isabel. What did he tell you?"

"He said you were a lesbian and had sexually molested several girls in Port Isabel," I told her, laughing, letting her know that I never believed the words of a nut, least of all a Port Isabel nut. "I told him you were one of our best teachers and he had no right to criticize you or call you names. He got mad and left."

Gloria sat across the desk from me, hands folded in her lap, legs crossed, expecting, she told me later, to be fired. She had never had a school administrator stand up for her, never mind how ridiculous the accusations. She gave me a fleeting smile and got up to go.

"I've got to get back to my students," she said, walking out quickly before I could say any more.

The trust between Gloria and me was mutual. Although we each made mistakes in working with the other—we had our misunderstandings over the years—that trust held us irrevocably together. Gloria knew that Andrea and I cared about our students as much as she did. When I began to take students on field trips to Big Bend National Park and other places along the border, I asked Gloria if she would come along as the other adult leader (Andrea hates to camp). Although Gloria Montoya was a single Mexican female, raised in a tradition in which one must carefully guard one's reputation against the intentions of all males, she never doubted that I would behave in an honorable way.

The second teacher we hired was Mrs. Slatsky. She was our science teacher, as different from Gloria in her background and personality as night from day. Mrs. Slatsky was from Vermont, had taught in New England public schools for many years, and had finally come to the Valley to retire on her modest pension. At least thirty years older than Gloria Montoya, she had soon become bored by retirement, and she longed to go back into the classroom. Mrs. Slatsky—I never recall calling her by any other name—brought a strong will and energy to her classes, at the same time intellectually challenging her students in a nonthreatening way. Her major weakness, as it turned out, was her discipline in the classroom, especially of the younger boys. The director's office usually had at least one twelve-year-old boy sitting outside the door, a constant gift from Mrs. Slatsky.

"Okay, Jorge, what was it this time?" I asked him.

"Nothing much. I was trying to get Mario's attention and Mrs. Slatsky caught me."

"How were you trying to get Mario's attention?" I asked, having a pretty good idea of the answer I would get back.

"I shot him in the head with a paper clip," Jorge said, producing the rubber band and a handful of projectiles.

We hired a language teacher from Mexico City and a part-time art teacher who had recently received her degree at the University of Texas– Austin. There were six of us, including Andrea and me, that first year.

At the same time we were hiring teachers, I was frantically advertising for students. We had a very diverse group. About one-third were Mexicans from Matamoros and had attended private schools in that city. The majority, however, were Mexican Americans and Anglos from Brownsville who had spent most of their years in public schools, although we did have a handful from the local Catholic prep school. Our students were mostly middle-middle and lower-middle class; several were from wealthy Brownsville and Matamoros families and we also had two students on partial scholarships.

Andrea and I interviewed each of the seventh, eighth, and ninth graders, attempting to gain insight into their motivation and character. The students were usually very honest.

"Why do you want to come to our new school?" I asked one eighth-grade girl who sat primly in front of me, her mother and father eyeing her anxiously.

After some hesitation she said, "Because my parents are making me."

I asked one ninth grader what he hoped to do in the future. "I'm going to be a tax lawyer and also play tackle for the Dallas Cowboys, sir," he told me, giving me a crunching handshake at the end of the interview.

"What didn't you like about your old school," I asked a small seventh-grade boy with large brown eyes and jet-black hair.

"I got tired of getting beat up every day," he said in a quiet voice.

We needed students to have a school and, that first year, students were in short supply. We took students who were rejects from other institutions; they had flunked out, been expelled for too many absences, been fighters and troublemakers, or more often than not, just did not fit into the rigid structures created by the Valley system. We also took students who were looking for a real change, an educational alternative. We turned down only a few, those who were in serious trouble with the juvenile justice system and were looking at doing time, those who had serious psychological problems, and those who had drug problems. Although we tried to screen out the extreme troublemakers, in the belief that those students required special help we could not provide, we were not entirely successful; one or two went undiscovered until well into the first semester.

In a few short months Andrea and I had created a school out of our dreams and hard work. By September 1, 1982, we had a new school building, six teachers counting ourselves, and thirty-eight students. School began Monday morning at eight-thirty. That same Monday morning was the last time I ever felt I had real control of the school.

The school took on a life of its own; it was far greater than the sum of its insignificant parts. Time sprinted furiously by, each day bringing long lists of confusions and contradictions, of unfinished business that was unfinishable. It was enough each day that Andrea and I made it until the clock struck five; there were students to talk to, parents with long lists of questions, bills to pay, teachers to shore up, a thousand and one things that had to get done, but never did. At the end of the day Andrea and I sat slumped in our chairs gasping for breath, unable at times to face yet another minor crisis. The school was like a three-hundred-pound toddler who has its hands grasped tightly around your neck, its large, brand new head in your face, demanding your immediate and full attention.

It was also a very rewarding time. There were days when I swore I actually saw comic-strip light bulbs switch on over the heads of particular students, that moment when they finally understood a particular idea or value for the very first time. These students' reactions to their education were often direct and immediate, as was their parents' feedback. I knew when we were doing the right thing, and when we messed up; there was rarely a middle ground.

Our school was never the way I wanted it to be. The school was always struggling against me, resisting immediate and direct control, as if on its own educational, and leaderless, mission. At the same time, I constantly felt uniquely challenged and uniquely reaffirmed by our school; I rushed with purpose from my morning classes at TSC to my own school, a school I helped to create, and recreate, each day. I became less sour, less cynical about my teaching at TSC and about the educational future of Brownsville and Valley students. The four years Andrea and I ran our school in Brownsville were in many ways the fullest of my life.

The Devil Student

"James has a problem," his mother told me, rearranging herself in the chair before my director's desk, already gazing awkwardly at the wall behind me. Outside the window of my small office, under a hot October sun, sprinklers fed the newly sodded lawn that surrounded the asphalt parking lot.

A minute of silence wallowed uncomfortably between us. James—I could hear him talking to Maria just outside my door—had seemed a likable seventh grader in his interview, a little small for his age, distracted and nervous, but nothing out of the ordinary.

"What is the problem?" I finally asked James's mother, realizing the words were sticking in her throat.

Again the woman, blond and attractive, well-dressed, moved around in her chair uncomfortably. Then finally, after several moments more of silence, she blurted out, "James is evil."

"He's what?" I said, thinking I had not heard the woman correctly.

"He's got the devil in him," she said in clear, precise words which obviously pained her.

"The devil?" I said, incredulously. Little James, blue-eyed and blond-haired like his mother, reminded me in no way of a seventh-grade Lucifer. I knew the woman was quite serious, but it was still difficult to hide my disbelief.

"You don't know him like I do. He's evil, pure evil. He's destroying my marriage, Dr. Maril, wrecking my relationship with my husband." Tears began to flow, from what kind of emotion I could not tell. I offered the woman some Kleenex, which she accepted.

"Maybe our school is not what you and James are really looking for,"

I finally said, wondering why Brownsville seemed to produce so many crazy people and why, in turn, these crazies sought out our school like flies attracted to sugar.

"He's pure evil," James's mother said yet once more, dabbing her eyes with the tissue. I thought of green pea soup, spinning heads, and flying objects.

"Does he have any other problems you want to tell me about?" I asked her, feeling a little like I was caught up, against my will, in a "Saturday Night Live" sketch.

"No. James is a good student. Sometimes he's a little lazy, but he is smart, like his father. You know," she said as an aside, "I'm not James's real mother. I married his father last year. It's my first marriage, his fourth."

I didn't know what to say to that, so I just nodded my head in a friendly and understanding way. James's mother left after a few more minutes. I talked the situation over with Andrea; we doubted, despite the mother's confession, that James could be the new Antichrist. What was more likely was that James's mother was a little bit flakey, a condition with which we were willing to contend. We admitted James the following week.

The problems didn't really start for another month.

"He's totally ruining my classes," Mrs. Slatsky told me as we sat comfortably in my office one Thursday afternoon. I offered her a Coke but she declined. As had become my habit, I was sipping on a Tab, enjoying the caffeine after another very long day.

"Who?" I asked, puzzled.

"James, the new boy. He's got everybody angry at each other. Ford — now you know Ford wouldn't hurt a flea — actually tried to punch Oscar in the nose. And Maria Susan, she started yelling at Yolanda who has been her best friend since school began."

"But what has James got to do with this?" I said, not understanding at all.

"I'm not sure, except before he came that class was my best. And since he came it's been all downhill." I thanked Mrs. Slatsky for her news and told her I would keep an eye on James. In truth, I wondered if the woman was beginning to slip.

Ten minutes later Gloria Montoya sat in Mrs. Slatsky's still warm chair.

"Dr. Maril, it's that James. There's something wrong with that child."

"What do you mean?" I said, becoming at last uneasy. Gloria's judgments of students were seldom different than my own.

"I can't put my finger on it. It's a feeling. He disturbs people, makes them act mean toward each other. Then he just steps back and watches it all. There's something wrong with him."

"How's he doing grade-wise?" I asked.

"He's above average. Hands in his work on time, participates in class discussions, seems really interested in the salt maps we are making right now. But I'm not talking about his academic abilities, that's not the problem. You know Rudy and Bruce?" she said.

"Of course."

"Well, he had them about to kill each other. I swear, if I hadn't intervened they would have busted each other over the head with chairs. And they are not violent kids."

I thanked Ms. Montoya, as I had Mrs. Slatsky, and thought briefly about James as I began locking up the school for the night.

I watched James closely over the next several weeks. In truth the boy did have some unique abilities I had never seen before. Time and again I observed a youngster who, both in the classroom and while playing soccer or baseball, could stir up trouble in less than five minutes. James was a master manipulator. He could read the emotional needs of his peers like a book, then in clever twists he could turn kids against themselves and others. He pulled their psychological strings as easily as an experienced psychotherapist, but always for the bad. When accused of initiating the conflict, he played the role of the innocent victim, his thin voice registering a high whine.

Tuesday afternoon I had to break up three fights on the soccer field. James was a part of starting these fights, although he did not participate in the actual blows. He was so slight of frame that the bigger kids considered it dishonorable to attack him. Given their growing furor at him, he could easily have ended up in the hospital, but as it was, his cherubic head remained free of black eyes and bruises.

James's father came alone to Parents' Night. Rumor had it that Wife Number Four, the woman who had enrolled James, had hit the road and Wife Number Five was waiting anxiously in the wings. But it was only a rumor and there were many rumors that came and went at the school. I told James's father I wanted to talk with him alone. I pulled him over to one side of the hall outside my office, away from the noise and confusion of students, parents, and teachers.

"We're having some problems with James," I began, smelling the whiskey fumes immediately. James's father was full-bore drunk; he leaned heavily against the wall to keep from falling. His words were slurred, difficult at first to understand.

"James is a very bright kid. None of his teachers at his other schools have appreciated him. He's too smart for them. I was hoping your school would be different."

"I'm not talking about academic problems." I said, trying to keep out of the range of the fumes. I was not against drinking, but I did judge it foolish for him to come to Parents' Night drunk as a skunk.

"The boy has had a hard life. My wife is not his real mother. He needs protection and love." Then James's father seemed to shift gears. He lit a cigarette, took several long puffs, then motioned me closer to him.

"If my boy is harmed in any way I will personally sue you into bankruptcy. I know a lot of people in this community. The right kind of people. Do you get my drift?"

"A lawsuit?" I said, confounded.

"You bet your life a lawsuit. I'll take you for every cent you're worth."

Without a word I walked away from the man, left him there in his own fumes and smoke. I knew where James must have learned his social skills.

Exactly five days later, on a Tuesday, I drove into the lot at our school, parked the car, noticed with pleasure that the new grass was at last beginning to grow, then stood dumbfounded as I gazed at the front door. Three squad cars surrounded the school entrance, red lights ablaze, driver's-side doors open, the sounds of the police dispatcher rumbling through the hot afternoon air.

I rushed into the school, fearing someone had been murdered or, at the very least, stabbed. Maria was staffing the front office. She was filling out a school form with one hand, talking into the phone she held with the other. She put down the phone when she saw me.

"They're in the back," she told me hurriedly, motioning me in the right direction with her free arm.

Andrea and three Brownsville policemen were moving towards me down the hall. Andrea looked worried, but certainly not overwhelmed. She shook hands with the policemen outside the director's office, then I closed the door behind us.

"What happened?" I said, listening to the squad cars begin to drive away.

"I'm not exactly sure of the details but, basically, Mrs. Slatsky's science class decided they had had enough of James. After lunch some of the bigger boys surrounded him in the backyard, pulled his jeans off, then threw them over the fence."

"That's all?" I asked, relieved. James was lucky that all he had lost was his pants. I was afraid they had, out of their frustration with him, torn one of his arms out of its socket. I'm not sure I would have blamed them that much if that was what they'd done. James was much more than an annoyance.

"No, that's just the beginning. Mrs. Slatsky and one of the other students retrieved James's jeans and James, who was very embarrassed, began crying. He demanded to be taken home. I called James's father to come get him. As soon as I had explained to him over the phone what happened, he started yelling that his son had been sexually assaulted. He called the police, who just left."

"But all they did was yank his pants off. Granted it was a stupid thing to do, but what's all the stink?"

"Charges of sexual assault are no joke. The police had to assume the worst. They charged in like gangbusters. I explained the situation to them. It turns out I knew one of them from when I worked for the Department of Human Services. They agreed that there was no foundation for the charges, that it was just a school prank, but they have to fill out a report. And they still have to interview Mrs. Slatsky and one or two of the students who witnessed it all."

James's father showed up thirty minutes later. I heard him arrive as he slammed on the brakes of his new Mercedes and skidded into a parking space thirty feet from my office window. He stormed across the asphalt and into the school. Luckily, by then most of the students had gone home for the day. Maria showed him into my office.

Before I could get a word in, James's father began yelling that he was going to sue the school, sue me, send everyone to jail including the bullies who had attacked his son.

"No one was attacked," I told him in a firm voice. I was determined not to get into a yelling match with the man. I was going to give him his fifteen minutes, then send him back to his clinic. I felt little sympathy for James or his bombastic father. I could not allow the boys who had thrown James's pants over the fence to go unpunished, but I certainly understood their motivation. The fact that James's father seemed more intent on suing us than helping us educate his son also did not sit well with me.

"My son was sexually attacked on your school property," he yelled back at me. "He has suffered great harm from all of this. I paid you to take care of him, and you have betrayed that trust. You have. . . ."

I'd heard and seen enough. From the smells coming from his direction and from his actions, I knew James's father was drunk again. While he certainly had reason to be angry, he showed no intention of wanting to discuss the matter in a reasonable fashion. The man was simply looking for someone to yell at, his own problems perhaps even greater than his son's.

"Get out of my office," I told him.

"What? What? You can't make me get out. I paid my tuition at this school and I bought your time."

"Get out of my office," I said again, keeping my voice low in pitch. "When you want to discuss this in a reasonable way, then make an appointment with my secretary. Now get out."

"You can't kick me out. I've never been kicked out of anybody's office in my life. Do you realize I'm a prominent doctor in this community? If I take James out of this school, half the parents will yank their kids out faster than you can blink an eye. I have a lot of pull in Brownsville. Come on," he waved at me with his arms, growing even more belligerent, "just try to make me leave."

It was tempting. I knew I could easily throw the man through the front door. He reminded me of someone, but I couldn't put my finger exactly on who. Maybe I should have just punched him out, one quick blow to the stomach and he would have folded like an accordion. Or I could practice all that I learned from Mando's Karate Academy on his face. Then it struck me. James's father was doing a damn good impression of his son. Father Devil.

I picked up the phone on my desk and buzzed Maria.

"Maria? Call the police. Tell them to come over right away. We have an emergency. James's father refuses to leave my office and is threatening me. Tell them to hurry."

James's father eyed me carefully as I put the phone back down. He still sat in his chair, one hand held stiffly in front of him as if cocked to hit me should I charge him.

"I'm staying right here. Remember this exactly because you're going to be testifying to a jury about what happened today." He crossed his arms over his chest, stared at his two feet outstretched in front of him.

"I'm going to meet the police," I told him, reconsidering a final time whether or not I should personally escort James's father to the parking lot. I thought once more of James-the-boy and closed the office door behind me.

Two minutes later, as I stood talking to Maria, James's father dashed out of my office and sprinted for his car in the parking lot. His new Mercedes had barely hit the street pavement before the squad car rolled up in front of the school and a Brownsville police officer carefully unfolded himself from the front seat.

Towards dusk, after the police had left for the second time that day,

I called my lawyer to tell him to prepare for an onslaught from James's legal staff. Oddly, we never heard a word about a lawsuit. Perhaps James's father woke up the next morning and, in a sober moment of reflection, reconsidered his position.

James returned to school the following week and managed to survive in one piece until the end of the year, at which time we promoted him on to the next grade, but did not invite him to rejoin the school in the fall. We "disenrolled" him, as the TSC dean loved to say.

We, the students, teachers, and administrators, also managed to survive James, although just barely. The talk we'd had with the students after the "sexual assault" did much to persuade them either to ignore James or, at the very least, to take a closer look at James's manipulations, his ability to create havoc while playing the innocent victim.

James was the most unlikable child I'd ever met, but he was not the devil, nor did he have the devil in him. Our school allowed me for the first time to see students, including James, as windows to their families. These children, who turned into our students as soon as they passed through our front door, were often vivid reflections of their families' loves, hates, frustrations, and other warts. To my surprise, the most difficult parents, although James's family was an extreme, expected us not only to right the wrongs of years of shoddy education, but to heal their kids emotionally. All in a semester.

In the end, I did not feel sorry for James; he and his father had posed a serious threat to our school. A lawsuit, even one without merit and sure to fail in court, would have created much negative publicity for the school during its beginnings, perhaps enough to have sunk it. I also did not excuse James for the responsibility he bore for his own behavior, regardless of his upbringing. His father, meanwhile, had, according to the *Brownsville Herald*, moved on to Wife Number Five. In a city as poor as Brownsville, it seemed more than ironic that an affluent family could have such serious problems, while many of those families who lacked financial stability managed themselves far better.

In the fall James's father placed him in a public junior high school not far from our school. One or two afternoons out of the week James was forced to walk past our school on his way home. If he was spotted by our students, they usually jeered at him as he walked briskly by. One afternoon I saw him, books in one hand, a new, as yet unsigned, cast covering his other hand, wrist, and arm.

Rudy, one of many students James had antagonized, also spotted him from a distance and approached me on the sidewalk near the school parking lot as I stood gazing in James's direction.

"Looks like somebody finally got tired of all his bullshit and busted him one, Dr. Maril," Rudy said, upon seeing James's heavy plaster cast. "Serves him right," Rudy added.

"Hey, *pendejo*, it serves you right," Rudy shouted at James as James sought to put some distance between himself and our school grounds.

A few other students aimed their own opinions in James's direction. I joined their impromptu chorus as James quickly retreated down the street.

Breakers

Andrea and I closed our school the following year. A series of disastrous peso devaluations rocked Mexico and the economic impact was quickly felt on the north side of the Rio Grande. Over the course of only one weekend our Mexican families lost the value of almost one-fourth of their salaries and assets because of the fall of the peso on international markets. The devaluation of the peso also closed businesses in Brownsville, especially in the downtown area which was normally filled with Mexican shoppers. I knew that it was a matter of time before the parents of our students on both sides of the river could no longer afford our modest tuition.

I held out awhile longer in hopes of a financial miracle. When none came, we had no choice but to close our doors. We sold what we could and took our losses. For a time I was angry at this turn of events, but never really dejected. As never before, I valued the time I spent with my family and friends, enjoyed my work, and focused on the positive aspects of living in the Valley. At the same time, I was determined to find ways in which the poverty around me, and the problems it created, could be alleviated.

On balance, I felt a lasting satisfaction with what was accomplished at our school. We took students with limited skills, some with very negative, and understandable, attitudes towards learning, and helped them — by their own efforts and support from their families — down the right educational road. We had our failures, but there were a number of students who seemed to deeply and lastingly benefit from what we offered; they continued to keep in touch with us after the school was closed.

Nevertheless, I found it difficult to drive by our school and its new tenant, the Brownsville School of Cosmetology. Backed by Federal tuition dollars, the Brownsville School of Cosmetology thrived even as the rest of the Valley continued to reel from the falling peso. I knew from my work at TSTI and TSC that the Valley needed more cosmetologists about as much as it needed more gasoline engine mechanics.

I kept my teaching position at TSC, but spent more and more time conducting funded research. In my research I studied the causes of and solutions to poverty in the Valley; I began to work with those who wanted basic changes made in the system, who had grown tired of the social and political inequalities. At the same time I also began to explore other parts of the Valley which I did not know. I retook to combing the beaches of South Padre Island, to sailing the Laguna Madre in light and heavy winds, to watching the sun set lazily over Port Isabel.

South Padre Island had dramatically changed since I had first known it. In the early 1980s the island had sprouted large numbers of condo high rises and retail strip malls. Then the oil bust, coupled with Mexico's peso devaluation, had sent real estate prices plummeting and construction on the island had ground to a violent halt. To attract new business the island tourist industry began an annual advertising blitz of Midwestern colleges and universities. In a few short years the number of spring-breakers increased by tens of thousands.

The hordes of breakers, encouraged by promises of free rock concerts, free t-shirts, and enough beach contests to fill their dance cards, descended on South Padre with an increasing ferocity during the months of March and April. I knew the college students were very good for the island economy but, along with the rest of the local regulars, I grew to resent the annual invasion. I also worried about their safety.

One Saturday morning in late March I stood in line for more than thirty minutes at my favorite island restaurant. Living in the Valley had spoiled me; I wasn't used to waiting to eat my breakfasts. Almost all the tables in the small restaurant were filled with breakers, although there were a few snowbirds scattered among them, remnants of last winter's hard snows.

I read the local paper as I stood there in line, trying to keep my patience. Ten feet from where I stood, six sunburned breakers were stuffing their faces from huge plates of food. I tried very hard not to think of their food as my food; after all, it wasn't as if I owned the restaurant or was even their best customer. Still, I found the breakers' comments between mouthfuls to be irritating.

On the island weather: "It's too cloudy. I wish we were back in Iowa."

On the island females: "Too many dogs on the beach."

On the island beer: "Everywhere you go they give it to you warm. Don't they have refrigerators around here?"

I was finally seated between two tables of breakers. Stomach growling, a large glass of ice tea in hand, I waited for my huevos rancheros, flour tortillas, and picante. The line at the door, to my amazement, continued to grow as the clock reached eleven, first doubling inside the restaurant, then snaking its way out the glass door, down the steps, and into the parking lot. I'd never seen anything like it.

The breakers to my right and left were dressed in the latest beach fashion, a cross between "Miami Vice" and the newest rap group. They sported combinations of luminescent pink, lime, purple, and orange synthetic shorts, t-shirts, sunglasses, swimsuits, and sandals. Beer logos were the leitmotif, Spuds McKenzie the overwhelming favorite. In contrast, the mute snowbirds, outnumbered ten-to-one, bore their plaid bermudas, sundresses, and gimme caps with a certain decorum. Seed companies and truck stops were their logos of choice.

The breakers at my elbows shoveled their food down their throats, pausing to make occasional comments among themselves, demolishing three-egg omelets, stacks of thick pancakes, barge-like subs, and mounds of biscuits with country gravy. Those who finished first looked vulture-like at the plates of their friends. Several ordered second rounds, smacking their lips, swallowing cup after cup of coffee with orange juice chasers.

A few tables away three snowbirds picked at their food, pushing it from one side of the plate to the other, measuring their sips from their coffee mugs, occasionally smiling off into the distance. I felt lost in the cultural gulf between twenty-year-old college kids working up a sweat as they downed their breakfasts and senior citizens stewing an extra week while the snow in their driveways back home melted a few extra inches.

I resented having my restaurant, and island, taken from me. I wouldn't have minded, sitting at my table chewing on the leftovers of my huevos rancheros, if a big old hurricane had come along and blown the island clear of all the t-shirt shops, the shell shops, the beer bars, and all the cruddy rest of it.

I paid up, fought my way through the crowd to the door, then dodged around the line that blocked my car in the parking lot. I drove down the island to the county beach, found a solitary parking space, and locked my car. I walked across the dune line to the beach, stared out at the Gulf's blue horizon, then turned north, as was my custom. I reached the brightly striped circus tents after less than a half-mile stroll. Giant replicas of cans and bottles of beer were tethered just outside the entrances to the tents. Spuds himself, ballooned to a full story-and-one-half in size, stood guard over the beer tents. A brisk wind from the southeast momentarily blew him over on his giant left haunch, but the party animal was quickly righted with a few adjustments of guy wires and ropes.

I walked inside one of the tents, its canvas walls tied back to catch the breeze. All around in the shade of the tent, tables were pitched in the sand, each full of beer mugs, t-shirts, hats, and other trinkets. Breakers grazed the tables, occasionally selecting a logo-bearing item to purchase.

I circled the display, then exited. Farther down the beach one beer manufacturer was sponsoring a recycling effort in the name of saving the environment. I watched a steady stream of breakers, almost all of whom were male, carry see-through, plastic garbage bags full of aluminum beer cans into the large tent. There the cans were dumped, weighed, priced, and the breakers received their bounty. From a distance I followed three male breakers as they recrossed the dune line, loped down a paved side street filled with expensive houses on stilts, then crossed the parking lot to the convenience store. Three minutes later they came out the door, each holding six-packs of their favorite beer. They each popped a top, took long draws. I could hear their sighs as they were carried along on the Gulf breeze.

I walked back to the beach and watched small groups of male breakers stand in the surf. They held cans of beer in their hands, taking sips at their leisure. The males postured and posed, biceps and deltoids tensed as female breakers walked by. Several waded out past the second surf line, water to their chests, hands high over their shoulders to protect the brew from pollution by Gulf seas.

Farther along a very large crowd was gathering to hear Stevie Ray Vaughn and the Fabulous Thunderbirds. According to the *Brownsville Herald*, there were twenty-five thousand breakers at the beach concert. Two days earlier, a crowd estimated at thirty thousand cheered to the comedy of Joe Piscipo and Jay Leno. Both shows were free and sponsored by major beer distributors.

The breakers seemed to me more intense than I had ever seen them, more collective in their actions as they traveled from their hotel rooms to the beach, back again to the hotels, then to the restaurants, bars, and music clubs. They seemed louder, more frenetic in their partying, as if they were competing at it, afraid to lose. They rushed the volleyball nets with fury in their eyes, dived recklessly over the hot sand for errant balls, kicked the hell out of hacky-sacks, danced the nights away on concrete club floors to the sounds of bands imported from Dallas, Houston, and Austin. In between, they sizzled in the sun, compared their tans with others', and publicly groomed themselves, not unlike my chimp friend Dale and his clan at the Brownsville Zoo. When it rained, they charged to the saunas and spas where they steamed and bubbled for hours, constant beers in hand.

When the serious spring showers came, I watched them queue up for the Mexican bar buses. The buses drove them in style to the new bridge in Brownsville, a block from my office at TSC, where they clambered off by the hundreds and headed directly for the border. They marched across the bridge in groups of five or more, quickly outdistancing their peers who had chosen to drive across the Rio Grande in the snail-like traffic.

In Texas, and on South Padre Island, you have to be twenty-one years old to drink beer, a recent change from eighteen. In Matamoros and all along the border there never has been an age limit; all that has ever been required was the money to pay for the drink. I saw breakers hit the Matamoros bars at ten o'clock on rainy mornings and not emerge until long after dark. They staggered in droves across the river and into the waiting buses, which whisked them safely back to their island hotels.

It was an efficient system. The kids, whether legal or illegal north of the Rio Grande, got to drink as much as they wanted, the businesses made money, and no one seemingly got hurt. But some of the breakers who didn't take the buses were not so lucky. That spring there were nine traffic fatalities that could be directly attributed to the breakers. In one fatal accident two breakers crashed their small truck into oncoming traffic on Highway 48 between Brownsville and South Padre. Beer cans, according to the *Brownsville Herald*, littered the scene of the accident.

Many breakers, well within the intended spirit of the American and Mexican business communities, ran trade routes of beer across the new bridge. Breakers bought cases of beer cheap in Mexican stores, then, for a dollar or two tip, paid young Mexican boys to carry their booty back across the river. The alcohol was transported back to South Padre, where it was consumed.

There were other related problems that emerged that spring. The streets of Avenue Obregón in Matamoros were filled with breakers, both those who arrived by bus from South Padre and those who came in private vehicles. The students milled around on street corners, sat under brightly colored umbrellas at the new sidewalk beer clubs, haunted the night clubs in the Zona Rosa where they heard Mexican bands play bad rock and roll.

When it got dark, the students who had drunk too much beer and margaritas urinated in the doorways and alleys of Avenue Obregón, on the front lawns of houses that face the busy street. They yelled at passing cars, made inappropriate remarks to Mexicans, and got a nasty kind of rowdy which would not have been tolerated by the police on South Padre Island.

None of this in its present form was exactly new, of course. College students have been seeking out Texas beaches since at least the fifties and Americans of all ages have visited the Texas border to enjoy a variety of vices, from drinking to prostitution and gambling, since the Treaty of Guadalupe Hidalgo in the mid-nineteenth century. Inevitably those Americans who fell into serious trouble blamed it on others. The suggestion by many that border towns should somehow carry the burden of moral responsibility for the actions of tourists who created demands for certain vices not tolerated elsewhere has to me always seemed seriously misguided.

I was once a beer-thirsty college student yearning for an isolated beach to lie on. In 1967 I rode by train through the cold, spring corn stubble of Iowa to the warm beaches of Galveston and Corpus Christi. Before that, I was a horny high schooler in Oklahoma City who had heard locker-room stories of the sexual pleasures of Nuevo Laredo, Matamoros, and other border towns. I badly wanted to drive the six hundred miles to the nearest border town, but never did.

Those who made the trip returned with exacting details, details which could excite the imaginations of a locker room full of adolescent males during gym class. Those voyagers to Nuevo Laredo became instant heroes who bore their sexual experiences, both the real and the imagined, with a newfound maturity which commanded instant respect. Even the nerdiest could return a prince, stringing his remarkable journey out for a semester's worth of stories to those, like me, who were chomping at the sexual bit.

But the numbers of college students who were enticed to South Padre Island grew and grew in the 1980s; it used to be ten thousand kids, now it was more than a hundred thousand breakers. The binge drinking, the frenetic collective consumption of alcohol in ritualized and rigid forms, these were real differences from my college days in the 1960s. The businesses of South Padre Island and the border towns reaped the profits, as did the beer manufacturers and distributors who spent large sums of promotional dollars in the hopes of building brand name loyalty. Breakers were no longer individual college students out to enjoy themselves before finals. Breakers became an industry.

Recently a Texas college student was kidnapped from the parking lot of one of my favorite Matamoros restaurants. He had been walking back to the new bridge late at night, according to the newspaper accounts, when he mysteriously disappeared. After several weeks of fruitless searching, the Mexican authorities began digging on a small ranch outside Matamoros, where they found the college student's dismembered body along with fifteen others.

The bizarre tale rode the national wire for more than two weeks. A Mexican drug ring was involved, a small group of young men and women who became members of a twisted Santería cult under the alleged leadership of Adolfo de Jesus Constanzo and Sara Aldrete. Aldrete was a student at TSC—I did not know her—an honor student who earned part of her tuition as a work-study student in the gym. Eventually, after an intensive manhunt, most of the cult were gunned down in an apartment building in Mexico City and those who survived, including Sara Aldrete, were thrown into a Mexican jail.

The national and international media flocked to Brownsville in droves, coming from as far away as Japan. They pronounced Brownsville, Matamoros, and the entire border to be rife with strange and murderous drug cults. Out of their own ignorance of the border and its peoples, the media frequently confused regional folk beliefs and customs with their own notions of mysticism. They made outlandish statements about the nature of Santería and its adherents, confusing all those who practiced this religion with the crazed actions of the mass murderers who had been killed or captured.

In a week's time the media turned South Padre Island, Brownsville, and Matamoros from a playground for college students into the killing fields of cannibalistic drug lords. The college students evacuated their hotel rooms by the thousands, local restaurants and bars soon completely emptied. Phenomenal rumors flew in the wake of the media blitz; thousands of parents on both sides of the border kept their children home from school in the weeks that followed because they feared members of the drug cult might kidnap their kids in revenge for the death of their leaders.

The tourist industry has no memory, no conscience. The next spring, breakers returned to the border in their usual hordes, again attracted by the handouts, posters, and ads that appeared in university and college newspapers throughout Texas, Oklahoma, and the Midwest. The heinous crimes of the drug cult, in spite of the contentions of the national media, were rarities, no more typical of this border region than Charles Manson and his gang could be said to be average Southern California criminals.

The real problem was not drug-crazed cannibals who preyed on American college students; nor, at the other extreme, was it the breakers' rudeness, especially to island locals who, like me, desired nothing more than to be left to their normal routines. In fact, those locals who can manage it have begun to desert the island during March and April, returning again when the students have gone back to their university classes.

The real problem, the lasting problem, was college students who drank too much, who climbed into their cars when they consumed too much alcohol, who killed each other and those who were unfortunate enough to be near them. Then grieving parents and families blamed the border towns for the maiming or death of their sons and daughters, the same parents who financed their offsprings' trip to the border as if they were vacationing in Disneyland.

The Texas-Mexico border is not a safe place for college students in search of a drunken vacation in the sun. To make matters worse, it will be just a matter of time before the citizenry of Matamoros and other Mexican border communities, grown tired of the insults of drunken American students, of the gringo tourists who urinate on their lawns, break some tourist dollar heads . . . what passed as mere rude behavior on the north side of the Rio Grande will in the near future easily be interpreted as a personal or cultural insult on the southern bank. Petty as well as more serious crimes against American students have also increased dramatically, even as public drunkenness has taken another dangerous bent; several students recently fell from the heights of South Padre Island condo balconies onto the concrete below.

There was only one Charles Manson and there will be no more Constanzos or Aldretes. But come next spring, it is an idiot who bets, one way or the other, against more dead breakers.

Larry

Larry Adams was stabbed to death last week. He died at eighteen years of age from multiple knife wounds to his heart and lungs.

He spent the night drinking with friends in Matamoros. Two blocks from the new bridge, on the Brownsville side of the Rio Grande, he stopped at the traffic light. It was one o'clock in the morning. Another car pulled up beside him and the passenger in the front seat looked at Larry in the wrong way.

Larry looked back hard at the guy. Larry didn't know his name, but he'd seen him around town. The other boy, who just turned sixteen, kept looking at Larry in a way Larry didn't like. The light changed, but the two cars didn't move. Larry jumped out, ready to fight.

When he was fifteen Larry roared up to the front door of my school on his big motorcycle. The motorcycle was a red and white Yamaha that Larry said could do a hundred and twenty on a straight piece of Texas highway. He parked the monster on the grass ten feet from the school's front door, where he could keep an eye on it from his classroom window.

Larry earned some of his reputation during my physical education class, although his good looks and his motorcycle didn't hurt him any. He was only five six or seven; many of the other tenth-grade boys were already beginning to leave him behind. Larry wore his light brown hair very long, but he got away with it because no one was stupid enough to ask him about it. Everyone knew about his explosive temper.

In the fall and winter we played football and soccer in my P.E. class. During the spring I gave them the choice of softball or a homemade version of kickball. When the field was too muddy, we played volleyball or basketball in the parking lot. Larry Adams played each sport with a certain ferocity. He hurled his body around as if every play were the last. He wasn't that big, but he was strong for his size, coordinated, and very determined.

Larry hated to lose any game. He was more than willing to sacrifice his body on a play that everyone else would have forgotten by the next day. We played touch football, one hand below the waist; Larry played the game as though he were in the NFL. He made diving receptions for footballs thrown beyond his reach, crashed countless times into the fence that bordered the field.

If Larry couldn't win fairly, he'd cheat. When I caught him at it, I could see his facial muscles clench in frustration. He'd loudly complain against the unfair call (although he knew it to be fair), then five minutes later he forgot all about it.

More rarely, Larry walked off the field, cursing silently. I let him cool off for ten minutes on the sideline. By then he'd be itching to get back into the game.

"It was a bad call," he'd say later. "He never touched me. Should have been a touchdown."

"You know he got you. I was standing five feet away from you and saw the whole thing," I said, not mad but always surprised he could so easily deny the obvious.

"If you say so," Larry said, heading back to class. He seemed to store up his hurts and grudges, until something would set him off again. When he lost his temper, he was virtually out of control. His friends were careful around him.

At the same time, Larry was a stickler for honesty in others. Nothing seemed to make him angrier than when an acquaintance or friend cheated in class or in the middle of a basketball or soccer game. He had a strict moral code; that he himself could never seem to live up

to it, although he expected others to, was one of his most obvious contradictions. Sometimes we talked about it, although he found it difficult to talk to an older male.

Larry was very good at football, but only mediocre at soccer. He
had rarely played the sport but, nevertheless, daily threw himself into
the game with his usual intensity. Pablo, on the other hand, was one
of our Mexican students who had played soccer all his life in Matamoros. Pablo had suffered through football season, knowing that his
time would eventually come. When he finally began playing soccer,
Larry was relegated from the status of football hero to average soccer
player, while Pablo was always picked first by the team captains.

Perhaps it was inevitable that Larry and Pablo would eventually come
to blows. It happened one December afternoon, as both rushed for
the soccer ball in the middle of the field. Larry kicked at the ball as
it skittered by, but struck nothing but Pablo's leg. Pablo, in full stride,
almost seemed to be expecting the blow. The two boys charged at each
other, fists flying, and fell to the dirt in a heap.

When Pablo could finally talk, he said, "Did you see what that ass-
hole did? Dr. Maril, he did that on purpose. You should have let us
fight it out."

Fifteen minutes later I had Pablo in my office, his father sitting in
the chair next to him. I asked Pablo to explain to his father what had
happened. His father was a wealthy businessman from Matamoros. Pablo
was his only boy and the apple of his eye. Still, as Pablo began de-
scribing the circumstances of the fight, I could see his father getting
very angry.

"Why did you do such a disgraceful thing in this school?" he finally
yelled at his son. "School is not where you fight, not here. I've always
told you to talk first, then if it doesn't work out, there is always time
for fighting."

Pablo lost the use of his brand-new Mustang for the next month.
He was forced to come to school with his younger sister; she'd just gotten her Mexican driver's license although she was only fourteen. Pablo
was very embarrassed that he had to have his sister drive him to school.
It was a good punishment.

An hour later Larry was in my office.

"I missed the ball, that's what happened. I didn't mean to kick him.
But Pablo's been after me since the day I got here. You can't run away
from someone like him. If you run away, then they'll just jump on you
harder the next time. That's just the way it is."

"You've got a shitty temper," I told him, not mincing my words.
"You've got to learn to control it. There are some things that are worth

fighting about, and some that aren't. You've got to be able to tell the difference."

"Pablo likes to push people around, intimidate them," he finally said. "The fight wasn't about soccer, it was about Pablo pushing me around." That made some sense to me, but it seemed that Larry also did his own share of pushing other people around.

With Larry sitting in front of my desk, I called Larry's mother on the phone. She was not surprised about the fight, she said, because Larry always seemed to get into fights. To a background of parrot squawks (she ran a pet store in San Benito), I asked her what she thought would be a good punishment for her son. The parrot squawks grew louder in the silence. She couldn't think of anything, but she promised she would talk to her husband, Larry's stepfather, about it at dinnertime. She never did call back and Larry never was punished by his parents for the fight.

I found out from other students and a teacher that Larry lived with his stepfather, who was Anglo, and his mother, who was Mexican American. His stepfather beat his mother regularly. His stepfather also beat on Larry until he was big enough to fight back. Apparently Larry didn't get along with his real father any better than his stepfather.

About three months later, in the spring, I walked into my office to find Larry and three other tenth graders seated and scowling. Andrea told me they had picked a fight with an eleventh grader. I talked to all the boys individually until I was able to get the facts straight.

"So what you're telling me is that the four of you decided Bruce was showing off. Right?"

The four boys in front of me nodded their heads.

"Then what happened?" I asked, already knowing the answer.

"We took turns hitting him," said Larry.

I looked over at him, my own anger growing. "What about a fair fight? You're always talking to me about a fair fight and honesty and that stuff, then you gang up on Bruce."

"He had it coming," said Larry, without apology.

Larry began dating Jodie, one of the most popular girls in school. From all appearances they made the perfect teenage couple. She rode around town on the back of his motorcycle, her long blond hair blowing in the wind. They held hands in the school hallway, whispered in each other's ear, and did all the other things couples in the tenth grade do.

But the relationship turned sour after only a few months. Larry, face contorted and full of anguish, would storm out the front door of the school, then dramatically roar away on his Yamaha. They seemed to spend most of their time arguing, breaking up, then getting back together. Later I found out that Larry had taken to hitting Jodie when he lost his temper. She hid the bruises from her parents and friends.

I thought Larry had a good chance of making it after high school, of avoiding any blunders that would scar his life. Sure, he had a violent streak, drove his motorcycle too fast, and beat on his girlfriend when he drank too much. He could be very mean, especially when his temper exploded and he lost control. But I knew Valley teenagers who were much worse than Larry. Much worse. And Larry was far from stupid; when pressed by his teachers he did good work.

Larry decided to skip college and work for a year at his parents' store. Then he was going to enlist in the marines, like his real father had done. Maybe if he had made it as far as the marines, it would have been enough to make a difference.

But those are just what-ifs. The fact is that when I read in the paper that Larry had been murdered, it came as no surprise. No one who really knew Larry could have been genuinely surprised.

Still, you always think about the what-ifs. Pablo is running one of his father's businesses in Matamoros now. He drives around town in a brand new Mercedes, a gift from his father, and is engaged to be married. Jodie went off to Austin to play in a band; the band folded soon after and Jodie enrolled in classes at the university.

When I think of Larry, I like to remember him at his best. I like to remember the afternoons when his determined legs sent his body hurling through the air, fingers stretching for, and catching, the leather football in the end zone. I like to remember him getting up slowly off the ground, holding out the football in one hand to show everyone that he'd caught the pass. I like to remember Larry tearing out of the school parking lot on his cycle, Jodie clinging to his back, the Yamaha giving off a bass growl that vibrated through the streets of the neighborhood.

I like to remember Larry talking about driving out north of Raymondville, in Willacy County, late at night. He'd hunker down over the gas tank and handle bars of his big cycle and roar down Highway 77 at more than a hundred twenty miles an hour, past mesquite and prickly pear, brush and buffel grass, past mile after mile of rusty barb wire fence. It was his way of letting off steam.

I like to think about what Larry said when I asked him how it felt to go faster than two miles a minute on a motorcycle, the wind blasting against his helmet, all alone out on that endless stretch of Valley concrete.

"Nothing's sweeter," he'd told me, a rare smile crossing his young face. "Nothing's sweeter."

Seminole Canyon

The Valley is only a small part of the Texas-Mexico border. The Rio Grande struggles through more than eight hundred miles of mountains and deserts before it reaches the Gulf of Mexico, twenty miles east of Brownsville. I decided to follow the Rio Grande from its mouth near Brownsville to El Paso, the largest American city on the Texas-Mexico border. I wanted to see what other places were like along the border, to see how the Valley compared. At first I traveled with friends who knew the region, but later I traveled by myself. Eventually, I began taking small groups of my students on summer trips to various parts of the border, including Big Bend National Park.

This particular afternoon I was on my own, thirty miles east of Del Rio, just outside Brackettville. I had spent several pleasant hours in an Indian cemetery. The graves that interested me most were those of Seminole Scouts who had fought bravely with the U.S. Army along the border. As a reward for their efforts, the Seminole Indians and their descendants had been buried in a cemetery that bore their name.

I leisurely went from one tombstone to the next, reading the names, writing down information about them that seemed important. The names on the oldest of the larger stones contained their own lyricisms: Pompey Perryman, Johnny Shields, Isaac Warrior. I spent several hours among the tombstones, soaking up the sun in the lonely cemetery, listening to the hum of a tractor in a nearby field, dodging the large bees that roamed among the wild flowers.

I lost track of time among the gravestones. Now, as I passed the familiar green sign that announced Seminole Canyon State Historical Park, a sign I'd passed many times before on my way to Big Bend, it suddenly occurred to me that the park must have been named, like the cemetery, in honor of the Indian scouts who had fought against Mexican bandits and Apaches.

I'd never before bothered to stop at the park. I knew that, in comparison with the vistas of Big Bend, Seminole State Historical Park was strictly in the minor leagues. But according to my map the park had a campground and I was in no condition that evening to drive the two hundred additional miles to the campgrounds at Big Bend.

I hung a U in the highway and headed back to the entrance of the park. I crossed a speed bump on a narrow park road and rolled sedately along a curving lane. The road led south, towards what would have been the Rio Grande, but was now a very, very large manmade lake, Lake Amistad (Friendship). I counted ten long, brown millipedes in the road by the time I reached the park headquarters. I'd never seen the creatures before. I carefully swung my car around each of them, although I was tempted to run them over. I assumed that they were poisonous; only later did I learn from the park ranger that they were perfectly harmless.

The park headquarters were closed. I walked up the sidewalk to an abode-like structure, much more interestingly designed than most buildings in Texas state parks, and squinted through the glass doors. Inside I saw a number of display cases. There was a pamphlet tacked to a bulletin board just outside the doors to the museum. Tours left twice a day for the canyon; entrance to the ancient rock dwellings was otherwise not permitted. The pamphlets described a series of unique pictographs that were to be found on the walls of the Indian shelters.

I got back in my car and followed the arrows to the campgrounds. The campgrounds weren't hard to find because there was only one way to go. The only other campers in sight were a middle-aged couple in a pickup at the far northwest corner of the grounds. I waved a friendly hello their way and set my tent up on the best spot I could find. I unpacked the rest of my gear, first checking for scorpions and snakes. The sun put itself to sleep in a magnificent fashion, with only the couple and me there to appreciate the spectacle. At a little after ten I climbed inside my tent, checked once more for unwanted wildlife, then fell asleep peacefully in the quiet desert.

After a quick morning run along the lone park road, then a light breakfast from my pack, I drove back to the park headquarters. On the way I passed a woman and a boy. I nodded and they waved back, after a slight hesitation, as I drove slowly and carefully around the millipedes and jack rabbits that filled the narrow pavement. Although I caught only a brief glimpse of them, the woman and child seemed peculiar. She was tall and angular, her face gaunt, hair pulled tightly back against her skull. The boy, perhaps seven or eight, seemed not quite right. I puzzled on it as I drove farther on, deciding it was his clothes that set him off, they appeared brand new and several sizes too large for his slight frame.

I put the two quickly out of my mind as I parked my car, laced on my hiking boots, grabbed my canteen, and headed for the small museum. Directly inside the door a patient park ranger sat ensconced behind a desk. He told me that the tour of the canyon left in fifteen minutes. I asked him a few questions, then briefly surveyed the museum displays, staring into each case, skipping the sixteen-millimeter movie that was offered, keeping an eye to the time.

Soon I joined six or seven people on the rear veranda of the museum. The veranda looked out over the small canyon. Among those who were gathered I saw, to my mild surprise, the woman and boy I had seen earlier.

I listened carefully as the ranger gave a short speech about the tour, but I could only hear fragments because of the boy. The child talked in a very loud voice and, in spite of sharp looks from the other adults, kept asking his mother foolish questions, one right after the other.

The group trudged down a path that led from the veranda to the bottom of the canyon. The ranger told us that at the bottom of the canyon we would find the dwellings of the ancient Indians and their famous pictographs. It was not a steep path, but the older couples took it very slowly. Along with these two couples who, I understood from their conversation, were traveling together from the Midwest, there were two college students, both males. I was a little surprised that two twenty year olds would care to tour the canyon; I was beginning to judge unfairly all college students by the breakers who visited South Padre Island.

I didn't want to match my pace to that of the rest of the hikers, so I waited a few minutes until they had cleared the trail before I started off again behind them. The trail was well-marked and I followed it easily as it wound gradually down the face of the bluffs overlooking a broad stream. It was a beautiful morning, no clouds in sight, the heat at nine o'clock not yet taking control of the day. Bees and butterflies worked the small, bright desert flowers that were spread among the cactus and the boulders. Below me I could hear the sounds of birds singing in the clear desert air. Very soon tree tops came into sight along with the sounds of running water.

Five minutes later I reached the bottom of the canyon. The group stood bunched up around the park ranger, listening carefully to his words. Then the young boy appeared from along another path and began asking, again in a very loud voice, another series of questions to whoever would listen. He saw me coming down the trail and immediately ran over to me.

"Did you know that the Indians used to eat cactus?" he asked me.

"Yes," I said.

Not stopping to hear my answer, the boy was off again, this time to bombard the ranger with more questions. To the ranger's credit, he tried to honestly answer each of the boy's questions. Soon the boy's attention was drawn elsewhere, this time by a millipede. The boy again interrupted, asking if millipedes were dangerous, if they were insects or snakes, and on and on. The older couples, whom I took to be grand-parents, lost patience with the child after he continued to bother them; out of frustration, they ignored him. No one, except for his mother, wanted anything to do with the boy.

The small boy was beginning to spoil the place for me. I got along well with most kids. I was used to a certain amount of kid noise and interruption. But this child's constant demands for attention in such a beautiful, quiet place were distracting, irritating. The mother was either unable or unwilling to do much with her son.

I drew up to the rest of the small group as they rounded a large rock and stopped by the stream that flowed through the small canyon. I thought fleetingly of President Humberto at TSC and his love of rocks, especially the ones on his desk. It would have been nice to have him there to explain the geology of Seminole Canyon.

The stream flowed lazily over and around large boulders. The can-yon walls echoed the call of the mountain crows that cruised above us. The ranger began telling us, as we walked along single file, about the prehistoric Indians who had lived in the shelters and caves of Semi-nole Canyon. I listened carefully, grateful that for a brief moment I could hear him clearly. The boy, who had been directly in front of me, darted off into the bushes. I found myself staring at the long arms of his mother who walked right ahead of me.

The veins on the mother's arms protruded from beneath her skin, long blue trails amongst pale, tight folds of skin. Along every inch of the tubes lay indentations, the veins partially collapsed from overuse, from frequent penetration. Staring at luminescent blue veins held close to the woman's sides, against a backdrop of limestone and millipedes, I heard again the impatient voice of the ranger.

"Son, don't go looking under that rock or you'll find more than you bargained for."

"Like what?" asked the boy.

"A rattlesnake. They're all over here."

"Will they bite me?" The boy started off on another marathon of questions, first to the ranger, then anyone who looked his way.

"There it is," the ranger told us, ignoring the noise from the boy.

Above us, jutting into the canyon wall not more than a hundred feet, was the Fate Bell rock shelter, a large overhang of rock that stretched for several hundred feet. Underneath the limestone roof, blackened by the smoke of countless fires, was a narrow cave that opened onto the canyon. Within stood waist-high piles of earth; archeologists had sifted through the many layers of the cave floor in search of artifacts. There were three or four large rooms in the cave, each partitioned off by the natural walls of the cliff. Inside the larger rooms were the remains of human-made walls, some less than a few feet tall, which framed smaller rooms and storage spaces.

The ranger led us through the cave, over woven floor mats that were placed to protect the cave floor from the wear and tear of tourists. The mats muffled our footsteps, allowing the sounds of the lazy stream and the birds to reach our ears. We followed a path bordered by a rope rail, at times placing our feet in grooved foot steps in the rock. The young boy, I noted thankfully, bounded ahead of the ranger and was temporarily out of sight.

The park ranger gave a short talk about the pictographs. At first I had not even noticed them. Faded, without frames, gallery track lighting, or the other paraphernalia that usually accompanies works of art, the paintings blended into the background rock, shade, and ceilings blackened from thousands and thousands of cook fires. There were small stick-like figures of hunters, their game, birds, and other designs and patterns. The paintings seemed to be randomly spread around on the walls, at various heights.

Among the pictographs were a few ringers. There was a large, white cross, which the ranger told us was probably the work of railroad workers who used the rock shelter as a supply dump in the 1880s. There were also several "Jane Loves George" tributes, already badly faded and well on their way to oblivion.

The more I looked at the pictographs, the more I found them to be restful, even reassuring. It was amazing that the work of these Indians had not been destroyed by the careless hands of previous visitors to the cave.

The ranger led us along a bit farther, down steps cut into the rock. Then he stopped. I assumed he wanted to show us more pictographs, so I looked around to find them. Instead, the ranger pointed to a large hunk of rock that stood off to one side of the cave, near a ledge that overlooked the stream a short distance below us.

The boulder was perhaps four feet in height, five feet long and wide. At first glance, the rock seemed little different from all the others around us. There were three shallow holes on its flat top. According to the ranger, the Indians used this rock to grind their grains and to prepare their other foods. On closer inspection, I saw that part of the surface of this rock was covered by layers of what appeared to be a twentieth-century epoxy resin, a thick, translucent substance. Several inches deep in some places, the resin had flowed like lava in random directions, reaching into several small crevices and cracks.

I touched the surface of the resin, expecting it to give in slightly, like the linoleum that covered my kitchen floor. But the surface of this resin was rigid, in spite of its appearance.

The ranger explained to us that the oils from the hands of the Indians who lived in the cave had, over eons of time, mixed with the rock itself. As the Indians worked their grains and other foods into edible mixtures, the interaction of human chemicals and rock crystals had created something new.

One of the college students rubbed his hand carelessly across the surface of the liquid rock. When he did, he added his own body oils to those already embedded in the rock, to those which had gone before him. The ranger pointed this process out to the student; the twenty year old self-consciously withdrew his hand from the rock.

As the others went farther into the cave, I stood looking at the boulder, gazing at its liquid cap of human and rock molecules blended and mixed by time. Finally I heard the ranger announce that lunchtime was approaching, that we needed to start back up the trail.

As we left the cave, our group walked single file by the grinding rock. Each, as he or she passed by the rock, brushed a hand against its hard, translucent surfaces. The two older couples did not hesitate as they walked by, in turn sweeping their fingertips lightly over the contours. The two college students walked briskly along, but then one of them turned at the last second to touch the rock a final time.

The woman with the tracked veins, her son nowhere to be seen, did not hesitate. She swept her hand along the surface of the rock, staring into its clear textures as if she expected an immediate, healing miracle.

I followed last. I waited until the others were out of sight, until they were just voices in Seminole Canyon. I drew my hand slowly along the top of the rock, feeling the resin that covered the individual fissures and bumps upon which the grain had been ground for many thousands of years, where generation after generation of my species had performed a routine necessary for their survival.

The unseen chemicals in my hand blended with those of Indian families no longer held in human memory, of the two elderly couples from the Midwest, of the college student, of the woman, ageless, who bore her personal history engraved into her arms. And of all those tourists before me. A modicum of my own living juices, as well as those of people both like and very different from me, became part of the liquid crystal joined to the rock.

Something new.

Forever.

Return of the Cowboy Son

"Pop, is it really you?" Laurio, genuinely surprised and pleased, answered back over the phone line.

"Sure is. Andrea and I are on our way back from Austin and we thought we'd give you a call. We're at the Holiday Inn, just off Highway 83. You know where it is? I know it's kind of late."

"Let me think a minute. You kind of got me at funny time. I'll be right over."

"Room two zero six," I told our foster son. "If it's a bad time, we could meet you in the morning for breakfast. How's Lupe and the kids?"

"Just fine, Pop, just fine. I can't believe this. How long's it been?"

"Two years maybe? Remember, you were going to come down that one Christmas, but something came up at the last minute. Listen, I know this is kind of unexpected, so if you are in the middle of something, Andrea and I will just get a good night's sleep and see you in the morning."

"Pop, my place is only five or six blocks from the motel. Let me get a few things organized and I'll be right over."

Laurio and I talked a few minutes more, then hung up. I looked out through the thick, plastic curtain, down into the parking lot one story below. I had a good view and would see Laurio's Camaro as soon as he drove up.

I turned the air conditioner to maximum and Andrea and I soaked in the coolness. It was past ten o'clock, but still very hot and humid. I switched on the television to catch the local news and weather. I learned that Kingsville's school system was having financial problems and that it was eighty-nine outside, cooling to a low of eighty-two for the night, with no rain in sight.

We hadn't seen Laurio in several years. Usually he would call when we least expected him and we'd have a chance to catch up on what he was doing. He'd been in Kingsville for seven years, first living with his mother and half-sisters, then on his own in an apartment, a trailer, and then a house. In between times he'd worked on a pipeline in Pampa, his mother's hometown, and for an air conditioning contractor in Corpus Christi. It was always small jobs, nothing to get excited about, but it seemed to me that he was working steady and staying out of major trouble.

Laurio had always lusted after a Camaro and bought one in Kingsville just after he moved back. I counted three, in fact, since he'd left

Brownsville. He showed up in his first one about six months later, on a Saturday afternoon. The car was all air scoops, fancy carburetors, and four tail pipes sticking out the rear end. It was the car of his dreams.

"Nice car," I told him, knowing he'd want me to appreciate every inch of it. In truth, the banged-up Camaro was seven or eight years old and had seen better days.

"Actually it's not exactly mine yet, Pop. I'm test driving it, making sure it's a good deal. I've sort of got it on loan from one of my cousins who can't use it right now. I'm thinking of buying it from him in installments. Maybe five hundred down, then the rest when I can get the money. He needs the money more than he does the car."

We drove around Brownsville, Laurio checking out his old haunts, asking me about his friends, who was still around, who wasn't.

"Seen Amy recently?" I asked him as we cruised by the former site of the Brownsville Boys' Home.

"Naw. She was awful stuck up, Pop. I'm back with Lupe, my regular from when I was in high school. I guess Kingsville is my home now and always will be. It just feels right. Where is it?" he asked me, staring at the new bank.

"They tore it down, moved it four blocks east of here. The new director found a building that they renovated. It's nicer than when you were there."

"Pop, I hated that place, really hated it. The other guys were okay, most of them, but the counselors were two-faced. You couldn't trust what they told you."

We picked up some Cokes at a convenience store and continued to cruise. After an hour I had figured out, from bits and pieces of conversation, that Laurio was working as a busboy and dealing dope small time. He was trading out some of his product for a down on the Camaro. Laurio looked good to me then, still had that cowboy in him, his own way of walking, of charming. And he still had his dreams, what he wanted to have, what he wanted to be.

The news on the Holiday Inn television ended and the "Tonight Show" came along. Andrea and I waited for Laurio, knowing when he said fifteen minutes, it meant an hour. Andrea took a shower and, when she came out saying she was finally cooled off from the day's travel, it convinced me that I needed a cold shower too.

Not so many years ago I would have begun to worry about Laurio, to know that he had gotten into another fight, been picked up by the police, or some other trouble. But time spent living in the Valley, on top of thinking long and hard about the meanings of a recent life-threatening fall while hiking in Big Bend, had provided me a clarity

of perspective that I had long missed. Laurio was twenty-six years old, married, the father of two kids. He was an adult and had to take care of himself. Laurio would show up when he damn well pleased and, if he didn't appear tonight for some reason, then Andrea and I would visit him in the morning.

In the meantime, just because I was bored, I paced the walkway outside our room for ten minutes or so, circled the motel, located, for no particular reason, all the candy and drink machines. Then, nothing left to do, I returned to our room.

"Did he call?" I asked Andrea.

"No," she said. "But you know how he is."

"But it's close to an hour and a half since I talked to him. It's almost midnight and I'm getting tired. I'm going to bed."

"Let's give him another half-hour, then call him up and tell him it's gotten too late and we'll come by to see him in the morning," Andrea reasoned. I agreed, growing a little cranky because of the time.

That's when I noticed the late-model Bronco park next to my car and turn its lights off. I didn't move until I saw Laurio and Lupe, his wife of three years, unpack their kids, one of whom looked fast asleep. After hugs and slaps on the back, I walked them up to our room. Their two year old quickly cozied up on a corner of one of the beds and went back to sleep. The five year old, however, was wide awake and he quickly settled in front of the television with a candy bar bribe.

"You look good," I lied to Laurio, as we sat facing each other in chairs, a small table between us. Laurio was still thin and tall, had that cowboy look that was a big part of his upbringing, but his extra flash, the flash that attracted the women and let him slide by in life, was gone. His jeans and cowboy shirt were worn and faded and his boots, on which he always prided himself, were cheap and unpolished. But more important than the clothes on his back was the look in his eye, a look of complete defeat. Laurio was going down, hard and fast.

"You haven't changed a bit, Pop, except for that gray in your hair," he smiled at me, his old charm resurfacing for a brief second.

"So what are you up to these days?" I asked him.

"Well, I'm not exactly working right now, but I expect something to come up next week, a job over in Corpus Christi. You know it's been tough times around here since the oil bust and jobs aren't as easy to get as they used to be."

"What happened to that security guard position you had at the hospital?" I asked him, not wanting to push him.

"I had it for about six months, I guess. Then they started raising the hours on me but wouldn't pay overtime. So I told them to forget it. But I'm doing okay. What do you think of Lourdes and Laurio, Jr.? Would you believe how they've grown?"

"They're good-looking kids. You've got a good family," I praised him.

"What's Lupe been doing?"

"She's decided to go back to school," Laurio told me, looking over at his wife as she talked quietly with Andrea. "Can you believe that? I never graduated high school and she's going to college."

"Sounds good to me," I said. Lupe was an intelligent woman and I wasn't surprised she was going back to school.

We talked on for another hour or so before they finally left. I walked them down to their truck as we made arrangements to visit them the next day.

"I can't believe you're driving a Bronco," I kidded Laurio as they climbed into the big truck.

"It's not mine, it's Lupe's," Laurio said, rolling down the window so he could talk to me as he sat warming up the engine.

"Still got your Camaro?" I asked, a little confused.

"No. I've got my eye on one, but the engine needs some work. I've got me a motorcycle, but I lost my license so I've got to keep an eye out for the cops. One more time and they try to put me in jail."

We said our goodbyes and I climbed up the concrete stairway to my motel room.

The next morning, after a lazy breakfast, Andrea and I drove over to Laurio and Lupe's house, following their directions. Off of 14th I swung my car down a back alley, then onto a dirt driveway that led to several trailers set up on cinder blocks.

I didn't think Laurio and Lupe would be living in a Kingsville condo, but I was surprised by the condition of their home. The small trailer was at least twenty years old, its siding long since faded, broken windows patched with tape, cardboard, and plywood. The screen door was full of holes and about to fall off its hinges. I knocked loudly, but no one answered. Finally Laurio, Jr., peeked through the doorpane, then scampered away. I knocked again, beginning to hear noises from the far side of the small trailer.

Laurio appeared in his faded jeans, rubbing his eyes, apologizing for oversleeping. Shirtless, his thin shulders and neck made him look very vulnerable. He greeted us and motioned us inside. Clearing away dirty clothes and diapers from a torn plastic sofa, he told us to sit down. He sat cross-legged in a big old chair, its foam stuffing spread at its base like dandruff. Down a short hallway I could hear a shower running.

"I got to tell you something," Laurio said first thing. "You know I don't like lying to you so it's better that I just tell you straight out. Lupe and I are separated right now. When you called here last night, I had to call Lupe up at her parents and get her to come over with the kids. That's why it took us so long to get over to your place." He stopped, not knowing how to continue.

"Things aren't working out?" I said, in a low voice, not wanting to embarrass him. Andrea was playing with Laurio, Jr., getting him to talk to her.

"No. Not for about a year. Finally she told me she was leaving with the kids, about two months ago. She wants to be a teacher. I get to see the kids some, but since I lost my license it's hard for me to get over there. I got a friend who's got a car, but he's not around that much so I don't get to see my kids like I want to." Again he stopped, stared down at the floor.

"I thought I'd have more by now," Laurio said, looking up at me, wanting an answer I couldn't give him.

"What do you mean?" I said, but I knew what he meant.

"I thought I'd be living better. You know, with a house like you have, a good car, some extra things that make life better. I had some of those things, but I lost them."

"One of the times you drove to Brownsville you told me you had bought a house," I said.

"Yeah, I did. Not a big house, but nice, clean, over on the south side of town. I got it with the money they gave me from my motorcycle accident. I got twenty-five hundred bucks. Then when I got hurt on the pipeline, my other leg, my lawyer gave me nine thousand for it, plus paying the hospital bills. I bought that house, made the downpayment and paid the first year on it. But the owner had to take it back because I couldn't keep the payments up. The Bronco, that belongs to Lupe. Her father gave it to her last week."

"How are your legs?" I said. I hadn't heard about his accidents before, or his surgery, or his legal settlements.

"They're okay. Both of them get a little stiff when it's cold, but I can work on them fine. Only thing I'm not supposed to do is any climbing or heavy lifting."

Lupe appeared, freshly dressed, her hair still wet from the shower. As bad as our foster son looked, I thought Lupe never looked better.

"Coffee?" she offered. Andrea and I nodded.

"This trailer is a dump," Laurio said, unprompted. "It was real nice when Lupe and I first moved in. We fixed it up real good. Lupe's uncle rents it to us for almost nothing. We've been here six, seven years. Lupe, how long we been in this trailer?"

"Seven years," said Lupe, making coffee in the small kitchen.

"But you've stayed out of jail," I told Laurio, trying to find something positive to say. "You've kept out of big trouble."

"Pop, except for weekends and a couple of times that really shouldn't have happened, I have never been in jail. See, a couple of years ago, just when I got back from Brownsville, they had this special program where the cops take you over to a real prison and show you what it's like. They introduce you to the guys that are doing hard time. I got the point of it real quick. There's no way, no way ever, that I'm going to prison. So don't worry about that."

I looked around the small trailer, at the broken furniture, the patched and dirty carpet, the plywood in the windows. I didn't know what to say.

Laurio saw me looking at the small glass etchings on the shelf over the television. He showed me his handiwork.

"They're easy to do, Pop, really easy, just takes some time and patience. This one was my first."

With pride he showed me the American bald eagle, then searched out his tools to demonstrate how he had done it. I admired his work.

"Take this one. It's not my best, but it was the first one I ever did."

"I can't do that," I said, protesting.

"No, really, take it. I want you to have it." He handed it to me. I couldn't say no.

The four of us talked for a while longer, until the trailer began to heat up and Laurio turned on a window unit that didn't do much good, but made a lot of noise. Lupe sat next to Andrea and me, across from Laurio, and wouldn't look at him.

"Lupe will pull through with the kids," I told Andrea as I backed slowly out of the driveway and into the alley.

"Yes. She's really excited about college. She's working part-time and has got some financial aid from the school. She said she finally had enough, that Laurio was getting worse and worse. She wants to protect her kids."

I pulled back onto 14th and found Highway 83. Soon we were whizzing down the pavement at sixty-five, one hundred and twenty miles from home.

I didn't know what to tell Laurio just before we left. I'd given him a hard hug, a slap on the back, and told him to take care of himself. We said our final goodbyes and he promised to call soon.

The condition of the trailer didn't really bother me; I'd seen much worse in the Valley. Neither did Laurio's unemployment, or the scars on his knees, or his brushes with the law, or his oblique references, after he gave me his glass etching, to his drug use. Or even the eventual divorce, though I thought Lupe was the best thing that had ever happened to him.

What troubled me most was that Laurio, by his own standards, had failed. At twenty-six he'd lost his cowboy charm, his good looks, his youth. He'd butted heads with life in Kingsville and come away a major loser. He'd told me, just before we left, about his half-sister, the one he fought with the hardest and liked the least; she had become a successful lawyer in Corpus Christi. Laurio couldn't figure how she had done so well, while he was still stuck in a shit trailer he didn't even own.

Laurio realized that he was failing in his life, bits and pieces at a time. It hurt him deeply. But what I think scared Laurio the most, what gnawed at him daily, was that he knew that it was only going to get worse.

El Viejo

The first day El Viejo (the old man) moved into the house next door to us he became the full-time manager and publicist for the Enchilada Gang. El Viejo herded the crew together for a pep talk in his backyard. Then he ran them through weenie drills and mini-parades, barking orders at them in Spanish. When they strayed into my yard, El Viejo yelled at them. Tails in tow, they returned to their own territory in enchilada disgrace. When they raised their usual group song at midnight, El Viejo ran screaming at them, throwing beer cans at their sausage tummies, laughing as they scattered unharmed into the acacia. Singlehandedly, with never a shot fired, El Viejo tamed the Enchilada Gang.

El Viejo had been a migrant farm worker all his life, worked the fields from Texas up to the Canadian border. The years of work made him look far older than fifty-eight. Like many migrants, he and his wife were not in good health. But El Viejo managed over the years of hard work in the fields to save his money, to buy a house. He also bought a new nine-passenger van. El Viejo upon first glance may have looked like many of the poor peasants who just crossed the Rio Grande, but he wasn't. El Viejo was a successful Mexican American, stubborn, calculating, disarming. I guessed that he didn't have many years left in his life.

El Viejo and his wife soon packed their son-in-law Rodríguez, El Estupido, off to a house on the other side of Brownsville. It was El Estupido who had allowed the Enchilada Gang to ride roughshod over the neighborhood, forever changing my life. El Estupido appeared every now and then, first in the uniform of a Federal Express truck driver, later as a Domino Pizza delivery specialist.

In gratitude I waved at El Viejo in a neighborly fashion whenever I saw him in his yard. He always stopped whatever he was doing, leaned heavily on his rake or shovel, then waved back, mopping his brow with his red handkerchief.

I wanted to thank El Viejo for reining in the Enchilada Gang and deporting El Estupido, but I didn't know how. Of course the gang had not completely reformed. That was too much to ask. They continued their nightly commando raids to various parts of the neighborhood, stealing anything that was left outside. The acid in their conjoint urine had, over the years, eaten away at the fibers of my steel-belted tires, one molecule at a time, and at the thin outer skin of the rocker panels; my white car was now a quarter yellow. In the early mornings, when there was a heavy dew, I easily made out the trail of paw prints which led from my yard back to Enchilada Land.

I was working at the desk in my study one day, engrossed, when I saw El Viejo's profile just outside the window. I put down my pen and walked out onto the front steps.

"See this tree?" he asked me right off, not bothering to explain what he was doing in my yard.

"Yes, I see it," I told him, looking at the mess of mangled limbs and leaves that rubbed against the window screens of my study every time the wind blew.

"It's a peach tree," El Viejo said. "These are little peaches. There are so many of them that they're pulling the tree down, making it fall over. It's killing the tree."

"Oh?" I said, not seeing his point. One of my goals in life was to do as little yard work as possible. When the grass grew too high, I reluctantly mowed it. I also picked up branches after a storm, swept the gutter clean in front of the sidewalk when it backed up, that kind of thing. But, basically, I hated yard work.

"I'll brace the trunk up like this, fix it for you. Then you will have peaches every year." He pointed to some stakes and string he had in his hand.

I thought that El Viejo was angling for some peaches in return for the favor, so I offered him some. El Viejo shook his head, told me he hated peaches.

I went back inside, quickly returning to the papers that were before me. Later that evening, when the sun had set behind the palm trees on Palm Boulevard, I surveyed the peach tree. El Viejo had set it straight again, hooked up ropes to keep its limbs off the ground, trimmed back the heavy branches. He'd also watered the tree and all my front yard. A few months later my lawn mower, a cheap machine I'd originally gone halves on with my brother-in-law, gave up the ghost. The grass in my yard grew steadily higher, in spite of the fact that I refused to water it. El Viejo knocked on the front door one afternoon to ask me if I wanted my lawn mowed.

I told El Viejo I'd pay him five dollars for the front, five for the back, which I knew was the going rate around the neighborhood, except for the teenagers across the alley who charged more and also did a lousy job. El Viejo mowed my lawn within the hour. He also cut back the vines that were overrunning the ebony and sour orange trees, trimmed the hedges, and hacked down the jungle behind the back fence with his machete, which I saw he kept razor sharp. He asked me if it was okay for him to water the front and back yards and I told him to go ahead.

Over the next year El Viejo took over all the odd jobs around my house and yard that I hated. Not only did he do a better job than I would have done, but I had more time to work in my study and to spend on the back of my sailboat. El Viejo swept piles and piles of ebony pods, microleaves, branches, and thorns into large plastic garbage bags, then dragged the heavy bags over to his house where he used them for mulch in his garden. He dug little trenches around our flower beds, after cleaning them out, hammered my old wooden fence into shape so animals from the alley couldn't get at our trash, and trimmed back all the trees and the flowering poinsettias and acacias that covered the windows. El Viejo spent hours setting up odd arrangements of hoses and sprinklers to water my lawn, while carefully tending the peach tree and the other plants. In a short time he brought our yard back to life.

El Viejo longed to clean the mess in the garage. I had grown used to the confusion and wanted to keep it the way it was. Andrea's protests to the contrary, I had watched our garage fall apart for almost ten years and, in a way, the slow collapse of the plaster, wall studs, roof beams, and shingles had nudged my imagination, given me some insights I found difficult to explain to others. I didn't want to interrupt the process of urban decay that had been set in motion.

El Viejo also gazed up at the roof of my house, shook his finger at the branches and leaves that covered the rain gutters and tore at the shingles. I told him no, that I didn't want him climbing on my roof at his age; I was afraid he would fall on the slippery mesquite leaves and hurt himself badly.

El Viejo always took the money I paid him and immediately walked up to the neighborhood grocery store, up on the corner of Palm and

Boca Chica boulevards, where he bought beer and other personal supplies. Then he sat for hours in his backyard chair, under the shade of a big mesquite tree, listening to his radio. While he listened, he worked. He tinkered with radios, sharpened his tools, whittled, made minor repairs. Often he also worked in his garden, weeding, hoeing, stopping frequently to talk to his friends who came by to share a beer. Although he seemed to enjoy his beer, I rarely saw El Viejo drunk.

I returned from teaching a class one spring afternoon to find El Viejo up on the roof of my house, chopping away at tree limbs with his machete. I could see he was sweating hard under the sun, oblivious to all but his work. He wore his usual clothes, a tattered white t-shirt rolled up to his rounded shoulders, a broad leather belt holding up his baggy, cut-off trousers, a red bandana across his forehead.

I waited until he had climbed down his homemade ladder before I talked to him. I was more than half mad at him. He could easily have fallen from the roof or suffered a heart attack in the intense heat of the day. I thanked him first for the work he had done, but then told him I didn't want him up on my roof again. I told him, in my anger, that I didn't want him to work anywhere in my yard, not until I asked him to. El Viejo nodded, wiped his forehead with his red bandana, then walked slowly back to his yard. A few minutes later I saw him washing his new van with his hose.

El Viejo kept his word for almost two weeks. Then I noticed that the garbage cans I set inside my back fence were miraculously finding their way into the alley on their own. Twice on Tuesday mornings, hearing the leitmotif of the Enchilada Gang against the groaning labors of the garbage truck, I raced out the back door to toss the garbage bags on the other side of the fence. Twice I found the bags had vaulted the fence under their own power.

El Viejo, on his own initiative, also started to tend my yard again. But thinking I might be still mad at him, which I wasn't, he always worked in the mornings when he knew I taught classes at TSC. By the time I returned home for lunch, he was already back in his yard, innocently weeding his garden. I had lived in the Valley long enough to know what had to be done. I gave in to him, but not before I made him promise to stay off the roof of my house and to keep his shovel and broom far away from my decaying garage. He nodded his head in agreement, but I didn't believe him.

About that time Andrea decided she wanted a small garden in one corner of the backyard. She asked El Viejo to help her. He broke the tough sod, worked it with a hoe, weeded, watered, worked it some more. Andrea planted lettuce, carrots, spinach, and tomato sprigs. But over the summer she lost interest in the garden and, in a matter of days, the sun burned the delicate carrot tops, the leaves of the little spinach plants turned brown, and even the hardy tomato plants withered. El Viejo stood next to Andrea's parched garden, on the other side of our wooden fence, shaking his head at me as he surveyed the dead plants.

"It's not my fault," I told him.

"You should have watered it more in this hot sun," he said, scolding me.

El Viejo, for some reason, was one of the first people I told about my new job. Again, he was standing on the other side of our back fence, tending his roses. El Viejo planted about ten roses in his front and back yards, all in a random pattern. Like everything he planted, the roses thrived.

"My family is moving. I got a new job. We're going to leave Brownsville, maybe be back in a year or two. Maybe not. I don't know yet. It all depends on how things work out."

"Where?" he asked me.

"Alabama," I told him. "About eight hundred miles from here, along the coast. Mobile, Alabama."

"I've never been there. Been to lots of places, but never there."

Telling him, I felt stupid. I knew it couldn't make much sense to him. A man shouldn't leave his home for nothing, just pick up and move on, not when he had a steady job, a good house, family, friends, a town he felt comfortable in. But if I had learned anything from living in the Valley, it was to trust my instincts. It was time for Andrea and me to go, painful as I knew it could be. Unsolicited, they'd called me in July about a position and a week later, after flying in for the interview, after late-night talks with Andrea, both of us weighing the pros and the cons of it, I'd accepted the job. It was not an easy decision, but I knew it was the right one. I took a leave of absence from TSC so we could come back to Brownsville if things didn't work out. Andrea knew better, knew we'd never move back. She was right.

We had a yard sale on a Saturday morning. Andrea put an ad in the paper. We had lived more than ten years at 24 Poinsettia Place and in that time we had collected an incredible amount of things, many of which weren't worth transporting to Alabama. Our front yard was covered with bits and pieces of our lives in Brownsville: plates, broken toys, pieces of furniture from the *mercado* in Matamoros, copies of books, electric cords, kitchen appliances we never used, stupid Christmas presents, and on and on and on.

The professional buyers came at seven-thirty in the morning, picked through our junk, and were gone in less than fifteen minutes. Others drifted by in carloads. Neighbors came to chat, politely looking over our possessions with a careless eye.

El Viejo arrived about ten with one of his granddaughters in tow behind him. He was very drunk, which was unusual for him. He carefully picked through the sale, finally sat down hard on our front steps. From his perch he spoke in a loud, slurred voice about the people who came to look at our yard sale and the items they purchased. Some were lazy and stupid, others paid too much. Everyone ignored him.

Finally El Viejo turned to me and asked me why we were selling our things. I told him once more that we were moving north, that the van was coming next week. El Viejo wished me and my family good luck. A few minutes later, holding his granddaughter's hand, he walked back to his own yard. The Enchilada Gang eagerly surrounded him, yelping their greetings to his shoelaces.

The moving van came on Thursday. It was a typically hot and humid day in Brownsville. It took the two men from Chicago most of that day and part of the next to load all of our belongings onto the eighteen-wheeler. Around eight-thirty the next evening we were finally ready to go. The house was completely empty. I walked through the rooms a final time, growing disoriented, dizzy. Andrea shed more than a few tears. Mine came later when I pulled off the road somewhere south of Kingsville.

I followed closely behind the moving van as I passed slowly down Poinsettia Place one last time, before we hit Highway 83 north to the Great Beyond. I saw El Viejo sitting in his backyard, busy with a big iron chisel and a piece of wood. The Enchilada Gang lay scattered about at his feet. El Viejo waved a slow hand in my direction, then returned to his work.

Epilogue

Dallas International was as busy as ever. I rushed down the crowded corridors, dodging travelers and their luggage, jumped to the side to let the carts full of the sick and aged zoom electronically by. I checked my watch every five minutes to make sure I reached the gate in time. As usual I made the last call for the flight to the Valley and, as usual, the plane left the gate twenty minutes late, then spent another twenty in line on the runway.

It had been only a year since my last visit to the border, but it seemed like much longer. At first I had kept in close touch with Valley friends and relatives, following Valley events through the papers. But of course it wasn't the same, couldn't be the same, as being there. I faithfully subscribed to the *Brownsville Herald*. They would not send me the daily paper for weeks, then one morning I would check my faculty mailbox and it would be stuffed full of issues. I read, then, every paper I could get my hands on. But later I threw them all out, saving only the Sunday edition. After a year I received a subscription renewal form, but I never returned it.

As the plane began its long descent a little south of Corpus Christi, I looked out the window in anticipation. From twenty thousand feet the Valley was a vast and smooth carpet of brown foliage dotted with watery mirrors, crisscrossed by thin roads going nowhere and irrigation channels leading inevitably to the sea. In ten minutes' time I picked out Port Mansfield, a lonely fishing village clinging to a wide expanse of sand and bay stretching to the horizon. To the west I caught a quick glimpse of Raymondville through the window across the aisle.

I told myself, once again, that I should have driven my car, that jet parachuting into the Valley was stupid because it gave me no time to make the necessary adjustments. I did not want to feel like a tourist again, foreign to my own skin. To ease the transition I had, this time, a definite purpose in returning: I had been asked to testify as an expert witness at a trial. Although I arranged for Andrea and a colleague to take my classes, I had only three days. Deep down I knew I should have taken a week off and driven the long miles, stopping frequently along the way, adjusting gradually to South Texas, appreciating the familiar changes as I neared the border.

The plane landed roughly on the ground at Harlingen and the passengers filed slowly out into a bright terminal corridor. I followed the crowd, staring in amazement at Harlingen's fancy new airport, a big improvement over its original three gates. They'd moved the rentals, but I followed the signs to them with little difficulty, filling out the necessary forms. Then I walked out the new airport entrance into a twenty-five-mile-an-hour gritty south wind, humidity at eighty percent, temperature in the mid-eighties, all about usual for a February afternoon. I found my rental, tossed my one piece of hand-carried luggage into the trunk, and stripped off my coat and sweater while I let the car cool down. Across the street the palms in front of Texas State Technical Institute swayed in the brisk breeze. In front of the administration building I saw three grackles grazing in the grass, but they were down-wind from me and I couldn't hear their crazy calls.

I headed straight for South Padre Island, along the way briefly stopping at a Burger King for a large ice tea. It felt good to be on the ground again. I sped quickly along the back roads from Harlingen to Port Isabel, avoiding the speed traps and enjoying the day.

I knew the Valley would have changed since I last saw it, but I was not ready, ever, for the specific changes. Like the new building standing where a lot had stood empty, or a business gone broke and moved out, or a bit of a fence line or a tree well-known to me suddenly rearranged or obliterated. Not to mention the changes in my friends, family, colleagues, neighbors, acquaintances, all the people who had surrounded me each day and whom, for many years, I had taken for granted in the ways one often does. I told myself I was no longer a tourist because I knew just where to look and what I would find. But I also realized that time played its little tricks, mutating, readjusting, even erasing those people I closely knew as if they were nothing more than a part of the Valley landscape, a brown and withered palm or a corner grocery gone bust.

Port Isabel and South Padre were, as usual this time of year, putting on their spring breaker game faces. Store fronts had been recently painted, palms planted, signs set out like so much bait to reel in the college catch.

I took the causeway to the island, checked in at one of my favorite small hotels along the bayside, and unpacked in five minutes. I grabbed a pair of faded shorts, a worn Hawaiian shirt, and old thongs that had walked many beach miles. I carried a chair, much against its will, out onto the small patio that faced the bay and, dark lenses perched on my pale face, greedily soaked in the tropical sun.

I remained on the patio until the sun set behind Port Isabel, until twilight brought out the nightbirds which began systematically sweeping the bay skies. I made a few phone calls to friends and family, checked in with the lawyer, then ate dinner at a favorite restaurant, which had managed to change in only very small ways. I left the sliding glass doors open that night, listening to the bay sounds as I stared at the white plaster ceiling of the bedroom.

The next morning I dressed up again in a suit and tie, met with Rolando the lawyer at his Brownsville office at nine-thirty sharp, then spent an hour testifying on the third floor of the Cameron County Courthouse. The other side in the case decided, a little after lunch, that the trial wasn't going the way they had planned it and they made motions to Rolando that they wanted to settle. The trial suddenly stopped, the jury was dismissed, the courtroom cleared, and the lawyers made ready to sign the final legal agreements. I hastily shook hands with Rolando a final time—he no longer needed me—and recrossed the railroad tracks to the parking lot directly across the street from the courthouse.

It was only a few miles from the courthouse to my old neighborhood. I drove past 24 Poinsettia Place several times, each time more slowly than the time before. I didn't want the new owners to see me. I didn't want to be given the obligatory tour of my former home, didn't want to see all the things they had done to the house since we had sold it to them. It had not been an easy sell. The market was almost dead; prices had, in fact, never recovered from the peso devaluations in the early 1980s, and no one was buying except a few winter tourists from the north. For a while Andrea and I feared we would never sell the place. But finally a Mexican-American couple took a serious interest and we worked out a deal. I had no doubt that Mimi and Chuey Galarza would take good care of our former home. I also knew that Mimi and Chuey would paint and decorate 24 Poinsettia in ways I could not tolerate. They would, in the process, make our home distinctively theirs, as was their right. But I preferred to preserve my memory of it free from contact with contemporary reality.

From the outside the house appeared the same, although I did notice that the paint was beginning to peel in some places and that the

Galarzas' curtains gave it a different look from the curb. The lawn was, to their credit, in good shape. I saw no signs of the Enchilada Gang or El Viejo next door, although the dust stood in puddles by their front door, as if waiting to be stirred into clouds by the tiny feet of the sausage herd. It was almost three o'clock by then, not too late for El Viejo to be deep in his siesta, not too late for the gang to be lounging about in the backyard, gathering strength for their nighttime exploits.

I parked the rental in the Texas Southmost College library parking lot and walked across International Boulevard, breathing in the diesel fumes from the bridge traffic which was already beginning to back up along the very busy avenue. I found the empty lot I was looking for in less than ten minutes. It wasn't much; all that remained of the disaster was a stretch of concrete on a corner lot not too far from where Mando had had his karate academy. Almost twenty shoppers, the majority poor women and children from Matamoros and Brownsville, had been crushed to death in the rumble of the collapsing building. The top story had allegedly been constructed without the proper supports and, for years, the city inspectors had allegedly looked the other way. One rainy afternoon in the fall the roof caved in; the story made national news for three days until, finally, it was clear that the rescue workers would uncover no more survivors. Then the national reporters disappeared as suddenly as they had arrived, leaving Valley papers, like the *Brownsville Herald*, to cover the impact of the tragedy on the people of Brownsville and Matamoros. But the national media were soon back again. A busload of school children crashed into a caliche pit near Alton in Hidalgo County; it was the worst school bus accident in Texas history.

I recrossed Boca Chica Boulevard and spent the next hour inspecting the changes to the TSC campus. All the major buildings displayed a new coat of paint, and the abundant flower beds, oversized plants, and palms had been carefully nurtured and groomed. A brand new complex of buildings dominated the campus. Three tiers of classrooms, offices, and conference rooms sheltered tiled and green courtyards from the wheezing noises of Boca Chica Boulevard. Morning classes were long since finished and evening classes would begin in less than two hours; the halls of the new buildings were empty. I walked up and down the new stairways and corridors, found familiar names of friends and colleagues posted to office doors, peeked through the windows at their desks, papers, and books within. I noted the long lists of donors who had given to the fund that had in part paid for the new TSC buildings; the plaques were attached waist-high to the walls. Nearby a new addition to the library was already in progress, fenced off for safety reasons.

TSC needed much more than these new facilities, but I drove away from the campus feeling that the college had taken a large and positive step towards a better future.

I spent the rest of the evening visiting family and old friends. By the time I headed the rental towards Padre Island, around eleven, I had grown very tired, part travel weary, part worn out, engulfed by Valley memories. On the way back to the hotel I fueled up on cheesecake and coffee, ordered more coffee to go, then later at the hotel gratefully threw my courtroom clothes to the floor in exchange for shorts and thongs. I plopped down heavily into the patio chair that faced the bay waters.

There was no moon tonight, no heated Valley moon, just the bright stars over the bay and the lights of Port Isabel reflected against the quiet waters. I sat comfortably in my chair for a time, thinking of Andrea and my kids in our new home in Oklahoma; we'd stayed two years in Mobile, Alabama, but not found it to our liking. At night on the Oklahoma prairie I could walk out the back door, down the hill to the little pond that was surrounded by oak trees. I knew that there were deer somewhere near me in the shadows of that little pond, along with the other animals that made the prairie grasses wave gently even when there was no wind. During the winter months my children helped me build the nighttime fires that warmed our hands and feet. The temperature dropped to below zero the first winter as Arctic blasts blew through central Oklahoma, one right after the other. Ice a half-inch thick formed on all surfaces, on the driveway, my aging white and yellow car, the barbed wire fence, the treeline that sheltered us from the north wind. Andrea and I bought parkas, wool sweaters, thick socks, gloves, and snow boots for the kids and us. The kids did fine, but Andrea and I took the cold badly. Oklahoma was at first as foreign to our time in the Valley as China. Our new home was not an impoverished frontier and border, but a land long since settled and civilized, at least partly, by several generations of homesteaders and oilmen.

I missed my family in our new home in Oklahoma but I knew I would see them in a short while. It was time now, I had two days more, to retrace my steps in the Valley. Not to reminisce for the sake of nostalgia, but simply to remember correctly and well just how it was to live on the edge of America. I shifted in my chair, took another sip of coffee from my styrofoam cup, and recalled my first days at TSTI, when Guero ruled my class of gasoline engine mechanics and, by night, I shot hoops at the Harlingen High School gym.

Over those thirteen years in the Valley I had grown used to the limpid heat, the smell of possum sweat in the moonlight outside my bedroom window, to Laurio, La Boca, Humberto, and Evangelina, to palm fronds groaning in a burning wind, to bulging pink gecko eyes under the porch light, to Mando's Karate Academy, Arnoldo and his flies, El Viejo and La Boca, cockroaches the size of baseballs, a madman grinding his teeth in the back row of my TSC classroom, to Berta's small but important victories, the devil student, all of these and more backdropped by the thorns and tangles of the leathery mesquite in a neighborhood ordered by the Enchilada Gang.

The Valley, every living and inanimate part of it that had touched me, had long since fused to my living tissues, like the clear resin mixture of human oil and rock in Seminole Canyon, like the roots of the mesquite cemented in deep Valley earth. I knew now that it didn't matter if I made my home on an Oklahoma prairie or an ice pack off the Alaskan shore. The Valley was forever within me, a part of my heart.

Living on the Edge of America was composed into type on a Compu-graphic digital phototypesetter in ten and one-half point Goudy Old Style with one and one-half points of spacing between the lines. Goudy Bold was selected for display. The book was designed by Jim Billings-ley, typeset by Metricomp, Inc., printed offset by Thomson-Shore, Inc., and bound by John H. Dekker & Sons, Inc. The paper on which this book is printed carries acid-free characteristics for an effective life of at least three hundred years.

TEXAS A&M UNIVERSITY PRESS : COLLEGE STATION